Cooperative Learning in Mathematics

A HANDBOOK FOR TEACHERS

Neil Davidson, Editor

University of Maryland, College Park

ZEPHYR PRESS

3316 North Chapel Avenue
Tucson, AZ 85716-1416
P.O. Box 13448
Tucson, AZ 85732-3448
(602) 322-5090
FAX (602) 323-9402

Addison-Wesley Publishing Company

Menlo Park, California • Reading, Massachusetts • New York
Don Mills, Ontario • Wokingham, England • Amsterdam • Bonn
Sydney • Singapore • Tokyo • Madrid • San Juan

Cooperative learning in
mathematics

ACKNOWLEDGMENTS

This book is sponsored by the International Association for the Study of Cooperation
in Education and the Math in Action Project of the San Francisco School Volunteers.

Chapter 1, "The Math Solution: Using Groups of Four," appeared in *The Math Solution*
by Marilyn Burns, © 1984 by Marilyn Burns Education Associates. Reprinted with
permission of Marilyn Burns.

Design: Seventeenth Street Studios
Cover Design: Seventeenth Street Studios

This book is published by the Addison-Wesley Innovative Division.

ISBN 0-201-23299-5   BK $32.⁰⁰

5 6 7 8 9 10 AL 9594939291

Contents

Introduction and Overview

NEIL DAVIDSON

Small-group cooperative learning provides an alternative to both traditional whole-class expository instruction and individual instruction systems. The procedures described in this volume are realistic, practical strategies for using small groups in mathematics teaching and learning. These methods can be applied with all age levels of students, all levels of the mathematics curriculum from elementary school through graduate school, and all major topic areas in mathematics.

Systematic and frequent use of small-group procedures has a profound positive impact upon the classroom climate; the classroom becomes a community of learners, actively working together in small groups to enhance each person's mathematical knowledge, proficiency, and enjoyment. Frequent use of small groups also has an enlivening and invigorating impact on the professional lives of mathematics teachers.

To avoid confusion, I would like to clarify a point of terminology. During the late 1960s, the pioneering workers in this field tended to use terms such as *small-group learning* or *small-group teaching*. In the 1980s the term *cooperative learning* became more prevalent. Cooperative learning involves more than just putting students together in small groups and giving them a task. It also involves very careful thought and attention to various aspects of the group process, as will be explained. We have chosen the name *cooperative learning* for this volume. However, at times we will talk about "small-group learning," "small-group teaching," or "group work." No distinction in meaning is intended.

This handbook is the first comprehensive work devoted to small-group cooperative learning methods in mathematics. It is designed for all those who wish to expand their repertoire of available instructional strategies in mathematics: classroom teachers, mathematics professors, teacher educators, mathematics supervisors, staff developers, curriculum specialists, and researchers.

This volume is truly a cooperative and interdisciplinary effort. A variety of perspectives on small-group cooperative learning in mathematics are provided by a set of expert practitioners, staff developers, and researchers. The set of authors includes professionals who work with a diversity of age levels and who assume varying responsibilities. Whereas the majority of the authors are mathematics educators or classroom teachers, there are representatives from such fields as pure mathematics, teacher education, special education, staff development, educational research, social psychology, and anthropology. Several of the authors have 15 to 20 years of experience with cooperative learning.

This introduction has been designed to set the stage for the viewpoints that follow. It provides a rationale for the use of cooperative learning, a brief description of cooperative learning procedures in mathematics, a quick overview of research outcomes, and a set of key questions to consider when reading chapters 1-12.

Rationale

Since authors of various chapters also address this topic, the case for cooperative learning methods is stated only briefly here. Young people have tremendous energy, yet school learning situations often require students to sit quietly and listen passively. The teacher must then exert strong control to keep the students quiet and on the task at hand; this takes an inordinate amount of time away from instruction and learning. Instead, why not mobilize students' energy levels by engaging them actively in the learning process? Moreover, human beings have strong affiliative needs for contact and communication with others. Indeed, many students are motivated to come to school in order to be with their friends; they have a strong need to be accepted, to belong, and sometimes to influence others (Glasser, 1986). Yet school "discipline" is often designed to prevent students from talking to one another in class. In contrast, by setting up learning situations that foster peer interactions, the teacher meets a basic human need for affiliation and uses the peer group as a constructive force to enhance academic learning. How can active engagement in learning be combined with peer interaction? By letting students work together in small cooperative groups. This argument is summarized in the following diagram.

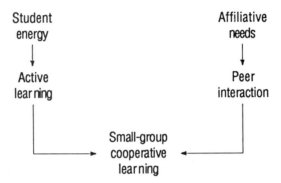

As demonstrated above, cooperative learning makes use of basic characteristics of human nature. Hence, it is not likely to be just another passing fad on the educational scene.

Cooperative Learning in Mathematics Instruction

Why does cooperative learning have a place in mathematics instruction? The learning of mathematics is often viewed as an isolated, individualistic matter. One sits alone with paper, pencil, and perhaps calculator or computer and struggles to understand the material or solve the assigned problems. This process can often be lonely and frustrating. Perhaps it is not surprising that many students and adults are afraid of mathematics. In contemporary language, they are troubled by math avoidance or math anxiety. They often believe that only a few talented individuals can compete successfully in the mathematical realm, whereas most of humanity is fit only for a life of mathematical mediocrity or incompetence.

Small-group cooperative learning addresses these problems in several ways.

1. Small groups provide a social support mechanism for the learning of mathematics. Students have a chance to exchange ideas, to ask questions freely, to explain to one another, to clarify ideas and concepts, to help one another understand the ideas in a meaningful way, and to express feelings about their learning. This is part of the social dimension of learning mathematics.

2. Small-group learning offers opportunities for success for all students in mathematics (and in general). Students within groups are not competing one against another to solve problems. The group interaction is designed to help all members learn the concepts and problem-solving strategies.

3. Unlike many other types of problems in life, school mathematics problems can actually be solved in reasonable lengths of time, such as a class period. Moreover, mathematics problems are ideally suited for group discussion in that they have solutions that can be objectively demonstrated. Students can persuade one another by the logic of their arguments.

4. Mathematics problems can often be solved by several different approaches. Students in groups can discuss the merits of different proposed solutions and perhaps learn several strategies for solving the same problem.

5. Students in groups can help one another master basic facts and necessary computational procedures. These can often be dealt with in the context of the more exciting aspects of mathematics learning through games, puzzles, or discussion of meaningful problems.

6. The field of mathematics is filled with exciting and challenging ideas that merit discussion. One learns by talking, listening, explaining, and thinking with others, as well as by oneself. Buck (1962, p. 563) puts it this way:

> *Let me remind you that* student-student *interactions are also important in learning, and that at the professional level, much*

mathematical research springs from discussions between mathematicians. Moreover, a test of understanding is often the ability to communicate to others; and this act itself is often the final and most crucial step in the learning process.

7. The role of small groups in mathematical communication is addressed in the *Curriculum and Evaluation Standards for School Mathematics* by the National Council of Teachers of Mathematics (1989):

    Teachers foster communication in mathematics by asking questions or posing problem situations that actively engage students. Small-group work, large-group discussions, and presentation of individual and group reports—both written and oral—provide an environment in which students can practice and refine their growing ability to communicate mathematical thought processes and strategies. Small groups provide a forum for asking questions, discussing ideas, making mistakes, learning to listen to others' ideas, offering constructive criticism, and summarizing discoveries in writing. Whole-class discussions enable students to pool and evaluate ideas; they provide opportunities for recording data, sharing solution strategies, summarizing collected data, inventing notations, hypothesizing, and constructing simple arguments.

8. Mathematics offers many opportunities for creative thinking, for exploring open-ended situations, for making conjectures and testing them with data, for posing intriguing problems, and for solving nonroutine problems. Students in groups can often handle challenging situations that are well beyond the capabilities of individuals at that developmental stage. Individuals attempting to explore those same situations often make little progress and experience severe and unnecessary frustration.

There are many additional reasons for using cooperative learning both in general and in the field of mathematics. Further elaboration is presented by the various authors in this volume.

Classroom Procedures

The following brief discussion of instructional procedures is expanded upon in later chapters. A class period might begin with a meeting of the entire class to provide an overall perspective. This may include a teacher presentation of new material, class discussion, posing problems or questions for investigation, and clarifying directions for the group activities.

The class is then divided into small groups, usually with four members each. Each group has its own working space, which might include a flipchart or section of the chalkboard. Students work together cooperatively in each group to discuss mathematical ideas, solve problems, look for patterns and relationships in sets of data, make and test conjectures, and so on. Students actively exchange ideas with one another and help each other learn the material. The teacher takes an active role, circulating from group to group, providing assistance and encouragement, and asking thought-provoking questions as needed.

In each type of small-group learning, there are a number of leadership and management functions that must be performed. These are generally handled by the teacher, although some of them may be explicitly delegated to the students. The list of functions includes:

- Initiate group work

- Present guidelines for small-group operation

- Foster group norms of cooperation and mutual helpfulness

- Form groups

- Prepare and introduce new material in some form: orally to the entire class; orally to separate groups; via written materials— worksheets, activity packages, text materials, and special texts designed for groups

- Interact with small groups in various possible ways: observe groups, check solutions, give hints, clarify notation, ask and sometimes answer questions, give specific feedback, point out errors, provide encouragement, reinforce social or group skills, help groups function, furnish overall classroom management

- Tie ideas together

- Make assignments of homework or in-class work

- Evaluate student performance

Each of these functions can be performed in various ways and to varying degrees, depending upon the model of small-group instruction in effect. Additional ideas, advocated by some of the authors, are as follows: structured positive interdependence, equal status interaction, assigned social roles, explicit processing of academic and social skills, perspective taking, and team building.

Research Outcomes

The outcomes of cooperative learning methods have generally been quite favorable. Reviews of research have been presented by Sharan (1980), Slavin (1980, 1983a, 1983b), and the Johnsons (1974, 1981, 1983). Reviews by Davidson (1985; 1989), and by Webb (1985; 1989) specifically address cooperative learning in mathematics.

Research has shown positive effects of cooperative learning in the following areas, which are described in more detail in later chapters:

- Academic achievement

- Self-esteem or self-confidence as a learner

- Intergroup relations, including cross-race and cross-cultural friendships

- Social acceptance of mainstreamed children

- Ability to use social skills (if these are taught)

Davidson (1989) reviewed more than 70 studies in mathematics comparing student achievement in cooperative learning versus whole-class traditional instruction. In more than forty percent of these studies, students in the small-group approaches significantly outscored the control students on individual mathematical performance measures. In only two studies did the control students perform better, and both these studies had design irregularities. This evidence might be reassuring to teachers who are concerned about the potential effects of cooperative learning methods on their students' achievement in mathematics.

The effects of cooperative learning of mathematical skills were consistently positive when there was a combination of individual accountability and some form of team recognition for commendable team achievement. The effects of small-group learning were nonnegative (that is, not significantly different from traditional instruction) if the teacher had no prior experience in small-group learning, was not aware of well-established methods, and did very little to foster group cooperation or interdependence.

Defining Characteristics

What are the defining characteristics (critical attributes) of small-group cooperative learning in mathematics? Our definition includes the following characteristics:

1. A mathematical task for group discussion and resolution (if possible)

2. Face-to-face interaction in small groups

3. An atmosphere of cooperation and mutual helpfulness within each group

4. Individual accountability

The authors represented in this book would generally agree on these first four points. However, certain authors would advocate including one or more of the following points:

5. Heterogeneous or random grouping

6. Explicit teaching of social skills

7. Structured mutual interdependence

To illustrate the range of differences among the authors, we have included a brief discussion of the controversial points 5, 6, and 7.

Point 5. There is a debate about the requirement of heterogeneous or random grouping. Most of the authors advocate teacher-selected heterogeneous groups based on mathematical performance, race/ethnicity, and gender. However, some authors advocate random grouping; others prefer student choice of group members. Most would agree that homogeneous groups consisting of all slow learners or all high achievers do not work well for either range of performance.

Point 6. Similarly, there is debate about the teaching of social skills: Should these skills be explicitly modeled, practiced, and discussed? Does this depend on the extent to which students are already well versed in social skills?

Point 7. Finally, there is controversy about the degree of structuring mutual interdependence. How much interdependence is necessary for a group activity to be considered truly cooperative? Perhaps there is a continuum involving greater or lesser degrees of interdependence. At one extreme are tasks that require input from all members—if one person withholds information, the task cannot be completed. At the opposite extreme are tasks that can be resolved by individuals—for example, individuals solving the same exercises and comparing results with their group members. Interdependence (called "positive interdependence" in the literature) can be structured in several ways, which are described in later chapters.

Key Questions

To assist the reader, we have identified a set of key questions to keep in mind while examining the various chapters. These are the questions most frequently asked by teachers interested in implementing small-group cooperative learning. Each author addresses many (but not all) of the questions from his or her own perspective. While there are many points of commonality, there are also differences, depending on the authors' viewpoints, on such variables as:

- The age level of the students
- The type of small-group process

- The mathematical goals of the model
- The beliefs about the nature of mathematics
- The philosophical basis for small-group learning
- The importance of nonmathematical goals, such as learning communication skills and fostering intergroup relations

We shall present two versions of the set of key questions. The first is a brief set of basic questions, suitable for an initial reading of the chapters. The second list is greatly expanded; it is designed to facilitate an in-depth study of the chapters.

Basic Set of Key Questions

1. What is the rationale for small-group cooperative learning in mathematics?

2. How does a teacher begin group work in mathematics?

3. What factors motivate students to learn and explore in small groups?

4. How are groups formed, and how frequently should group membership be changed?

5. How does one foster cooperative behavior among students?

6. What are appropriate leadership styles for the teacher?

7. What types of mathematical activities are most appropriate for small-group learning?

8. How frequently do group activities occur?

9. How are students held accountable and graded?

10. What management issues does group work raise for teachers, and how can these be handled?

11. What types of physical room arrangements are used with small groups?

12. How can group work be used in combination with other instructional methods?

13. How is group work adjusted to meet the needs of different types of students?

14. What are the outcomes of cooperative small-group learning in mathematics?

15. What do students and teachers perceive as the strengths and limitations of cooperative learning in mathematics?

Expanded Set of Key Questions

These key questions are arranged in categories to facilitate indepth study.

Rationale

- What is the rationale for the use of cooperative learning in general?

- What is the specific rationale for small-group cooperative learning in mathematics?

- Are there different reasons for using different models of group work?

Beginning

- How does a teacher begin group work in mathematics?

- Does a teacher ease slowly into group work or attempt to implement it quickly on a full-scale level?

- How can initial student or teacher uncertainty about group work be handled?

- Will there be a transition period during which groups have not yet learned to function effectively? What can be done to ease this transition?

Motivation

- What factors motivate students to learn and explore in small groups?

- Is motivation regarded as extrinsic or intrinsic?

- Are the sources of motivation assumed to be in the mathematical task, in the group discussion, in the group-reward structure, or in a combination of these and other factors?

Group Size and Formation

- What is the optimal number of members for a cooperative work group in mathematics?

- How are groups formed?

- How frequently should group membership be changed?

Group Dynamics and Behavior

- How does one foster a sense of cooperation and interdependence among students?

- What are appropriate guidelines for behavior in small groups?

- Are social skills (relationship skills, communication skills) explicitly taught?

- Do students practice certain social skills in their groups and then reflect upon the effectiveness of their use of these skills?

- Are students assigned specific roles in their groups? If so, what are these roles?

- Does every small group have a leader?

- Can leadership in a group be shared among its members?

- Is competition (between groups) ever desirable?

Teacher Behavior

- What are the most important skills of a teacher in cooperative learning?

- What are appropriate leadership styles for the teacher?

- How active a role does the teacher play in facilitating small-group learning?

- How much direction or guidance does the teacher offer to the groups?

- When and how does a teacher intervene in a group?

- How long does the teacher stay with any one group?

- Under what conditions does the teacher directly answer a question from a group member?

- How does the teacher extend the learning that is going on in a group?

Curriculum

- What types of mathematical activities are most appropriate for small-group learning?

- Are there any mathematical topics that cannot be presented in some form with small-group learning?

- In lesson design, what is the appropriate balance between tightly structured activities and open-ended explorations?

- What is the "fit" between the small-group activities and the underlying philosophy of the instructional approaches being employed?

- What are characteristics of an effective problem set designed for small groups?

- How challenging is it for the teacher to design suitable group activities?

- What resource materials are available to the teacher?

- What is the role of a standard mathematics textbook in small-group learning?

- What is the place of small-group cooperative learning in dealing with the following:

  1. Different levels of cognitive outcomes such as learning facts, skills, simple applications of rules or procedures, concepts, principles, or generalizations

  2. Various mathematical processes including:

     a. Problem solving

     b. Developing techniques for solving whole classes of problems

     c. Use of heuristics

     d. Logical reasoning

     e. Seeing patterns or relationships in data

     f. Making conjectures

     g. Inductive or deductive discovery/inquiry

     h. Constructing examples or counterexamples to propositions

     i. Proving propositions

     j. Making mathematical models of real-world situations

     k. Posing problems

  3. Use of manipulative materials or technology, such as calculators or computers

Timing and Pacing

- How frequently do group activities occur?

- What percentage of a class period can be devoted to group work?

- What is the appropriate balance between group work and other instructional activities?

- Do all groups proceed at about the same rate?

- How much of the mathematics curriculum can be "covered" when using groups?

Evaluation/Grading/Assessment

- What grading procedures are used with groups?

- How are students individually held accountable and individually graded?

- How is group grading handled for a project or a group test (if these are given)?

- Should students' mathematical performance during group activities be graded?

- Are students evaluated for their group behavior? If so, how?

- How are small groups used as a diagnostic assessment tool?

Classroom Management

- How many small instructional groups can a teacher handle?

- What is the role of an instructional aide during cooperative group activities?

- How does one handle transitions between whole-class instruction, group activities, and individual work?

- What management issues does group work raise for teachers and how can these be handled (for example, noise level)?

- What is the effect of group work on classroom discipline and vice versa?

- How can the teacher discuss and problem-solve with the students about management concerns?

Classroom Ecology

- Do groups work at the chalkboard, at small tables, with desks pushed together, or on the floor?

- Do all students have a copy of all instructional materials, or are materials limited or divided up among the members?

- Do students work together using one huge piece of paper for the whole group?

- Do students take notes individually (or use individual record sheets)?

- Does time have to be allotted to move furniture before and after group work?

Instructional Flow

- How does one establish a regular cycle of classroom activities involving, for example, a combination of whole-class instruction, group work, and individual work?

- Does every class period include an overview or anticipatory set and end with some type of synthesis, summary, or closure step?

- How do different groups present their solutions or findings: to the whole class? to the teacher? to other groups?

- How is homework addressed?

Individual or Group Student Differences

- How is group work adjusted to meet the needs of high achievers, average students, and slow learners?

- How can teachers make sure that low achievers are as involved in the task as the more successful students?

- How is group work used with racially or ethnically diverse students, mainstreamed students, or language-minority students?

- How can teachers handle students who prefer not to work in a group?

- What can teachers do for students who are disliked by all their classmates?

- How does group work take into account differences in learning styles?

Evaluation of the Method and Research Outcomes

- What are the outcomes of cooperative learning in mathematics in terms of:

  a. Student achievement

  b. Problem-solving ability

  c. Attitude toward learning mathematics

  d. Self-confidence as a learner

  e. Intergroup relations

  f. Social acceptance of mainstreamed children

  g. Ability to use social skills

- What do students and teachers perceive as the strengths of cooperative learning in mathematics?

- What do students and teachers perceive as the limitations of this approach?

Concluding Remarks

In addition to the set of key questions, a few other comments for the reader may be useful. First, there is bound to be some repetition in a book of this type, where diverse authors address similar issues from different perspectives. The reader may wish to read the entire volume or to select chapters aimed at particular age groups or types of strategies. The reader should, however, read the final chapter, which provides a balanced perspective on a number of practical implementation issues.

We would also like to call the reader's attention to the following additional items of special interest in the appendix:

1. Sponsoring Organizations: A statement by the International Association for the Study of Cooperation in Education (IASCE) describing global and regional networks that foster the use of cooperative learning; and a description of the Math in Action project of the San Francisco School Volunteers.

2. Teachers' responses to questionnaires about their use of cooperative learning.

3. A list of resource materials for cooperative learning in mathematics.

The main goal of this volume is to help teachers expand their repertoire of useful and positive instructional strategies in mathematics. This involves building upon skills and techniques already used successfully by capable teachers. We realize that making some changes in teaching style is not a quick and easy matter. Change is a gradual process; it involves both trying out new strategies and techniques and also considering carefully the goals for which those practices are intended. With patience, persistence, and the right kind of support, teachers can and do make constructive changes in instructional practice.

Teachers are currently faced with a variety of challenges: large class size, diverse student populations, management problems, accountability pressures, legal issues, curriculum changes, and new technology, to name only a few. We are not trying to add professional burdens to anyone's life. Rather, we believe that use of the cooperative-learning strategies described here can make classroom life for teachers and students more supportive, engaging, intellectually stimulating, creative, mathematically productive, and fun.

References

Buck, R.C. 1962. Teaching machines and mathematics programs: Statement by R.C. Buck. *American Mathematical Monthly* 69 (6): 561–64.

Davidson, N. 1985. Small-group learning and teaching in mathematics: A selective review of the research. In *Learning to cooperate, cooperating to learn,* edited by R. Slavin et al. New York: Plenum Press.

———. 1989. Small-group cooperative learning in mathematics: A review of the research. In *Research in small-group cooperative learning in mathematics,* Monograph of the *Journal for Research in Mathematics Education,* edited by Neil Davidson and Roberta Dees.

Glasser, W. 1986. *Control theory in the classroom.* New York: Harper and Row.

Johnson, D.W., and R.T. Johnson. 1974. Instructional goal structure: Cooperative, competitive, or individualistic. *Review of Educational Research* 44: 213–40.

Johnson, D.W., R.T. Johnson, and G. Maruyama. 1983. Interdependence and interpersonal attraction among heterogeneous and homogeneous individuals: A theoretical formulation and a meta-analysis of the research. *Review of Educational Research* 53: 5–54.

Johnson, D.W. et al. 1981. Effects of cooperative, competitive and individualistic goal structures on achievement: A meta-analysis. *Psychological Bulletin* 89: 47–62.

National Council of Teachers of Mathematics. 1989. *Curriculum and evaluation standards for school mathematics.*

Sharan, S. 1980. Cooperative learning in small groups: Recent methods and effects on achievement, attitudes, and ethnic relations. *Review of Educational Research* 50: 241–71.

Slavin, R.E. 1980. Cooperative learning. *Review of Educational Research* 50: 315–42.

———. 1983. *Cooperative learning.* New York: Longman.

———. 1983. When does cooperative learning increase student achievement? *Psychological Bulletin* 94: 429–45.

Webb, N.M. 1985. Student interaction and learning in small groups: A research summary. In *Learning to cooperate, cooperating to learn*, edited by R. Slavin et al. New York: Plenum Press.

———. 1989. Student interaction and mathematics learning in small groups. In *Research in small-group cooperative learning and mathematics*, Monograph of the *Journal for Mathematics Education*, edited by Neil Davidson and Roberta Dees.

Neil Davidson *is Associate Professor of Mathematics Education in the Department of Curriculum and Instruction at the University of Maryland, College Park. He is the coauthor of* Abstract Algebra: An Active Learning Approach. *Dr. Davidson is currently president of the Mid-Atlantic Association for Cooperation in Education (MAACIE) and a member of the board of directors of the International Association for the Study of Cooperation in education (IASCE). Dr. Davidson first developed procedures for small-group discovery learning more than twenty years ago.*

1.

The Math Solution: Using Groups of Four

MARILYN BURNS

The Math Solution in-service program is dedicated to the improvement of mathematics education—to the teaching of mathematics as a way of thinking and a tool for solving problems. Children who are taught to think mathematically can apply their mathematics understanding and skills to solve problems. They can see relationships and patterns and use numbers confidently to make decisions. Because they are mathematically secure, these children enjoy their mathematical explorations and are challenged and stimulated by them.

Powerful young mathematicians such as these develop when mathematics is taught through a problem-solving approach, with the goal of classroom instruction to help students make sense out of the mathematics they are learning and perceive its usefulness.

The Math Solution approach to reaching this instructional goal is based in a theory of learning consistent with ideas of Piaget and Bruner. In order for children to learn mathematical concepts and see relationships among these concepts, children must construct these concepts and relationships in their own minds.

In much of mathematics instruction, children are expected to accept an entirely organized intellectual discipline, usually presented symbolically. They may learn to deal with the symbols well enough to learn to perform arithmetic operations. However, learning arithmetic procedures does not ensure that children truly understand the concepts that those symbolic manipulations represent. It does not guarantee that children will be able to use those concepts in situations that require reasoning for solving problems.

The mathematics testing of the National Assessment of Educational Progress (1982) attests to this. Both 13-year-olds and 17-year-olds were given the following question:

Estimate the answer to 3.04 × 5.3.

a. 1.6

b. 16

c. 160

d. 1600

e. I don't know

This item tested students' abilities to estimate that if you multiplied a bit more than 3 by a bit more than 5, the answer would be about 16. That is the only possible answer of the choices given that makes mathematical sense. The following shows the percentages chosen for each answer in the two age groups:

		AGE 13	AGE 17
a.	1.6	28%	21%
b.	16	21%	39%
c.	160	18%	17%
d.	1600	23%	11%
e.	I don't know	9%	12%

Adding to this discouraging information are the results from the same test on items that required that the students perform computations with decimals. Almost three fifths of the 13-year-olds were successful with the calculation; more than four fifths of the 17-year-olds were able to compute correctly. That so many of our graduating high school students demonstrate such a disparity between following a rule in one situation and using their reasoning ability in another is alarming.

How Children Learn Mathematics

Because learning mathematics requires that students create and recreate mathematical relationships in their own minds, we cannot be seduced by the symbolism of mathematics when providing instruction. The Math Solution approach seeks to provide experiences that have the potential for students to develop mathematical understanding. Such experiences need to consider three ingredients in order for learning to occur: maturity, physical experience, and social interaction.

First, consider the maturity issue: The older children are, the more likely that they will have mental structures that act in more coordinated ways. It is senseless and often harmful to have children attempt to learn what is simply beyond their developmental reach. For example, a young child who does not conserve quantity may verify that two groups of objects have the same number of objects in each. However, when the objects in one group are spread out, the child then says that this group has more. This is what the child perceives. Such a child in kindergarten or first grade may be expected to learn sums and perform workbook exercises before he or she is able to conserve number. At all grade levels, teachers need to consider children's levels of maturity when structuring instruction.

Second, children need to interact with physical objects before abstractions in mathematics are introduced. The more experience that a child has with physical objects, the more likely that related understandings will develop. Many students are expected to learn about circles from a textbook or workbook page. They are taught an approximate value for pi as 3.14 or $3\frac{1}{7}$. They learn formulas to use to find the circumference, diameter, or area. They may perform these textbook exercises successfully. But without having had experiences exploring circular objects, measuring the diameters and circumferences, and examining and comparing these measurements, they may not develop understanding of what pi really represents and of what use it is beyond the school assignment. School mathematics experiences need to provide opportunities for explorations with physical materials.

Social interaction is the third key element in the learning process. The more opportunities children have for social interaction with their peers, parents, and teachers, the more viewpoints they will hear. Confronting others' thoughts provides children with perspective on their own ideas, stimulating them to think through their own viewpoints. From opportunities to verbalize their own thoughts, children have the opportunity to explain their thinking and clarify their thoughts, helping them move from their own subjective stance to a more objective view. It is important to encourage the communication of ideas in the classroom.

A teacher cannot talk a child into learning. Teachers cannot tell a child to understand. Learning is an internal process that happens in individual ways and on individual time schedules. Teachers need to plan instruction that is responsive to the maturity level of the students, provides for experiences with physical materials, and promotes social interaction in the classroom.

What Mathematics Should Children Be Learning?

Along with planning for instruction that is responsive to how children learn mathematics, The Math Solution carefully examines the mathematics that is being taught. The major emphasis of the elementary mathematics curriculum has traditionally been to teach children arithmetic—how to add, subtract, multiply, and divide whole numbers, fractions, decimals, and percents. What generally occurs in elementary classrooms is that children spend the bulk of their math time learning the arithmetic processes and practicing them with paper-and-pencil assignments.

Problem solving generally appears as an outgrowth of computation, with word-problem applications following the teaching and practice of each arithmetic skill. Though some attention is given to other topics in mathematics—geometry and measurement, most typically—such topics are developed in ways unrelated to the study of arithmetic and are often treated as optional or less important.

The Math Solution recommends that the study of mathematics at the elementary level give substantial attention to concepts and skills from all strands—number, measurement, geometry, patterns and functions, statistics and probability, and logic. These strands are not separate and unrelated mathematical topics but are arbitrary delineations that frequently overlap. Instruction in mathematics needs to incorporate concepts from all strands, presented to students so that their interrelatedness is emphasized. Mathematical rules and procedures should not be taught in isolation but in the contexts of problem-solving situations that require their use.

The Mathematics Framework for California Public Schools states: "Teaching for understanding emphasizes the relationships among mathematical skills and concepts and leads students to approach mathematics with a commonsense attitude, understanding not only how but also why skills are applied."

The Use of Cooperative Learning Groups

Students' learning is supported when they have opportunities to describe their own ideas, hear others explain their thoughts, speculate, question, and explore various approaches. To provide for this, learning together in small groups gives students more opportunities to interact with concepts than do class discussions. Not only do students have the chance to speak more often, but they may be more comfortable taking the risks of trying out their thinking during problem-solving situations in the setting of a small group.

The Math Solution seeks to establish classroom environments in which working in cooperative groups is part of the basic culture of the classroom learning process. Such classrooms maximize the active participation of each student and reduce the isolation of individuals. A setting that values and promotes social interaction provides students with an ingredient essential for learning.

Implementing Groups of Four in the Classroom

Organizing a class into small groups requires reorganizing the classroom physically, redefining the students' responsibilities, and considering the teacher's role in the class. The Math Solution recommends a system called *groups of four* to accomplish this goal.

The physical reorganization calls for students to be organized into groups with four students in each, seated together. Getting students into groups of four is simple enough; it can be achieved either by moving desks into small clusters of four each or by having students sit at tables. One of the goals of The Math Solution is to have students work in heterogeneous groups and learn to solve problems with *all* classmates. Thus, to benefit from the full range of thinking available in the classroom, students are randomly assigned to groups. Groups are changed on a regular basis, usually weekly or biweekly.

Using playing cards works well when assigning students. The tables or clusters of desks are labeled ace, 2, 3, 4, and so on, and the corresponding cards are removed from a deck. Groups are formed by shuffling the cards, distributing them, asking all the aces to go the aces' group, and so forth.

Using the cards mixes groups fairly well with each reshuffle and removes the responsibility of deciding who works with whom from the teacher. This is an advantage, especially in elementary classrooms where boys often feel unwilling to work with girls (or just the opposite) or where cliques of students like to work together to the exclusion of others. Using cards deals with these kinds of situations with the fairness of randomness.

There are three rules that should be in operation when students are in groups of four:

1. You are responsible for your own work and behavior.

2. You must be willing to help any group member who asks.

3. You may ask the teacher for help only when everyone in your group has the same question.

These rules need to be explained to the class, discussed at least the first half dozen times the students work in groups, and reinforced from time to time. The rules are only useful if they are understood and practiced in actual operation.

The first rule is not new for any student. Even so, it helps to clarify it with further explanations over time: "You have responsibilities in this class, and your job is to meet them. If you don't understand something, what you need to do first is to ask your group for help. On the other hand, it you do understand, don't take over and give answers. Listening to others' ideas is also a part of your individual responsibility. Sometimes, though you are sitting with your group, you will have an individual assignment to complete. Other times, your group will have an assignment to complete jointly, and then your responsibility is to contribute to the group effort."

Two comments help to clarify the second rule: "Notice that the benefit of this rule is that you have three willing helpers at your side at all times, with no waiting for help. Also, remember that you are to give help when asked." Students may need to by reminded not to be pushy, to wait for group members to ask, and to help not by merely giving answers, but by trying to find questions that would help someone focus on the problem at hand.

The third rule contributes greatly to the success of managing groups of four in the classroom. It eliminates most of those procedural concerns, such as: What are we supposed to do? When is this due? Can we take this home? This rule directs students to seek help from each other first, relieving the teacher of the tedium of having to give the same directions or information over and over again.

Staying true to the third rule requires discipline on the part of the teacher. Teachers are used to responding to children directly and offering help whenever possible. When working with cooperative groups, teachers need to ask students if they have checked with their group, reminding them that only when all group members have the same question will they offer assistance. Responding in this way may seem contrary to being a responsive, sensitive, helpful teacher. However, it needs to be viewed as a way to help students learn to rely more on themselves and each other so that they become more confident and independent learners.

The benefits of cooperative groups of four can be realized only when enough time and attention are given to implementing the groups in the classroom. There is nothing magical about seating students in groups of four and explaining the rules; success is not instantaneous. It takes practice, encouragement, and discussion for students to learn to work together successfully. Though students have heard much about cooperation, functioning cooperatively is not a skill with which they have necessarily had practice. Though students have always been told that they are responsible for their own work and behavior, meeting that responsibility independently does not come naturally for all. And though teachers may intellectually accept the educational and social benefits of responding to students in cooperative groups rather than to individuals, they may need to change long-standing teaching habits.

The Role of the Teacher

When organizing mathematics instruction that is responsive to how children learn mathematics and that is based in a curriculum that focuses on developing mathematical thinking in all the strands, teachers need to examine both the teaching and learning aspects of the classroom. In many areas of instruction, the teacher is the key person in the learning situation, providing information, explaining concepts or skills, and giving examples. Students interact with the teacher and with each other, but it is the teacher who directs the instruction, leads lessons, prompts responses, and paces the class.

Teaching in accord with The Math Solution problem-solving approach requires a different role of the teacher. Rather than direct a lesson, the teacher needs to provide the time for the students to grapple with problems, search for strategies on their own, and learn to evaluate their solutions. Though the teacher needs to be present, the primary focus in the class needs to be on the students' own thinking processes.

In order for this to occur, the teacher needs to support a shift in students' attitudes. Students need to develop the following learning characteristics:

- Interest in finding solutions to problems

- Confidence to try various strategies

- Willingness to risk being wrong at times

- Ability to accept frustrations that come from not knowing

- Willingness to persevere when solutions are not immediate

- Understanding of the difference between not knowing the answer and not having found it yet

This is not a casual list of qualities. Teachers need to model these attitudes in order to help develop them in their students. To this end, students must feel that their teachers value their attempts to solve mathematical problems. It is not enough for a teacher to provide for mathematical problem solving in the classroom. Teachers need to present themselves as problem solvers, as active learners who are seekers, willing to plunge into new situations, and not always knowing the answer or what the outcome will be. There is no place for "Do as I say, not as I do" in teaching mathematics through problem solving.

Teachers need to emphasize the importance of working on problems, not merely on getting correct answers. That means that errors should not be viewed as unfortunate mistakes but as opportunities for learning. The teacher needs to make the classroom a safe place so new ideas can be tried out and so students feel free to risk making mistakes. Teachers need to value persistence in thinking, not speed. Putting the value on quick right answers does not help to establish an environment that encourages the learning of mathematics.

Teachers need to urge students to find ways to verify their thinking for themselves, rather than relying on the teacher or on answer books. They need to encourage students to explain their approaches and results, even when they are totally correct. Often, teachers nod and affirm students' correct responses and question students only when they are wrong. Students soon catch on if teachers question only their incorrect responses.

It is important for teachers to remember that helping students develop understanding of mathematics concepts and skills cannot be a single lesson objective but needs to be thought of as a long-range goal. Time is often a concern for teachers. There is just a year to "get through" an enormous amount of material. Individual learning, however, does not happen on a time schedule and often requires more time than classroom instruction is organized to provide. Teachers must provide students with the time they need, letting the students push the curriculum rather than the other way around, and not slip into teaching by telling for the sake of efficiency.

Teaching a Cooperative Problem-Solving Lesson

When students are engaged in a cooperative problem-solving lesson, they need first to understand the problem situation, then to work toward finding solutions, and finally to evaluate the solutions they find. Specific teaching techniques are useful at each of these three stages. These techniques are described in the following categories: introducing, exploring, and summarizing.

Introducing

During the introducing stage, the teacher's goal is for the students to understand the problem, the scope of solutions possible, and whatever guidelines are necessary to record their results. At this stage, some or all of these teaching steps are needed:

1. Present or review concepts that are needed.

2. Pose a part of the problem or a similar but smaller problem for the students to try.

3. Present the problem to be solved.

4. Discuss to make sure students understand what they are to do.

The introduction is made to the entire class, with a focus on whole-class interaction to make sure that all understand what is expected of them. It is useful to have students give examples and restate the problem to check their understanding.

Exploring

Once the problem has been introduced, exploring begins. In this stage, students work cooperatively toward a solution. While the groups are working, the teacher has three responsibilities:

1. Observe the interaction, listening to each group's ideas, strategies, and work procedures for use in summarizing.

2. Offer assistance when needed, either when all members of a group raise their hands or if a group is not working.

3. Provide an extension activity for groups that finish early.

When offering assistance, the teacher's goal is to get the group working productively and independently. To that end, the teacher needs to determine the nature of the difficulty, offer assistance, and then move on once the group gets going. There are two types of difficulties that occur with groups, each calling for a different type of intervention.

One problem is difficulty with the activity itself. The group is either stuck or is pursuing an incorrect line of thought. If they are stuck, the teacher needs to help them restate what they know so far. Following this, it helps to pose a simple example for them to solve, reexplain concepts if needed, pose another example, have them restate the problem again, and, finally, have them return to work. If the group is pursuing an erroneous idea or has made an error, the teacher needs to confront the students, either by pointing out a contradiction that illustrates their erroneous thinking or by asking them how they arrived at a certain conclusion. The goal is to make students aware of their mistakes rather than giving them correct answers.

A second difficulty may be with the group rather than with the mathematics. This requires focusing the group on what they are to be doing by asking questions such as: *What are you supposed to be doing? How do you plan to organize your group? What materials do you need? How will you do the recording?* Though some groups may have more difficulty than others in working together, it is important that the teacher consistently reinforce the expectation that they are to work cooperatively. It may be helpful for the teacher to remind the students of the guidelines for working in the groups.

During the exploring stage, teachers need to have some extensions of the problem to offer to groups who have completed work before the rest of the class has had sufficient time to explore. These can be offered verbally or can be ready as written directions. It is also effective to structure the class so that groups move on independently to some other work once they have checked with the teacher for completeness of the current project.

Summarizing

When summarizing, there are three goals to accomplish:

1. Have groups share their processes, both group procedures and strategies used.

2. Have groups present solutions.

3. Generalize from the solutions.

When processes are shared, time needs to be provided for all groups to respond. The following questions are useful for summarizing their procedures: *How did you organize the work in your group? What difficulties did you encounter? Was your method effective, or can you think of a better way to have worked?*

For discussing groups' problem-solving strategies, it is useful to ask: *What strategy did your group use to solve the problem? Did any group use a different strategy?*

When presenting solutions, have groups present their findings. Groups should display their work whenever possible. Ask: *How did you decide if your findings make sense? How can you check your solution?*

Generalizing a solution involves extending it to other situations not necessarily dependent on the specific limitations of the problem. To explore generalizations, the following questions are useful: *Are there patterns or relationships you can see from your solution? Does this problem remind you of another problem you have solved? How are they alike or different?* Another way to encourage the students to generalize is to present an altered version of the problem and ask them how their solutions or methods of solution would change.

Before summarizing, it is important that all students have ended their explorations and that their attention has returned to a class discussion. It helps, if possible, to have the students come together in a single gathering place to help them focus. Students should be encouraged to listen and respond to each other's comments. It may be helpful for the teacher to record data on the chalkboard as it is presented.

It is from direct experience with their classes that teachers become more comfortable using these teaching techniques and learn about the time required in each of the three stages. In some situations, it is possible for a class to complete all three stages within one math period. Other situations may require that summarizing be delayed until all have had sufficient exploring time or because time has run out on a particular day.

It is also possible for a teacher to pose several problems at once, even a week's work, for groups to work on at their own pace. This is an effective way to structure a unit of study in a particular area or on a particular topic.

A Sample Geometry Lesson in a Sixth Grade Class

Gena St. Augustine's sixth grade class is accustomed to working in small cooperative groups. The desks are grouped into clusters of four, with groups of three or five as needed to accommodate all students. The students were told on the previous day that today's math lesson will be a problem-solving activity that will launch a unit on geometry.

The emphasis in the geometry activity to be presented by Gena is on the concrete and informal experience, not on the symbolism and formal definitions that are the focus in many textbooks. There are two aspects to this beginning activity. One involves searching for all possible arrangements of five squares, requiring students to visualize shapes. The other necessitates deciding when all possible arrangements have been found, requiring applying logical reasoning to a spatial task. This problem-solving activity creates a common base of experience upon which the students can build as they study congruence, symmetry, area and perimeter, and cubes.

The 31 students have already been seated randomly in eight groups (seven groups of four and one group of three). Gena distributes materials to each group—twenty 1-inch tiles, enough for each student to have five, and two sheets of dittoed paper ruled into 1-inch squares. Once the materials have been distributed, Gena introduces the lesson.

To begin, Gena tells the class that this problem-solving activity will involve their exploring shapes that can be made from five squares, using the tiles she has distributed to each of their groups. "These shapes made from five squares are called pentominoes," she explains, writing the word *pentominoes* on the chalkboard. Gena goes on to present the concepts that are needed, telling students that there are three ideas that they need to understand.

"First of all," she says, "there is a rule you will need to follow when making pentomino shapes in this activity. When you arrange the squares into shapes, the requirement is that at least one whole side of each square touches a whole side of another square."

She draws these examples on the chalkboard and labels them:

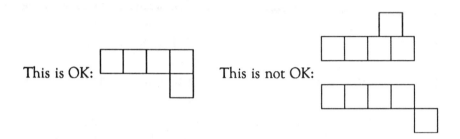

This is OK: This is not OK:

"Secondly," she continues, "you will have to decide if the shapes you create are the same or different. That's where the squared paper will come in handy. Here are two legal shapes." She draws on the chalkboard:

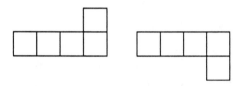

Then she cuts the shapes out of a sheet of squared paper and models how to use the cut-out shapes to compare them. "I can move these, flipping one and turning it like this so it fits exactly on the other. Even though they look different the way I drew them on the board, they can be moved to match each other exactly. Because of this, they are considered to be the same shape. Does anyone know the word that describes two figures that are exactly the same size and the same shape?"

A few volunteer responses are made: "Matching." "Equal." "Congruent." "Exact."

"The correct mathematical term is *congruent*," Gena tells them. She explains once again, "If two cut-out shapes fit exactly, they are called 'congruent' and count as only one shape."

Finally, Gena discusses the derivation of the word *pentomino*. She first draws a picture of a domino on the board and can tell from the students' murmurs that they recognize this shape. She explains, "A domino is made from two squares. The pentominoes you will explore are five-square versions. What do you think a three-square version might be called?" After several predictions, she writes *tromino* and *triomino* on the board, telling them that these are two possible names. Sara remembers a game called Triominoes that she received as a gift once. Gena also writes the word *tetromino*, telling them that this is what four-square shapes are called.

After this introduction, Gena poses a problem to the class that is similar to but smaller than the pentonimo exploration she will ask them to begin shortly. "Suppose we were trying to find all the different arrangements of three squares, all the different triominoes. What shapes could we make?"

One student volunteers immediately, "They could be in a straight row," and Gena draws this possibility on the board.

Another says, "You could make an L," and Gena draws this also.

"I've got one," Todd says. But when he looks up from his desk and notices what she has already drawn on the board, he corrects himself, "Oh, no, you've already got that L."

"I've got a different L," Leah offers. But Jennifer, one of her group members, tells her that it would look the same if she just turned it upside down. Gena notices that Leah looks up at the drawing on the board and back at the shape at her desk a few times, and finally rotates her shape on her desk to convince herself that the two L's are indeed the same. Merely looking wasn't enough.

"Cutting them out of paper will give you final proof whether two shapes are congruent," Gena reminds them.

Gena feels that the class understands what has been presented so far and decides to get them started on their problem. (If she thought they were at all shaky, she would have them search for the different tetrominoes, the shapes from four squares.) She presents the problem to be solved. "In your groups, you are to find all the possible ways to arrange five squares into pentominoes. You are to cut each of them out of the graph paper provided. Each group should make one set of pentominoes that are all different and that have all the possible arrangements accounted for. Are there any questions?"

"How many shapes are we supposed to find?" Scott asked. Gena and the class have learned to expect Scott to ask those kinds of clarifying questions.

"That's part of the problem for your group to solve, to find all the pentominoes and to convince yourselves that you have found all the possible arrangements there are. Let me know when you think you've done this and I'll come and discuss what your group has done."

There were no other questions. As the students got to work exploring the problem, the noise level rose in the room, but it was the productive kind of noise that was purposeful, not frantic. The class seemed focused and interested in the problem. Gena has noticed that whenever the students have the opportunity to handle materials, they seem to get interested more easily than when she presents some paper-and-pencil problems.

Gena circulates as they work, picking up the playing cards and table labels they used to form their groups. She checks on Leah to make sure she is moving along with the others and decides that she seems to be doing fine. During this exploring time, Gena stays out of their group interactions as much as possible. She listens casually to their comments, noticing how individual students are working. She notes ideas she overhears that will be useful for later discussion. She is ready to offer assistance when all group members raise their hands, as they've learned to do when they need help, or when she feels a group is totally bogged down.

After almost 20 minutes, a group calls Gena over. "We think we've found them all," they announce.

"How many do you have?" Gena asks.

They do a quick count of their cut-out shapes. "Nine. No, ten."

As Gena scans their shapes, a nearby group that overheard them chimes in, "We have 11." Gena tells them she'll be there in a moment and refocuses on the first group. She notices that two of their shapes are congruent. "Reexamine your shapes. I see two that really are the same. See if you can find those and then see if you can discover any new ones."

The group seems a little discouraged, but Mark gets them back on track. "I see them," he says, picking up the two congruent shapes. Mark is usually motivated to continue a search and is a good group member to keep a group probing.

Gena moves to the second group. "We found another," they tell her. "Now we have 12, and we think we have them all." Gena looks over their shapes and also notices in their arrangements two that are the same. "I see two that are congruent," she tells them, moving away. She hears Susie comment, "Let's find those and then look some more. There can't be just 11. There are never 11 of anything."

Another group calls her. It's often at this stage in a problem-solving activity that the class gets a bit hectic. This group had found 8 and seemed satisfied. "The group with Mark in it has found 9, and the group with Susie has found 11. Keep looking," says Gena. They groan a bit but get back to work.

One more group is ready. They have found 12, all different, and feel calmly secure and satisfied. "We think we found them all," they announce.

"Tell me why you think that," Gena asks.

Scott explains. "We know there is only one with all five in a row. Then we looked for shapes with four in a row. Then with three. There were lots of those. Then two. We threw out the doubles." This explanation is typically Scott. He usually provides the leadership in thinking, and Gena feels that the other students benefit from working with Scott.

"Do we have them all?" Sara asks, not having Scott's confidence and needing to know.

Gena answers them, "Yes, but don't announce this to others. Let's give them some more time to search. In the meantime, here's a puzzle you can work on using your pieces. See if you can get all 12 of your pieces to fit together into one large rectangle. How many squares are there in all with your 12 pieces?"

They think a bit. Kenny jots down 12×5 on a piece of scrap paper and comes up with 60. "So," Gena continues, "a large rectangle will use all 60 squares. What dimensions might it have?"

"Ten by six," Sara answers quickly. "Will that work?" she asks, again needing to know.

"I'm not sure," Gena responds honestly, "but I've fit them into a 5×12 rectangle and into a 3×20. I don't know how many different ways there are to do it. Maybe you can find out."

By this time, two other groups have their hands raised. One is the group with Susie in it. "We have 12 now," they say. Gena directs them to ask the group with Scott and Sara in it to explain the puzzle activity to them. When Gena approaches the other group, they wave her away, having gotten back to work. They probably heard Susie's group report that they had found 12 shapes and were willing to look some more.

One more group raises their hands to announce that they are done. They have 10 shapes, all different. "I've seen two other groups with those same 10 shapes, and more. See if you can find others," says Gena.

After another few minutes, Gena decides it is best to interrupt the entire class for a discussion. It takes her a bit to get their attention and settle them down.

"Let's summarize this activity," she announces when she has their attention. "Let's talk first about how you got organized as a group. I'd like you to hear from each other."

Sara started. "Scott organized us. He wanted us to look for the shapes in a system. We did it his way."

Gena asked, "Did you understand his system?"

"Not really at first," Sara answered, "but then as we got into it, I kind of caught on. I was able to find some shapes, though."

"How about another group?" Gena asked.

Jennifer responded, "We just all started working, and when someone found a shape, they told the rest and we looked to see if it was a new one or not. Then they cut it out."

"We did it the same way," Mike offered, "but Stephanie did all the cutting out."

"Why did you decide to do that?" Gena asked.

Stephanie answered, "We really didn't decide. I just did it." The class giggled.

"Did it work well for you?" Gena pursued.

The group looked at each other and nodded. "I think so," Mike said. "I liked it," Stephanie said. Stephanie likes being organized and often offers to do the kinds of chores that keep things orderly.

"Are there any other ways groups organized that were different?" Gena continued. She waited a bit. There was no further response. "What about the problem of finding the pentominoes? Was it hard, easy, enjoyable, unpleasant? How did you feel about searching for all the shapes? Do you think your group solved the problem?" No comments were immediately offered. Gena merely waited, having learned that the students need the time to think that a few moments of silence can provide.

Finally Jennifer raised her hand. "It started off being easy, but then it got hard to find more." Some murmurs of assent went through the class.

"What did you do when it got hard?" Gena asked.

Jennifer responded, "Oh, we just kept looking. I found that when I just kept moving the tiles around, I would find a new shape. Then we had to check all the ones we had."

Steve agreed. "It was real hard once we got 10. We knew there were more because you had said that Mark's group had 11."

"What did you do then?" Gena asked.

"We went and looked at his group's shapes," Steve confessed. Giggles again from the class.

"How did you tell which ones you didn't have?" Gena asked.

"That wasn't easy," Steve said. "It was hard to figure that out. We had to bring our pieces over."

"Where was I when all this was going on?" Gena asked, wondering how she had missed this. The class laughed.

Kirsten, also in Steve's group, offered an explanation. "Oh, you were talking to Scott's group. You were real busy."

"Are there really 12 shapes?" Leah asked.

"Yes," Gena replied. "How about one group that has found them all posting theirs so the other groups can see which they're missing. I want each group to have a complete set for tomorrow's activity. Also, I want each person to sketch all 12 shapes on a piece of centimeter paper as an individual record. You'll need this for tomorrow as well. There are lots of other geometry ideas I want you to investigate using your pentomino pieces. Who will post the pieces?"

Mark volunteered to do so, and Gena gave him a box of pins so he could put them up in a corner of the bulletin board. She put out a stack of centimeter paper for the students to use to make their individual recordings, suggesting that one person from each group come get enough for their group. She had Stephanie pass out a small envelope to each group for their pentomino pieces. "Take some time now to make your own recordings and clean up the scraps of paper," Gena instructed. "Label the envelope for your pentomino pieces with your group name. I'll keep the envelopes for tomorrow. If you have time and are interested in a puzzle, check with Kenny's group to find out one to do with your pentomino pieces."

The class got busy again, finishing up and organizing. Gena felt good about this lesson. The students were working well together and were approaching these kinds of problem situations more eagerly than they had when the year began. They were getting more used to her and to each other and seemed to be learning more about their own work habits.

Lessons such as this could become hectic, but Gena felt that the activity was worth the extra effort. Even the fact that the students suspended their need for the answer of the number of pentominoes was a valuable sign that good attitudes toward solving problems were being fostered.

As the students were finishing up, Gena thought about how she would structure tomorrow's lesson. She wanted the groups to sort their shapes into two sets, those that would and those that would not fold into a box. That way the students would experience relating these two-dimensional shapes to a three-dimensional one, a cube with one side missing.

She planned to introduce the activity with the shape that looks like the Red Cross symbol:

She would ask them to imagine how they could fold up the sides of this shape so that it would be a box without a lid. She would have them predict which side they thought would be the bottom of the box, opposite the open side. They would mark their prediction with an X on the appropriate square on their group shape and then actually fold it up to check. They would have to do the same for each of the other pentominoes, predicting whether or not each would fold into a box, discussing predictions in their group, marking the bottom for each with an X, and finally testing them. Some of the students were weak on these types of activities; this sort of experience could help them strengthen those skills and build their confidence.

Gena had other experiences planned using the pentomino pieces. She wanted groups to sort the shapes in some other ways. They would fold each of the pieces to decide which had mirror symmetry and which did not. They would sort them by their perimeters, providing a concrete experience with the notion that shapes with the same area do not necessarily have the same perimeter.

Gena planned to have them each make a set of pentomino pieces from sturdy paper along with a 5 × 12 in. sheet as a gameboard, with squares matching the size of the squares they used for the pentominoes. To use this as an individual puzzle, they would try and fit all 12 pieces onto the board, the puzzle some groups had already begun to explore. To use it as a two-person game, players would take turns placing pieces on the board with the object being to play the last possible piece, so that it is impossible for the opponent to fit in another. These games could go home as family gifts to help children communicate what sorts of things they are doing in their math class.

Gena planned to have the students save school milk cartons. She would have them rinse them well and cut the tops off so they were topless boxes. Then when there were enough so each student could have several, she would have them try cutting them to lie flat in the different pentomino shapes that they chose.

As long as the students' interest held, she would offer them activities that would give them experiences with different geometric concepts. It is this kind of investigation that can extend over time that Gena finds valuable for giving the students time to digest and process what they are learning. Not all days would go as smoothly as the initial day, perhaps, but the emphasis on problem solving in these particular activities would have good influence on their further math pursuits.

A Sample Fractions Lesson in a Third Grade Class

Dee Uyeda's third grade class had not had any formal instruction in fractions yet this school year. This was December, and Dee was interested in giving the students an opportunity to develop understanding of fractions and fractional equivalents. At the same time, she would be giving herself the opportunity to assess the students' present levels of understanding.

The children were told that they would be working together in groups for this activity. Dee settled the children into six groups, five groups with four in each and one group of five.

"I've cut many small circles that you'll be using for this activity," Dee explained, introducing the children to the materials they would be using. The circles were cut from ditto paper and were about 2 inches in diameter. "You'll also have worksheets on which your group will record your work."

Before passing out any materials, Dee posed the following question to the class: "If I gave each group of 4 children 4 cookies to share equally, how much would each person get?" As Dee had predicted, this was obvious to them. But it gave her the chance to discuss sharing equally, an important concept for dealing with fractions.

Dee then told the children that they would have a similar problem to solve in their groups. "Your first task will be to figure out how to share 6 cookies equally among 4 people. You are to use the circles I've cut as the cookies, and actually share them. Use scissors, and paste each person's share on the worksheet." The worksheet had space for the group members' names at the top and was divided into four spaces in which they could paste their "cookie shares." A question was written beneath these four spaces at the bottom of the sheet: How much did each person get?

"When you have shared the cookies," Dee explained further, "you are to discuss together how to record at the bottom of the sheet to tell how much each person got."

Dee also told the children that when they had solved the problem with 6 cookies, they should come and get another worksheet and try the problem with 5 cookies, then 3 cookies, 2 cookies, and finally with 1 cookie.

The goal of this lesson was to provide the children with a problem-solving experience that required them to interact with fractional concepts. The "cookies" gave them the opportunity to learn from physical materials. This way, rather than focusing on the abstract symbolization of fractions, they could verify their thinking in the actual material they were using. Asking them to record how much each person got would give Dee the opportunity to learn what, if anything, the children knew about how to write fractions. She was curious how they would answer that question on their worksheets.

Dee asked that one person from each group come up for their materials. She gave each of them 6 circles and a worksheet. During the exploring time, all groups were able to work with ease. Dee worried a bit that perhaps this was too easy for them, but the children were involved and interested.

The class worked for about half an hour. In that time, each group of 4 did all the problems, with 6, 5, 3, 2, and 1 cookies, and several groups asked for more problems. For an extension to those groups who finished first, Dee gave them the problem of sharing 7 cookies among 4 people.

When Dee offered the 7-cookie problem to one group, a girl in the group commented that it was too easy to do. "Let us do 8 cookies," she said. But then she continued thinking aloud, "But that's even easier; it would be 2 cookies." And then the group started to think aloud together. "What about 9 cookies?" "Easy, two and a quarter." "Ten would be two and a half." Dee left them and they didn't even notice.

Dee gave one particularly interested and speedy group the problem of sharing 7 cookies again, but this time she said she was going to attend their party also, so they needed to divide the cookies equally among five people. They did not feel this was difficult. Though they were satisfied with their solution, it revealed that they were unable to deal with these fractional parts. They had pasted Dee's share on the back of the paper and had recorded: "Everyone gets 2 halves, 1 quarter, and one sliver."

The group with 5 students had difficulty that Dee was not immediately aware of. They began by assuming that each person in their group needed a share, a decision that is commendable for its sense of fairness. But that meant they had to tackle the problem of sharing 6 cookies among 5 people as their first problem. This was difficult for them, and once Dee noticed their struggle, she suggested they include her and share 4 cookies among the 6 of them. They did fine with that, but it was all they had time for. Because of their different experience, the summarizing was not very valuable for them.

The lesson was a rich one for summarizing. First Dee discussed with the children how they organized themselves for working. The children reported the different ways they divided up the jobs of cutting, pasting, and writing, how they took turns, and how they helped each other. The children had worked cooperatively in a natural way. This occurred only because Dee had taken the time to develop the classroom atmosphere, working hard to develop the children's attention to the social skills needed for cooperation.

Dee began discussion of the fractions with 6 cookies. They had all reached the same conclusion—each person gets one and a half. Most groups wrote this in words; two groups had used symbols. "So," Dee concluded, "you all agree on each person's share. Here's how we write this." She wrote $1\frac{1}{2}$ on the board, and all the children nodded that they were familiar with this. In this way, Dee was connecting the standard symbolism to the thinking they had already done.

With the 5-cookie situation, each read what they recorded to indicate each person's share. "A whole cookie and a quarter of a cookie." "One and a quarter." "Everyone gets one and a quarter." None of the groups used symbols in their recording, however.

Dee took this opportunity to introduce the symbolism. "Does anyone know how to write the fraction for one quarter?" she asked.

Brad volunteered, hesitantly, "Three over one?" This response did not surprise Dee. Children do not always think that the symbolism is supposed to make sense and often resort to guessing.

Dee said, "Let me explain to you why one half is written as a 1 over a 2." She then took a circle and cut it into two equal pieces. "The 2," she said, pointing to the denominator, "tells us that we cut the cookie into 2 pieces. The 1 on top tells how many pieces I have. If I have half a cookie, I have just 1 of the 2 pieces." Dee did not introduce the words "numerator" or "denominator." Instead, she kept the cookies as the reference for the children.

She continued with fourths. "Here's how you divided a cookie into four equal parts," she said, cutting a circle into quarters. "To write how much one piece is, I need to write a 4 on the bottom. Who can explain why?" Several children volunteered. "And what do I write on top?" Dee continued. In this way, she showed them the symbolism for one fourth. She used "one fourth" and "one quarter" interchangeably as she did this. In this teaching, Dee was again connecting their experience to the standard fractional notation.

When Dee asked the groups to report how they shared 3 cookies among 4 people, most agreed that each person got a half and a quarter, and Dee wrote this on the board as $\frac{1}{2} + \frac{1}{4}$. One group, however, reported that each person got three quarters. They had cut each of the 3 cookies into 4 pieces and each student had taken a piece from each cookie. This gave Dee the opportunity to introduce the symbolism for three fourths: $\frac{3}{4}$.

"Though the answers are different," Dee asked them, "did each group divide up the cookies equally?" There was some initial disagreement before they were comfortable with $\frac{1}{2} + \frac{1}{4}$ being the same amount as $\frac{3}{4}$.

As Dee continued to discuss each problem, she wrote the fractions on the board to connect the children's findings to the symbolism. The most interesting variation came from one group's solution to sharing 2 cookies among 4 of them. Most groups solved this problem by giving each person half a cookie. But this group cut each of their halves into smaller pieces. First they cut each half in half and knew they had two quarters. Then they cut each quarter in half. Their final conclusion stated, "Each person gets four halves of a quarter." Complicated, for sure, but it was understood clearly by the group.

Dee feels strongly that the attention to the children's language is essential for helping them develop concepts and that working in cooperative groups provides many opportunities for this to occur. She was pleased and surprised by the quality of the children's thinking during this experience. Not only did the children seem to learn, but she gained useful insights into their thinking. Dee planned to follow this with additional fractional work using other concrete models.

Reactions from Classroom Teachers

Teachers are introduced to The Math Solution through in-service courses. These have been attended by more than 10,000 teachers across the United States. The courses help teachers develop the skills needed for teaching mathematics through a problem-solving approach. The use of small cooperative groups is an integral part of the courses, as is the use of concrete materials.

For responses to a questionnaire sent to teachers implementing The Math Solution approach, see the appendix.

References

Bruner, J. 1960. *The process of education*. New York: Random House.

Burns, M. 1987. *A collection of math lessons from grades 3 through 6*. Sausalito, Calif.: The Math Solution Publications.

Labinowicz, E. 1980. *The Piaget primer: Thinking, learning, teaching*. Menlo Park, Calif.: Addison-Wesley.

Mathematics framework for California public schools. 1985. Sacramento, Calif.: California State Department of Education.

Marilyn Burns *is the creator of* The Math Solution *in-service courses, now taught by the nationwide faculty of Marilyn Burns Education Associates. A former classroom teacher, Ms. Burns has written extensively for teachers and is the author of* A Collection of Math Lessons from Grades 1 Through 3 *and* A Collection of Math Lessons from Grades 3 Through 6. *She has also written nine children's books, including* The I Hate Mathematics! Book; The Book of Think; *and* Math for Smarty Pants.

2.

Finding Out About Complex Instruction: Teaching Math and Science in Heterogeneous Classrooms

RACHEL A. LOTAN AND JOAN BENTON*

A Classroom in Action

As we enter Mrs. Montoya's third grade classroom, we are struck by the lively and stimulating environment. Tall structures and bridges made of drinking straws, along with crystal gardens in baby food jars, are carefully arranged on the shelves lining the walls. We see beans, bottles and bunsen burners, maps, magnets and measuring cups—a long list ranging from aluminum foil to colorful yarn. Decorative mobiles of three-dimensional geometric figures are hanging from the ceiling. Some unusual posters catch our eyes. "No one of us is as smart as all of us." "You have the right to ask for help. You have the duty to assist." "Nobody is going to be good at all the abilities, but everybody is going to be good on at least one ability." "Everybody cleans up."

At first, the high energy level and the infectious excitement of the children take us by surprise. Around six swarming learning centers, children are noisily measuring and cutting, pasting and building, talking spiritedly, and working together comfortably. Wondering if there is a system to this "madness," we survey the

* All staff members working with the Program for Complex Instruction at Stanford University have contributed to the development of the instructional approach described in this chapter. The authors, who merely act as spokespeople, wish to acknowledge their contributions.

groups of children at the learning centers. Gradually, we begin to discern the patterns of organization in Mrs. Montoya's classroom. Four or five children work together at each learning center. Each child is wearing a brightly colored badge indicating his or her role in the group: facilitator, checker, reporter, safety officer, or cleanup. We focus our attention on the nearest group of children, listening in on their conversation.

Charles (facilitator): We are not doing it right. We have to read the card again. Who wants to read the card?

Amy (cleanup): You read the card. You're the facilitator.

Charles (facilitator): I don't have to read the card. I just have to see that somebody reads it. Remy, you read the card.

Remy (reporter): (Reads the activity card, which has the instructions to the task. Since there is only one such card at the center, the rest of the children crowd around Remy.)

Charles (facilitator): Okay, does everybody understand what to do now?

Manuel (checker): (Does not speak English well.) No, I no understand. What is lava rock? What is blueing?

Charles (facilitator): Here I'll show you. (Hands the lava rock to Manuel.) This is the lava rock.

Remy (reporter): (Picks up the bottle.) This label says "Blueing," so this must be blueing.

Lei (safety officer): Hey, you guys, be careful! Don't spill it.

Various things lie on the tables around which the children are gathered: illustrated instruction cards in English and in Spanish, student worksheets, and manipulatives. The latter seem to include everyday household items, tools, and utensils, as well as laboratory materials. Among the many items are test tubes, boxes of salt and sugar, mixing bowls, and lava rocks. Following the instructions on the activity cards, students busily manipulate these materials, observing, measuring, and experimenting. Listening to their conversations, we realize that the children are estimating, hypothesizing, inferring, and reasoning out how things work. At the center next to the sink, we hear the following conversation.

Tuyen:	Look, when you put Alka Seltzer® in the test tube with water, it bubbles all up.
Juan:	When I hold my finger over the test tube, the bubbles tickle it. How come the bubbles tickle?
Jesse:	It's because the bubbles are made out of Alka Seltzer®.
Margaret:	No, that's not the reason.
Juan:	Then what is tickling my finger if it isn't the Alka Seltzer® bubbles?
Margaret:	I think that the Alka Seltzer® and the water make something else, but I don't know what.
Jesse:	Hey, maybe it's like when water boils and you get vapor.
Juan:	But vapor doesn't tickle.
Tuyen:	I know. I bet it's a gas. Do you think it's a gas?
Margaret:	I don't know. Maybe we should ask Mrs. Montoya.
Jesse:	Well, Juan. You're the facilitator. Get the teacher.
Juan:	(Raises his hand to get the teacher's attention.)

After twenty minutes, Mrs. Montoya signals to the children that they have ten minutes left to complete the activities for today. Immediately, most of the children begin writing on the worksheets that they had been consulting all along. They still continue to discuss the tasks and confer about their answers. As the ten minutes draw to a close, reporters get ready to report, checkers begin to make sure that the worksheets are complete, and the cleanup officers urge everyone to put away the materials. We cannot fail to notice how expertly children handle many of the responsibilities traditionally handled by the teacher.

The teacher calls the children to gather on the rug at the front of the classroom. This is wrap-up time, and it is conducted like the orientation that occurred at the beginning of the lesson. Mrs. Montoya is addressing the class as a whole, complimenting the children on the way they worked together and on their exciting discoveries. She singles out Juan, Josie, and Charles, who performed particularly well in the role of facilitator. Next, Jesse, the reporter from Learning Center 2, is asked to describe to the class how his group conducted their experiment with the Alka Seltzer®.

Jesse:	We had to put Alka Seltzer® into a test tube with water and then we had to shake it up and make the Alka Seltzer® disappear. It made a lot of bubbles. The bubbles tickled. It was fun. Everybody did what they were supposed to do.
Mrs. Montoya:	Jesse, I noticed that your group was experimenting a great deal. Would you share with the class the different experiments you did with the Alka Seltzer®?
Jesse:	Well, we had to put so much water with half an Alka Seltzer®. (He holds up two fingers to show the amount of water.) But then, we wanted to know what would happen if we put in more Alka Seltzer® and less water, or less Alka Seltzer® and more water. So we did it, and we had fun.
Mrs. Montoya:	What did you discover from all your experiments?
Jesse:	The Alka Seltzer® disappears faster in more water. You get more bubbles for a longer time if you have more Alka Seltzer®.
Mrs. Montoya:	Yes, your group discovered that there is a relationship between the amount of water, the amount of Alka Seltzer®, and the way the Alka Seltzer® dissolves. Perhaps the next group will be able to tell us more about this relationship to-

morrow. For now, Jesse, I have one more question. Your group discovered that if you held your finger over the test tube you felt a tickling. What did your group decide caused that sensation?

Jesse: We decided it was gas coming from the Alka Seltzer®.

Mrs. Montoya: Good hypothesizing. Group 2 used the information about solids, liquids, and gases we discussed during orientation today. You discovered that a chemical reaction took place when you mixed the Alka Seltzer® and the water. Tomorrow, during orientation, I am going to talk some more about chemical reactions that create gas. Thank you, Jesse, and thank you, Group 2.

What Makes This Classroom Special?

Mrs. Montoya is using an instructional approach called complex instruction, developed at Stanford University by Dr. Elizabeth Cohen and her associates. There are a number of things that make complex instruction a unique educational innovation: the nature of the learning tasks (that is, the curriculum), the unusual features of the authority structure, the classroom management system, and the nontraditional role of the teacher—all of which is described further on. The activities in which the students engage are intrinsically motivating and highly challenging. While completing the tasks, the children not only read, write, and manipulate the materials, but they also use a number of other important skills such as reasoning, visual and spatial acuity, and precision in work. In addition, as we observed the children interacting, we could hear a mixture of Spanish and English. Some youngsters spoke no English, and others acted as translators. In this buzzing and bustling classroom, language is not a barrier to learning. Whether English, Spanish, or a mixture of both is being used, it is done so in a natural setting and in a meaningful context.

During learning-center time, the teacher is no longer the pivotal figure in this classroom. She delegates her authority and makes the students responsible for their own learning and task engagement. To fulfill these new responsibilities, the children are assigned various roles and learn new norms for classroom behavior. Instead of directly supervising the students, the teacher engages in asking probing questions, stimulating and extending the children's thinking, providing specific feedback, and treating any status problems in the classroom.

Most impressive in this classroom, where children have been made responsible for their own learning, is the high level of engagement and involvement of the students while working at the learning centers. Indeed, in Mrs. Montoya's classroom, the children were so thoroughly engaged in their tasks, they barely noticed our presence.

The Curriculum

In classrooms like Mrs. Montoya's, where the teachers and the students are using complex instruction, the curriculum being taught is a bilingual math and science curriculum called Finding Out/Descubrimiento.* This curriculum was developed by psychologist Dr. Edward DeAvila and his associates. The delivery of the curriculum through the complex instructional approach is designed to facilitate the development of thinking skills and to improve the linguistic and academic functioning of children in socially and culturally heterogeneous elementary school classrooms. The curricular materials include illustrated activity cards with instructions for the task, worksheets to be completed individually by each student, and manipulatives. The activity cards and the worksheets are available in English and Spanish. (The cards and the worksheets also have been translated into Vietnamese and Portuguese in one California school district using the curriculum.)

More than a hundred activities are organized around seventeen themes: measurement, change and measurement, shapes, crystals and powders, balance and structures, coordinates and measurement, clocks and pendulums, time and shadows, reflection/refraction and optical illusions, estimation, probability and estimation, sound, wa-

---

* The Finding Out/Descubrimiento curriculum is published by Santillana Publishing Company, 257 Union Street, Northvale, NJ 07646-2293.

ter, water measurement, magnetism, electricity, and heat. Children find these activities very interesting, motivating, and rewarding. The curriculum was developed on the basis of a Piagetian framework, emphasizing developmental readiness and providing experiential, step-by-step acquisition of concepts.

Evaluations of the implementation of the curriculum consistently show that, on the average, students in Finding Out/Descubrimiento classrooms demonstrate significantly better learning gains on standardized tests in reading and math, as compared with the normed student population (Cohen and Intili, 1981, 1982; Cohen and DeAvila, 1983; Cohen and Lotan, 1987). Significant development in the acquisition of English-language skills by students using the Finding Out/Descubrimiento curriculum has also been documented (DeAvila, 1981; Neves, 1983).

Meeting the language-acquisition needs of students who are limited- or non-English speaking is a particularly important aspect of Finding Out/Descubrimiento classrooms. In these settings, children continually use language, talking about their tasks and working together at the learning centers. Such interaction emphasizes natural and meaningful communication and the conveying of relevant information. Since the manipulatives used in this hands-on science and math curriculum provide nonverbal, visual, and experiential cues in addition to the verbal ones, Finding Out/Descubrimiento classrooms are particularly appropriate settings for task-related peer interaction. Thus, the Finding Out/Descubrimiento environment for learning language is different from and preferable to the drill and practice of formal language constructions traditionally associated with established English as a Second Language training. Researchers (Hatch, 1978; Richie, 1978; Neves, 1983) agree that peer interaction in natural settings is the optimal use of language necessary for successful acquisition of a second language.

When using the Finding Out/Descubrimiento materials, children explore the world around them and learn to use problem-solving strategies. By manipulating familiar items, gathering information, predicting possible outcomes, testing their hypotheses, and recording the results of their experiments, children discover basic laws and principles of mathematics, physics, and chemistry. The scientific concepts that are taught through the curriculum are presented in various contexts in the numerous activities. For example, students encounter the concept of measurement more than 50 times through-out the 17 units that comprise the curriculum. This deliberate re-dundancy in the presentation of a concept in varied situations, using varied materials, provides an opportunity for the children to acquire the concept at their own pace, given their individual capacities and stages of development as well as their existing repertoires of skills and problem-solving strategies (DeAvila, 1985).

One important feature of the activities in the Finding Out/ Descubrimiento curriculum is that many abilities or skills are needed for successful completion of a task. The tasks require that children be able to apply many more abilities than just the conventional academic ones such as reading, writing, and computation. Reasoning, visual thinking and spatial acuity, careful observation, and precise work are among the many important skills that members of the group contribute to the pooled effort. This is why these tasks have been called *multiple-ability tasks*.

An additional important feature of the curriculum deals with its instructional strategy. Ideally, when using Finding Out/ Descubrimiento, the teacher organizes the classroom into learning centers. At each learning center, no more than five children deal with an activity related to the central theme and concepts of each particular unit. Generally, since classroom size ranges between 28 and 35 students, there are six or seven different learning centers operating simultaneously in each classroom. In a typical Finding Out/Descubrimiento classroom, different groups of students work with different materials, performing different tasks. Sociologists have defined this kind of classroom organization as representing a highly differentiated instructional technology (Cohen, 1986a).

Delegation of Authority, Norms, and Roles

Sociologists of education have pointed out that when classroom technology is highly differentiated, direct supervision by the teacher becomes impractical and inefficient. In this situation, effectiveness and productivity are enhanced by the teacher's delegation of author-ity to working groups of students (Cohen and Lotan, 1987). When there are six different learning centers where children are simulta-neously engaged in six different tasks, the teacher cannot be everywhere at once, regulating, managing, and guiding the students' behavior and learning. In addition, if the tasks are discovery-oriented in nature, as are the Finding Out/Descubrimiento tasks, it becomes inappropriate for the teacher to lecture and instruct the class as a whole. Rather, it is essential that the teacher construct a learning environment that allows the children to experiment, make mistakes if necessary, and discover scientific principles by themselves.

In Mrs. Montoya's classroom, authority is clearly being delegated to the children by the teacher. At the learning centers, the children take full responsibility for their own and their groupmates' engagement and learning. The children know that they cannot move on to the next learning center unless all group members have completed the task and their worksheets.

The delegation of authority by the teacher is supported by a system of cooperative norms and assigned roles. This system allows children to manage and monitor their interactions at the learning centers. For example, children have the right to ask one another for help when they do not understand a step in the task; children who seem to understand have the duty to provide assistance. Children attempt to explain to each other what the task entails and why certain things might be happening. When turns need to be taken, children are concerned that everybody in their group gets the opportunity to contribute. It is the responsibility of the student acting as facilitator to see to it that members of the group use the cooperative norms that have been established. When substantive or procedural decisions need to be made—for example, extending an experiment or calling the teacher when the group is at an impasse—opinions are elicited from each child and a resolution is reached. A more detailed description of cooperative norms for group work and the training of children for implementation of these norms in the classroom can be found in *Designing Groupwork* by Elizabeth Cohen (1986b).

Delegation of authority by the teacher produces a need among the students for interdependence. Children find that they must act as resources for one another in order to complete a task successfully. Increased interdependence among the students in the small groups leads to increased rates of interaction. In turn, interaction is a significant precursor of learning; that is, the more the children talk and work together, the more they learn. This relationship between student interaction and learning has been a major focus of the research conducted by educators at the Program for Complex Instruction at Stanford (Cohen and Intili, 1981, 1982; Stevenson, 1982; Cohen and DeAvila, 1983; Cohen, 1984; Navarrete, 1985; Cohen and Lotan, 1987; Leechor, n.d.). Findings suggest that when the goal of instruction is conceptual learning, including the development of thinking skills and problem-solving strategies, children are more successful when they are given the opportunity to talk and work together in accomplishing their tasks. These results are conditional and are based on the assumption that the tasks have been well designed, as is the case with the Finding Out/Descubrimiento curricular materials.

In addition to the cooperative norms, the roles assigned to the children allow the teacher to delegate authority more effectively. For example, the facilitator has the responsibility of seeing to it that everyone in the group understands the instructions on the activity card that the children share at the learning center. The facilitator also is the one who seeks help from the teacher when the group cannot solve a problem. The checker makes sure that all the worksheets are completed. The cleanup person supervises the group as it puts away all the materials at the end of learning center time. The reporter summarizes the work accomplished by the group and comments on the way groupmates worked together. The safety officer makes sure that students take the necessary precautions in using the manipulatives at the learning centers, from striking matches and pouring water to cutting with knives and using ammonia. When there are only four students assigned to a group or when students are missing for the day, group members can assume more than one role.

New Role for the Teacher

After the initial orientation and before the final wrap-up, six or seven learning centers are in action and the teacher is no longer the focal element in the classroom. Moving from center to center, the teacher facilitates the interaction, helping students with their work and giving information only when absolutely necessary. Often, the teacher asks questions that stimulate and extend students' thinking about their tasks. He or she asks the children to describe and analyze what has happened in their experiments. The teacher encourages students to hypothesize about why and how certain phenomena occur. He or she pushes students to generalize scientific principles that they have discovered, and promotes further investigation and experimentation. When the children have difficulty working together, the teacher reminds them how to apply the cooperative norms and use the roles productively, so that they can then move on and complete their tasks.

When the management system is in place, that is, the children are working cooperatively and fulfilling their assigned roles, many opportunities become available for the teacher to provide sincere, well-timed, and specific feedback to the students as they work at the learning centers. Using the complex instructional approach, the teacher delegates authority and installs a cooperative management system in the classroom; then, he or she becomes a supportive catalyst of the learning process rather than an unconditionally available and easily accessible source of expected answers.

Status Treatment

One of the most important and unique contributions of the application of complex instruction is its capacity to address the growing heterogeneity in student populations found in American classrooms. Educators are well aware of the changing nature of school populations across the nation. Many children who enter school have limited or no proficiency in English. It is not uncommon for a teacher to have a class where a large percentage of the students are recent immigrants and where five to eight different languages are being spoken. In many of the Finding Out/Descubrimiento classrooms we observe, it is quite common to find children who speak Spanish, English, Hmong, Vietnamese, Cambodian, Mandarin, Cantonese, and Tagalog in the same setting. The instructional challenges generated by such language diversity among students, as well as academic heterogeneity, are compounded by the significantly different social and cultural backgrounds.

Concerned teachers are aware that traditional teaching methods and approaches are not adequate to provide access to learning for all children in their heterogeneous classrooms. Complex instruction proposes strategies to the teacher to handle and even benefit from the students' varied abilities and strengths. The installation of the management system, which includes cooperative norms and assigned roles, is the first step. When that is in place, the teacher finds the time to turn his or her attention to improving the quality of student-student interaction, which is, as explained before, a precursor of learning.

It is evident that student-student interaction in small groups is a critical feature of the complex instructional approach. However, as predicted by sociological theories of interaction in small groups (Berger, Cohen, and Zelditch, 1972) and as demonstrated in numerous empirical studies (for a summary, see Cohen, 1982), the interaction among students is not balanced; high-status students take and are given more opportunities to talk, to interact, and to make decisions and have them accepted by the group as a whole than do low-status students. Among students, high status is usually assigned to those students who exhibit better-than-average academic performance (for example, good at reading, good at math). These students are often chosen as friends by their peers and thus are considered as having social influence and power (Cohen, 1984).

In order to counteract the inequities of this situation and to increase the number of opportunities to interact for low-status students, a treatment of status problems is built into the instructional approach described in this chapter. This treatment has two aspects: *multiple-ability treatment* and *assigning competence to low-status students.*

Multiple-Ability Treatment. The *multiple-ability treatment* is a straightforward statement by the teacher, explaining to the students that there are multiple abilities needed for the performance of each task; while no one can possibly be good at every ability, everyone is going to be good at some of the abilities. Versions of this statement are repeated over and over again to the students by the teacher. He or she also spends considerable time identifying the many different abilities and skills required to complete the tasks.

Examples of the skills and abilities talked about by the teacher are: reasoning, observing carefully, mechanical inventiveness, asking key questions, being supportive or helpful to others, explaining clearly, being able to think visually, being able to reason spatially, recording data accurately, reporting concisely, thinking up and trying new ways to solve task problems, understanding word problems, being an intuitive thinker, working persistently, working carefully and with precision, and using ideas from other learning center experiences. This list can be elaborated upon and expanded by the teacher. Theoretically, as they come to understand the relevance of these abilities and their contributions to the performance of the tasks, the students gradually develop a varied and mixed set of expectations for competence on any set of tasks in which they are engaged (Cohen, 1982; Rosenholtz, 1977).

Assigning Competence. In addition to implementing the multiple-ability treatment, teachers are trained to use an additional method in their attempts to weaken the effects of status problems and thus equalize rates of interaction among the students. This method is called *assigning competence* to students exhibiting low-status behavior. It is one of the most powerful strategies that a teacher can use to treat status problems and expectations for competence in the classroom. While the children work in their groups to complete the tasks that have been explained to them as requiring multiple abilities, the teacher is busy observing his or her students. She pays particular attention to those students who, in general, tend to exhibit low-status behavior.

Generally, children who exhibit low-status behavior have poor reading and math skills. They often have few friends and are frequently perceived as "not too bright" by their classmates and by the teacher (Cohen, 1984; Rosenholtz and Wilson, 1980). Low-status children tend to interact less frequently with classmates than do high-status children. Low-status students are perceived as less influential and unable or unwilling to share ideas or help others. In the average elementary school classroom, the grouping of children into ability groups for reading and math exacerbates and intensifies status problems. Usually, low-status children are the children in the lowest reading group. The gap between the highest and the lowest groups in learning and achievement has been well documented (for example, Goodlad, 1984). The reasons for this gap are partly explained by the dissimilarity in the curricular content delivered to the different ability groups, the variability in the pace of the instruction, and the unequal access to learning materials and to the teacher.

In Finding Out/Descubrimiento classrooms, where children always work in heterogeneous groups, teachers look for incidents where low-status students make valuable contributions to the group. When they see students exhibiting reasoning, visual or spatial skills, or precision in manipulating, thinking, drawing, or reporting, teachers engage in status treatment by assigning competence. This process includes identifying, specifically and publicly, the particular skill on which the child has done well. The teacher, being a high-status participant in the classroom interaction, is a powerful source of evaluation for the students. Children exhibiting low-status behavior often respond to such favorable public demonstration of their competence by raising their expectations for their own performance. These children improve their task engagement and group participation and thus their learning outcomes. Indeed, this status treatment can be very rewarding to the teacher as he or she watches such students begin to achieve some measure of academic success as well as social integration.

Effective Treatment of a Status Problem. We would like to share with you a lengthy, yet dramatic, example of an effective treatment of a status problem in a second grade classroom. Alicia, a rather tall, bilingual Spanish-English-speaking second grader was the type of youngster whom people barely noticed. She was not a discipline problem; she did not make demands on the teacher or the other students, nor did she actively participate in interactions. Alicia seldom raised her hand to answer questions, and she rarely voiced her opinions.

One day in April, while videotaping group interactions in Alicia's classroom, we focused on students who frequently exhibited low-status behavior. While working on the coordinates and measurement unit, Alicia had teamed up with another child in her group, Aneke. Their task was to draw life-sized representations of their bodies. The girls took turns, lying on large sheets of butcher paper and then outlining each other's bodies with a thick, felt-tip pen. After making the outlines, the children had to cut out the replicas and then color in their features and clothing.

Aneke had possibly the highest academic status in this second grade classroom. She was petite, precocious, and popular. She knew the answer to almost every question the teacher asked. Her hand flew up at every opportunity. She was a delightful, outgoing child, who seemed to be skilled at everything that she was asked to do.

Among the important skills needed by students in the second grade is the ability to use scissors and to cut accurately. However, as Alicia and Aneke set about to cut out their butcher paper bodies, it became apparent that Aneke, who was so accomplished academically, did not know how to use scissors properly, nor did she know how to follow the outline of the body to cut it out accurately. Aneke was distressed. She feared she would cut off her paper arms and legs. Patiently and expertly, Alicia guided Aneke through the procedure, coaching her exasperated partner on how to use the scissors and follow the outline.

When Alicia's teacher viewed the videotape of this incident with one of the authors, the teacher commented on the fact that this was the first time since school started that she had seen Alicia show real mastery on a skill relevant to a classroom task. During the next orientation, the teacher shared her observation with the class. She wanted all the children to realize that Alicia was particularly skilled at using scissors and that if ever they needed help cutting, they could turn to Alicia as a resource.

Coincidentally, the school was getting ready to present a musical called "Let George Do It." This colonial play required that each class be responsible for making a number of three-cornered hats. The second grade teacher decided to put Alicia in charge of making these hats for her class. Alicia was to pick children to be on the committee, decide on what materials were needed, get the pattern from the teacher in charge of costumes, and see to it that the hats were made to specification. Since Alicia was perceived as the most accomplished "cutter" in her classroom, the committee looked to her for guidance.

Alicia took to the making of the three-cornered hats with tremendous enthusiasm. Again, it was the first time since September that her teacher had seen Alicia talking and working with other children in such an animated and empowered way. Alicia was now raising her hand more often during wrap-up, answering questions frequently and accurately. During this same period of time, the teacher also discovered that Alicia had good spatial reasoning and visual thinking skills. For example, when the task for her group was to draw a map of the classroom to scale, Alicia drew the map and then created an impressive three-dimensional model of the room. The teacher made sure that Alicia was assigned competence for this accomplishment also.

After the beginning of the next academic year, the opportunity arose to talk with Alicia's third grade teacher. This teacher said that she would have never guessed that Alicia had been a low-status student for a large part of her second grade. Particularly during Finding Out/Descubrimiento, but also during many other parts of the day, Alicia interacted frequently and effectively with her classmates, raised her hand and answered questions correctly, and expressed her opinions readily. Children listening to Alicia were often observed going along with her suggestions. Alicia was greatly valued by her teachers and her classmates for her artistic and organizational skills. It appeared that Alicia was also performing better academically in almost every curricular area.

Assigning competence is not miracle work. It requires effort, time, and commitment from the teacher to implement the treatment adequately, and the outcomes aren't always as obvious or immediate as illustrated in our example. It is important to see, however, how mastery of a skill as mundane as using scissors can provide a teacher with an initial opportunity to assign competence to a youngster who had appeared to be rather slow, unaccomplished and withdrawn—until the incident with the scissors. Being perceived as a resource by her classmates and taking on important responsibilities (such as preparing the three-cornered hats), Alicia now had the opportunity and the confidence to demonstrate her leadership qualities.

Relationship of Status, Task-Related Talk, and Learning. Cohen and her associates have investigated the relationship of status, task-related talk, and learning in Finding Out/Descubrimiento classrooms (Cohen, 1984; Cohen, Lotan, and Catanzarite, n.d.). They found that the effect of status on students' task-related talk was markedly weakened but not entirely eliminated by the installation of the classroom management system that uses cooperative norms and roles. These researchers also pointed out that a specific status treatment needs to be integrated into such a system. "The major implication of this work is the realization that the installation of cooperative learning is not sufficient to deal with the status problems that have been described. To the contrary, the fostering of interdependence (among students) may activate these very status problems.

Failure to deal with the status problem may shut off access to interaction for low-status children." (Cohen, Lotan, and Catanzarite, 1986). We cannot emphasize enough the importance of consistent status treatment as an integral part of the complex instructional approach. Having trained teachers to implement this approach in their classrooms, we also realize that it is one of the most difficult and sophisticated teaching skills required from a busy teacher. Benton (n.d.) has developed a training procedure called analytic video training, designed to have teachers attain mastery in assigning competence to low-status children.

Implications for Math and Science Teachers

When the Finding Out/Descubrimiento curriculum is used in the classroom, student learning gains documented in the program's research since 1979 are related to key features of the implementation of complex instruction: the differentiation of tasks, the delegation of authority by the teacher, the amount of student interaction, and the treatment of status. In turn, teachers' implementation of the approach is clearly affected by the amount and quality of their training, their understanding of the body of knowledge underlying the approach, and the organizational support available to them in their respective schools (Lotan, 1985). Thus, we propose that teachers use complex instruction as described in this chapter only after giving serious consideration to the following issues: (1) the adequacy of the match between the goal of instruction and the organization of the classroom; (2) the adequacy of the curricular materials; (3) the training needed for effective implementation of the approach as a whole; and (4) the presence of organizational support for the teacher.

The match between the goal of instruction and the organization of the classroom requires careful deliberation. No single instructional approach can be used to teach effectively all that needs to be learned in the classroom. For example, drill and practice are effective instructional techniques when the goal is memorizing or learning names and labels. Complex instruction is an effective approach when the goal is conceptual learning. We argue that the development of thinking skills requires increased amounts of task-related interaction, through which students have the opportunity to develop problem-solving strategies. This critical interaction is promoted by the installation of the management system and features of the curriculum as described in this chapter.

The way that curriculum materials for complex instruction are structured for presentation and delivery also requires careful design. For example, paper-and-pencil tasks used in drill and practice and textbook and workbook assignments in which answers are right or wrong are not compatible with complex instruction. Tasks that involve conceptual learning have variable and open-ended outcomes and require hypothesizing, estimating, and experimenting with manipulatives; these are the kinds of tasks that can be used with complex instruction. In addition, for effective treatment of status, such tasks need to be designed so that multiple abilities are required for their completion.

Activity-based classrooms, in which tasks designed for complex instruction are implemented, need management systems that can handle the complexity arising from the differentiated multiple learning centers and the uncertainty of the tasks. A key feature of such a management system is the delegation of authority by the teacher to groups of students. We acknowledge, however, that delegation of authority is easier said than done and that delegation of authority, by itself, is an insufficient component of any instructional approach. When the teacher understands this concept and is ready to let go and avoid unnecessary supervision, an alternative mechanism needs to be put in place in order to maintain the classroom system. The purpose of such a mechanism is to make sure that the tasks are being accomplished and that the children are engaged and learning. The system of cooperative norms and the assignment of roles represent such a mechanism. When "maintenance" is taken care of, the teacher is free to do higher level instruction: providing feedback, stimulating and extending thinking, and, most importantly, treating status problems.

Learning how to delegate authority, train students to internalize the roles and cooperative norms, and use the sophisticated teaching skills required in complex instruction is complicated. Implementing the model as a whole necessitates considerable training, on-the-job practice, continual examination, and systematic analysis of the process and the outcomes. Teachers involved in the Stanford program participate in a two-week summer training that includes learning about the theory, watching experienced teachers use the approach, practicing by teaching a class of students, and receiving feedback on their performance. We realize that many teachers would like to implement complex instruction yet do not have access to such thorough training programs. Many teachers have found that they can successfully implement certain components of complex instruction after carefully reading *Designing Groupwork* by Cohen (1986b).

Teachers who want to implement such a demanding program should have the benefit of support at the school-site level. Support from the principal includes making sure that the teacher has the necessary resources needed for successful implementation: adequate space where the noise level in the classroom does not interfere with other teachers' activities; the necessary materials; and time to prepare and meet with other teachers to discuss issues of implementation (Parchment, n.d). Ellis (1987) has shown that collaboration among teachers, and among teachers and their instructional aides, is related to the quality of the implementation of complex instruction. This collaboration has two elements. The first consists of regular, structured team meetings about problems that arise regarding implementation and maintenance of the program. The second pertains to feedback meetings that follow systematic classroom observations. When teachers attempt the implementation of a demanding instructional approach such as complex instruction, the necessity of organizational support cannot be overemphasized.

Conclusion

We have attempted to describe an exciting instructional innovation that has been implemented in more than a hundred classrooms in northern California. Teachers trained in the Finding Out/ Descubrimiento program at Stanford University have often expressed to us their satisfaction at being able to construct a classroom environment with the characteristics described here: Teachers can successfully deal with the academic, social, and linguistic heterogeneity among their students, and *all* students have the opportunity to become successful learners. We encourage teachers to investigate the possibilities of implementing the complex instructional approach. Although the professional as well as personal commitment may be difficult, the rewards are many.

References

Benton, J. n.d. Treating status problems in the classroom: Training teachers to assign competence to students exhibiting low-status behaviors. Ph.D. diss., Stanford University.

Berger, J., B. Cohen, and M. Zelditch, Jr. 1972. Status characteristics and social interaction. *American Sociological Review* 37: 241–55.

Cohen, E.G. 1982. Expectation states and interracial interaction in school settings. *Annual Review of Sociology* 8: 209–35.

———. 1984. Talking and working together: Status, interaction and learning. In *Instructional groups in the classroom: Organization and processes*, edited by P. Peterson and L.C. Wilkinson. New York: Academic Press.

———. 1986a. On the sociology of the classroom. In *The contributions of the social sciences to educational policy and practice: 1965–1985*, edited by J. Hannaway and M.E. Lockheed, 127–62. Berkeley, Calif.: McCutchan.

———. 1986b. *Designing groupwork: Strategies for heterogeneous classrooms*. New York: Teachers College Press.

Cohen, E.G., and E. DeAvila. 1983. Learning to think in math and science: Improving local education for minority children. A Final Report to the Johnson Foundation. Stanford: Stanford University School of Education.

Cohen, E.G., and J.K. Intili. 1981. Interdependence and management in bilingual classrooms. Final Report I, (NIE Contract # NIE-G-80-0217). Stanford: Stanford University Center for Educational Research at Stanford.

————. 1982. Interdependence and management in bilingual classrooms. Final Report II, (NIE Contract # NIE-G-80-0217). Stanford: Stanford University Center for Educational Research at Stanford.

Cohen, E.G., and R.A. Lotan. 1987. Application of sociology to science teaching: Program for complex instruction. Paper presented at the annual meeting of the National Association for Research on Science Teaching, April, Washington, D.C.

Cohen, E.G.,with R.A. Lotan, and L. Catanzarite. 1986. Treating status problems in the cooperative classroom. Paper presented at the American Educational Research Association Annual Meeting, San Francisco, Calif.

————. n.d. Can expectations for competence be treated in the classroom? In *Status generalization: New theory and research*, edited by M. Webster, Jr., and M. Foschi. Stanford, Calif: Stanford University Press.

DeAvila, E. 1981. Multicultural improvement of cognitive abilities: Final report to the state of California, Department of Education. Stanford, Calif.: Stanford University School of Education.

————. 1985. Motivation, intelligence, and access: A theoretical framework for the education of minority language students. In *Issues in English language education*. The National Clearinghouse for Bilingual Education.

Ellis, N.E. 1987. Collaborative interaction and logistical support for teacher change. Ph.D. diss., Stanford University.

Goodlad, J. 1984. *A place called school. Prospects for the future.* New York: McGraw-Hill.

Hatch, E.M., ed. 1978. *Second language acquisition: A book of readings.* Rowley, Mass.: Newbury House Publishers.

Lotan, R.A. 1985. Understanding the theories: Training teachers for implementation of complex instructional technology. Ph.D. diss., Stanford University.

Leechor, C. n.d. How high and low achieving students differentially benefit from working together in cooperative small groups. Ph.D. diss., Stanford University.

Navarrete, C. 1985. Problem resolution in small group interaction: A bilingual classroom study. Ph.D. diss., Stanford University.

Neves, A.H. 1983. The effect of various input on the second language acquisition of Mexican-American children in nine elementary classrooms. Ph.D. diss., Stanford University.

Parchment, C. n.d. The role of the principal in the implementation of a complex instructional program. Ph.D. diss., Stanford University.

Ritchie, W.C., ed. 1978. *Second language acquisition research. Issues and implications.* New York: Academic Press.

Rosenholtz, S.J. 1977. The multiple ability curriculum: An intervention against the self-fulfilling prophecy. Ph.D. diss., Stanford University.

Rosenholtz, S.J. and B. Wilson. 1980. The effects of classroom structure on shared perceptions of ability. *American Educational Research Journal* 17: 175–82.

Stevenson, B. 1982. An analysis of the relationship of student-student consultation to academic performance in differentiated classroom settings. Ph.D. diss., Stanford University.

Rachel Lotan is the Associate Director of the Program for Complex Instruction at Stanford University. In addition, she is a post-doctoral fellow of the Center for Policy Research in Education, Rutgers University. Her fields of interest are the sociology of the classroom and the organization of schools.

Joan Benton is a doctoral student at Stanford University School of Education. In her dissertation, she has evaluated the use of video to enable teachers to analyze and treat status problems in their classrooms. Previously, as a reading specialist, she directed an individualized/small-group instructional reading program at a high school in San Francisco.

3.

Student Team Learning in Mathematics

ROBERT E. SLAVIN *

Rationale

When I was an undergraduate, I took a course on educational psychology in which I read a book that had a considerable impact on me. The book was James Coleman's (1961) *Adolescent Society,* in which Coleman, a sociologist, wondered why it was that students were so motivated on the playing field and so unmotivated in the classroom, and why it was that students so valued their classmates' successes in sports but considered classmates who worked hard in academics to be teachers' pets or nerds. Coleman suggested that a large part of the difference between students' attitudes toward success in sports and success in school had to do with the *reward structures* of the two activities. In sports, a student's hard work is likely to benefit the team, and the team's success is valued by the school. Athletes know that the school is rooting for them, and they exert their best efforts accordingly.

Contrast this situation with that in the traditional classroom, in which students are in competition for grades, for teachers' approval, and for other rewards. If Suzy works hard, completes her homework, and knows the answers in class, does this make her popular? Hardly. Her success makes success more difficult for others in the class, so students express norms to one another against studying, against

* This chapter was written under a grant from the Office of Educational Research and Improvement, U.S. Department of Education (No. OERI-G-86-0006). However, the opinions expressed are those of the author and do not necessarily represent OERI policy.

working hard, or against appearing to enjoy academics. In industry, Suzy's behavior would be called rate busting, making life difficult for her coworkers by performing too well.

From elementary to high school, peer norms are very powerful. If peer norms say school isn't cool, most students will believe it. If peer norms say that only suckers do math and only nerds actually like it, most students will do only the minimum necessary to get by.

How can this situation be turned around? One answer is to try to capture some of the dynamics of the playing field and use them in the classroom. If students could work in teams, where hard work and achievement contribute to team success, perhaps peer norms could be made to work for, rather than against, academic efforts. Perhaps students could help each other learn if their teammates' learning was important for their team's success. Perhaps students could experience some of the excitement of the playing field in the classroom and learn that mathematics can be fun.

This simple idea, of bringing cooperation and teamwork into the mathematics classroom, lies behind the instructional methods described in this chapter. These are called *Student Team Learning* methods. Of course, the idea of using team activities in the classroom is hardly new; the spelling bee and many math games have been around since the one-room schoolhouse. What is new about Student Team Learning is making cooperation in learning teams a routine part of classroom organization, not an occasional fun activity. More importantly, carefully controlled studies have demonstrated that use of learning teams under specific conditions increases student achievement in mathematics and other subjects.

Student Team Learning

Student Team Learning refers to three instructional methods that have been used in mathematics: Student Teams Achievement Divisions (STAD), Teams-Games-Tournaments (TGT), and Team-Assisted Individualization (TAI). A fourth Student Team Learning method, Jigsaw II, has been used primarily in subjects other than mathematics. Brief overviews of these methods follow.

Student Teams Achievement Divisions (STAD). In STAD, students are assigned to four-member learning teams that are mixed in performance level, sex, and ethnicity. The teacher presents a lesson, and then students work within their teams to make sure that all team members have mastered the lesson. Finally, all students take individual quizzes on the material, at which time they may not help one another. Students' quiz scores are compared to their own past averages, and points are awarded based on the degree to which students can meet or exceed their own earlier performances. These points are then summed to form team scores, and teams that meet certain criteria may earn certificates or other rewards. The whole cycle of activities, from teacher presentation to team practice to quiz, usually takes three to five class periods. STAD has been used in many subjects and has been used in mathematics from grade 2 through college.

The main idea behind STAD is to motivate students to encourage and help each other master skills presented by the teacher. If students want their team to succeed, they must help their teammates to learn the material. They must encourage their teammates to do their best, expressing norms that learning math is important, valuable, and fun. Students are allowed to work together after the teacher's lesson but may not help each other with quizzes, so every student must know the mathematics. Students usually work in pairs and compare answers, discuss any discrepancies, and help each other with any roadblocks. They teach their teammates and assess their strengths and weaknesses because this is the only way they can help them succeed on the quizzes. Since team scores are based on students' improvement over their own past records, any student can be the team "star" in a given week, either by scoring well above his or her past record or by getting a perfect paper (which always produces a maximum score regardless of students' past averages).

STAD is more a method of organizing the classroom than a method of teaching mathematics; teachers use their own lessons and other materials. Worksheets and quizzes are available for most grade levels and subjects up to algebra 1 and geometry (see the resources at the end of this chapter), but most teachers use their own materials to supplement or replace these materials.

Teams-Games-Tournaments (TGT). Teams-Games-Tournaments, originally developed by David DeVries and Keith Edwards, was the first of the Johns Hopkins' cooperative learning methods. It uses the same teacher presentations and teamwork as STAD but replaces the quizzes with weekly tournaments, in which students compete with members of other teams to contribute points to their team scores. Students compete at three-person "tournament tables" against others with similar past records in mathematics. A "bumping" procedure changes students' tournament tables each week and keeps the competition fair. The winner at each tournament table brings six points to his or her team, regardless of which table it is; this means that low achievers (competing against other low achievers) have the same opportunities to contribute points to their teams as do high achievers. Middle scorers earn four points for their teams, and low scorers, two points. As in STAD, high-performing teams earn certificates or other forms of team recognition.

TGT has many of the same dynamics as STAD but adds a dimension of excitement contributed by the use of games. Teammates help one another prepare for the games by studying worksheets and explaining problems to one another. The same materials used in STAD are also used in TGT; the STAD quizzes are used as games in TGT. Many teachers prefer TGT because of its element of fun and activity, whereas others prefer the more purely cooperative STAD, and some combine the two.

Team Assisted Individualization (TAI). Team Assisted Individualization is the newest of the Johns Hopkins' cooperative learning methods and is quite different from STAD and TGT. It shares with these methods the use of four-member mixed-ability learning teams and certificates for high-performing teams, but where STAD and TGT use a single pace of instruction for the class, TAI combines cooperative learning with individualized instruction.

In TAI, students are placed in an individualized sequence according to a placement test and then proceed at their own rates. In general, team members work on different units. Each unit includes an instruction sheet reviewing the teacher's lesson, a set of skill sheets introducing skills step by step, two parallel checkouts, and a final test. Students work four problems on each skill sheet and then check with a teammate, who has their answer sheet. If all four items are correct, they may go on to the next skill sheet; otherwise, they may ask a teammate for explanations or help and then go on to work four more items on the same page. After completing all skill sheets, students take a ten-item checkout, which is also scored by a teammate. If they get at least eight items correct, they may go to the final unit test. These are taken without teammate help and are scored by student monitors. Because they know that they cannot help their teammates on the final tests, students make certain that their teammates have really mastered the material before they take the tests. At the end of each week, teachers total up the number of units completed by all team members and give certificates or other rewards to teams that exceed a criterion score based on the number of final tests passed, with bonus points for perfect papers and completed homework.

Since students take responsibility for checking each other's work and managing the flow of materials, the teacher is able to spend most of the class time presenting lessons to small groups of students drawn from the various teams who are working at the same point in the mathematics sequence. For example, the teacher might call up a decimal group, present a lesson on decimals, and then send students back to their teams to work on decimal problems. Then the teacher might call the fractions group, and so on.

TAI has many of the same motivational dynamics as STAD and TGT. Students are motivated to encourage and help one another to succeed because they want their teams to succeed. Individual accountability is assured because the only score that counts is the final test score, and students take final tests without teammate help. All students can succeed, because all have been placed according to their level of prior knowledge; it is as easy (or difficult) for a low achiever to complete three subtraction units in a week as it is for a higher-achieving classmate to complete three long-division units.

However, the individualization that is part of TAI makes it different from STAD and TGT. Individualization is especially appropriate in elementary arithmetic because so many arithmetic concepts build on earlier concepts. If the earlier concepts were not mastered, the later ones will be difficult or impossible to learn. For example, a student who cannot subtract or multiply will fail to master long division. A student who does not understand fractional concepts will fail to understand what a decimal is, and so on.

In TAI, as in any individualized mathematics program, students work at their own levels, so if they lack prerequisite skills they can build a strong foundation before going on. Also, if students can learn more rapidly, they need not wait for the rest of the class. However, individualized instruction in mathematics has generally failed to increase student mathematics achievement (Miller, 1976; Schoen, 1986), probably because the teacher's time in earlier models was entirely taken up with checking work, managing materials, and so on, leaving little time for actually teaching students. In TAI, students handle all the routine checking and management, so the teacher can spend most of the class time teaching. This difference, plus the motivation and help provided by students in their cooperative teams, probably accounts for the strong positive effects of TAI on student achievement, which contrast sharply with the effects of earlier individualized programs (research on TAI is described later).

Unlike STAD and TGT, TAI does depend on a specific set of instructional materials. As of this writing, these materials cover concepts from addition to an introduction to algebra and have been used for primary instruction in grades 2 through 8 and as remedial instruction at the high school and community college level. The TAI materials include specific concept lesson guides suggesting methods of introducing mathematical ideas, making extensive use of demonstrations, manipulatives, and examples. The curricular emphasis in TAI is on rapid, firm mastery of algorithms in the context of conceptual understanding and on applications of mathematical ideas to solution of real-life problems.

Research on Student Team Learning in Mathematics

The principal goal of Student Team Learning is to accelerate the achievement of all students. Of all cooperative learning models, the Student Team Learning methods have been most thoroughly evaluated and have been consistently found to be effective in well-controlled studies in regular public schools. These studies have taken place in urban, rural, and suburban schools over periods of 3 to 30 weeks, at grade levels from 3 to 9. Three studies of STAD (Huber, Bogatzki, and Winter, 1982; Madden and Slavin, 1983; Slavin and Karweit, 1984) found that students in this program gained significantly more in mathematics than did control students. In one of these studies (Slavin and Karweit, 1984), STAD was used over an entire school year in inner-city ninth grade mathematics classes and was found to increase student performance on a standardized mathematics test (the Comprehensive Test of Basic Skills) significantly more than either a mastery learning group or a control group using the same materials. Three studies of TGT (Edwards, DeVries, and Snyder, 1972; Edwards and DeVries, 1974; Hulten and DeVries, 1976) also found significantly higher achievement in TGT than in control classes, although one four-week study (Edwards and DeVries, 1972) found no significant differences.

The largest effects of Student Team Learning methods have been found in studies of TAI. Five studies (two in Slavin, Leavey, and Madden, 1984; one in Slavin, Madden, and Leavey, 1984a; and two in Slavin and Karweit, 1985) found substantially greater learning of mathematics computation in TAI than in control classes, while one study (Oishi, Slavin, and Madden, 1983) found no differences. Across all six studies, the TAI classes gained an average of twice as many grade equivalents in computation as traditionally taught control classes. For example, in one 18-week study in Wilmington, Delaware, the control group gained 0.61 grade equivalents in mathematics computation, whereas the TAI classes gained 1.65 grade equivalents. These experimental-control differences were still substantial (though somewhat smaller) a year after the students were in TAI. Results for mathematics concepts and applications have been positive but less consistently so than for computations. TAI has equally accelerated the achievement of students who were high, average, and low in prior performance.

Student Team Learning methods have had positive effects on many important outcomes in addition to mathematics achievement. One of these is race relations. Three studies of STAD, three of TGT, and two of TAI all found that these methods increased the number of friendships between black and white students, as indicated by sociometric measures. One of the STAD studies found that these positive effects lasted into the following school year, when students were no longer in the classes in which they had experienced the program (Slavin, 1983a). A study of TAI found that this method substantially improved white students' ratings of their black classmates' mathematics abilities (Slavin, 1985). Studies of all three Student

Team Learning methods have documented significant gains in student self-esteem, liking of mathematics, attendance, and behavior (Slavin, 1983a). These methods (especially TAI) are often used in classes containing mainstreamed students with academic handicaps and have been effective both for increasing these students' achievements and behavior and for increasing their acceptance by their classmates (Slavin, Madden, and Leavey, 1984b).

Component analyses of Student Team Learning methods have revealed that James Coleman was right in his prediction that if cooperative teams were brought into the classroom, students would express norms favoring academic efforts, would be motivated to achieve, and would, in fact, achieve more than would students in the traditional competitive system. Two elements have turned out to be critical to the effectiveness of cooperative learning: *group rewards* and *individual accountability* (Slavin, 1983b). That is, there must be some reward given to groups based on the achievements of their members, and there must be no way for students to ride on their teammates' coattails. Although students can help each other learn, their individual, unaided performances must be the basis for team success, so that the only way for the team to succeed is to concentrate on the learning of every team member. If students arrive at a single group solution to problems or complete one group worksheet, there is a danger that more able students will do all the work and provide answers rather than explanations to their groupmates. Cooperative learning methods in which students are simply asked to work with one another without any group goal or in which students complete a single worksheet or group solution have not been more (or less) effective than traditional teaching in increasing student achievement (Slavin, 1983b; Davidson, 1985).

Methodology: Using Student Team Learning in the Mathematics Classroom

The remainder of this chapter presents a guide to the use of Student Teams Achievement Divisions (STAD). For information on training and materials for STAD, TGT, and TAI, see the resources at the end of this chapter.

Overview

STAD is made up of five major components: class presentations, teams, quizzes, individual improvement scores, and team recognition. These components are described next.

Class Presentations. Material in STAD is initially introduced in a class presentation. This is most often a lecture-discussion conducted by the teacher but could include audio-visual presentations. Class presentations in STAD differ from usual teaching only in that they must be clearly focused on the STAD unit. In this way, students realize that they must pay careful attention during the class presentation because doing so will help them to do well on the quizzes, and their quiz scores determine their team scores.

Teams. Teams are composed of four or five students who represent a cross-section of the class in academic performance, sex, and race or ethnicity. The major function of the team is to prepare its members to do well on the quizzes. After the teacher presents the material, the team meets to study worksheets or other material. The worksheets may be materials obtained from the Johns Hopkins Team Learning Project (see the resources at the end of this chapter) or they may be teacher-made. Most often, the study takes the form of students discussing problems together, comparing answers, and correcting any misconceptions if teammates make mistakes.

The team is the most important feature of STAD. At every point, emphasis is placed on team members doing their best for the team and on the team doing its best to help its members. The team provides the peer support for academic performance that is important for effects on learning, and the team provides the mutual concern and respect that are important for effects on such outcomes as intergroup relations, self-esteem, and the acceptance of mainstreamed students.

Quizzes. After one to two periods of teacher presentation and one to two periods of team practice, the students take individual quizzes designed to test the knowledge gained from class presentations and during team practice. Students are not permitted to help one another during the quizzes. This ensures that every student is individually responsible for knowing the material.

Individual Improvement Scores. The idea behind the individual improvement scores is to give each student a performance goal that the student can reach—but only if he or she works harder and performs better than in the past. Any student can contribute maximum points to his or her team in this scoring system, but no student can do so without showing definite improvement over past performance. Each student is given a "base" score, derived from the student's average performance on similar quizzes. Then students earn points for their teams based on how much their quiz scores exceed their base scores (see page 87).

Team Recognition. Teams that meet certain preestablished criteria may earn certificates or other forms of recognition. Many teachers use bulletin board displays, class newsletters, special privileges, small prizes, or other rewards to emphasize the idea that doing well as a team is important.

Preparing to Use STAD

Materials. STAD can be used with curriculum materials specifically designed for Student Team Learning and distributed by the Johns Hopkins Team Learning Project, or it can be used with teacher-made materials. As of this writing, Johns Hopkins' materials are available in mathematics for grades 2 through 8, plus high school consumer mathematics, algebra 1, geometry, and elementary metrics education. An example of these materials (for algebra 1) appears at the end of this chapter.

However, it is quite easy to make your own materials. Simply make a worksheet, a worksheet answer sheet, and a quiz for each unit you plan to teach. Each unit should occupy three to five days of instruction.

Assigning Students to Teams. A team in STAD is a group of four or five students who represent a cross section of the class in past performance, race or ethnicity, and sex. For example, a four-person team in a class that is one-half male, one-half female and three-quarters white, one-quarter minority might have two boys and two girls, of whom three are white and one is minority. The team would also have a high performer, a low performer, and two average performers. Of course, "high performer" is a relative term; it means high for the class, not high compared to national norms.

Students are assigned to teams by the teacher rather than by choosing teams themselves, because students tend to choose others like themselves. You may take likes, dislikes, and "deadly combinations" of students into account in your assignments, but do not let students choose their own teams. Instead follow these steps:

1. *Make copies of team summary sheets.* Before you begin to assign students to teams, you will need to make one blank copy of a team summary sheet (Figure 3-1) for every four students in your class.

Figure 3-1 *Team Summary Sheet*

Team Name _____

Team Members	Weeks							
	1	2	3	4	5	6	7	8
_____								
_____								
_____								
_____								
_____								
Total Team Score ____								
÷ Number of Members ____								
Average Team Score ____								

2. *Rank students.* On a sheet of paper, rank the students in your class from highest to lowest in past performance. Use whatever information you have to do this—test scores are best and

grades are good, but your own judgment is fine. It may be difficult to be exact in your ranking, but do the best you can.

3. *Decide on the number of teams.* Each team should have four members if possible. To decide how many teams you will have, divide the number of students in the class by four. If the number is divisible by four, the quotient will be the number of four-member teams you should have. For example, if there are 32 students in the class, you would have eight teams with four members each.

   If the division is uneven, the remainder will be one, two, or three. You will then have one, two, or three teams composed of five members. For example, if there are thirty students in your class, you would have seven teams; five would have four members and two would have five members.

4. *Assign students to teams.* When you are assigning students to teams, balance the teams so that (a) each team is composed of students whose performance levels range from low to average to high and (b) the average performance level of all the teams in the class is about equal. To assign students to teams, use your list of students ranked by performance. Assign team letters to each student. For example, in an eight-team class you would use the letters A through H. Start at the top of your list with the letter A; continue lettering toward the middle. When you get to the last team letter, continue lettering in the opposite order. For example, if you were using the letters A–H (as shown in Figure 3-2), the eighth and ninth students would be assigned to Team H, the tenth to Team G, the next to Team F, and so on. When you get back to letter A, stop and repeat the process from the bottom up, again starting and ending with the letter A.

Figure 3-2 Assigning Students to Teams

	RANK ORDER	TEAM NAME
High-Performing Students	1	A
	2	B
	3	C
	4	D
	5	E
	6	F
	7	G
	8	H
Average-Performing Students	9	H
	10	G
	11	F
	12	E
	13	D
	14	C
	15	B
	16	A
	17	
	18	
	19	A
	20	B
	21	C
	22	D
	23	E
	24	F
	25	G
	26	H
Low-Performing Students	27	H
	28	G
	29	F
	30	E
	31	D
	32	C
	33	B
	34	A

Notice that two of the students (17 and 18) in Figure 3-2 are not assigned at this point. They will be added to teams as fifth members, but first the teams should be checked for race or ethnicity and sex balance. If, for example, one fourth of the class is black, approximately one student on each team should be black. If the teams you have made based on performance ranking are not evenly divided on both ethnicity and sex (they will hardly ever be balanced on the first try), you should change team assignments by trading students of the same approximate performance level but of different ethnicity or sex between teams until a balance is achieved.

5. *Fill out team summary sheets.* After you have finished assigning all students to teams, fill in the names of the students on each team on your team summary sheets, leaving the "team name" line blank. If your have six or more teams, divide them into two leagues. Teachers often name the two leagues (for example, American and National).

Determining Initial Base Scores. Base scores represent students' average scores on past quizzes. If you are starting STAD after you have given three or more quizzes, use students' average quiz scores as base scores. Otherwise, use students' final grades from the previous year, as follows:

LAST YEAR'S GRADE	INITIAL BASE SCORE
A	90
A–/B+	85
B	80
B–/C+	75
C	70
C–/D+	65
D or F	60

Getting Started

- Teach your first lesson (1 to 2 periods).

- Announce team assignments and have students move their desks together to make team tables. Tell students that they will be working in teams for several weeks and may earn certificates or other rewards based on their team's total performance. Allow students ten minutes to decide on a team name.

- Let students study worksheets in their teams (1 to 2 periods).

- Give the first quiz.

The first week of STAD is the hardest, but most students will settle into the pattern by the second week. Some students may complain about the teams to which they were assigned, but almost all students find a way to get along with their teammates by the second week. Do not change team assignments after you have announced them except under extreme circumstances, because it is students' realization that they will be in their team for several weeks that gets them to work on getting along with their teammates instead of complaining about them.

Schedule of Activities

STAD consists of a regular cycle of instructional activities, as follows:

- *Teach:* Present the lesson.

- *Team Study:* Students work on worksheets in their teams to master the material.

- *Test:* Students take individual quizzes.

- *Team Recognition:* Team scores are computed based on team members' improvement scores, and a class newsletter or bulletin board recognizes high-scoring teams.

These activities are described in detail next.

Teach

Time: 1 to 2 class periods

Main idea: Present the lesson.

Materials: Your lesson plan

Each lesson in STAD begins with a class presentation. In your lesson, stress the following (adapted from Good, Grouws, and Ebmeier, 1983):

- *Briefly review* any prerequisite skills or information.

- Stick close to the *objectives* that you will test.

- Focus on *meaning*, not memorization.

- Actively *demonstrate* concepts or skills, using visual aids, manipulatives, and many examples.

- Frequently *assess* students' comprehension by asking many questions.

- Have all students *work the problems* or *prepare answers to your questions.*

- Call on students *at random* so that they will never know whom you might ask a question—this makes all students prepare themselves to answer. *Do not* just call on students who raise their hands.

- *Do not give long class assignments* at this point—have students work one or two problems or prepare one or two answers; then give them feedback.

- Always *explain why* an answer is correct or incorrect unless it is obvious.

- *Move rapidly* from concept to concept as soon as students have grasped the main idea.

- *Maintain momentum* by eliminating interruptions, asking many questions, and moving rapidly through the lesson.

Team Study

Time: 1 to 2 class periods

Main idea: Students study worksheets in their teams.

Materials: Two worksheets and two answer sheets for every team

During team study, the team members' tasks are to master the material you presented in your lesson and to help their teammates master the material. Students have worksheets and answer sheets they can use to practice the skill being taught and to assess themselves and their teammates. Only two copies of the worksheets and answer sheets are given to each team to force teammates to work together, but if some students prefer to work alone or want their own copies, you may make additional copies available. During team study, stress the following:

- Have teammates move their desks together or move to team tables.

- Hand out worksheets and answer sheets (two of each per team) with a minimum of fuss.

- Tell students to work together in twos or threes within their teams of four or five. If they are working problems, each student in a pair or three should work the problem and then check with his or her partner(s). If anyone misses a question, his or her teammates have a responsibility to explain it. If students are working on short-answer questions, they may quiz each other, with partners taking turns holding the answer sheet or attempting to answer the questions.

- Emphasize to students that they are not finished studying until they are sure that their teammates will make 100 percent on the quiz.

- Make sure that students understand that the worksheets are for studying—not for filling out and handing in. That is why it is important for students to have the answer sheets to check themselves and their teammates as they study.

- Have students *explain* answers to one another instead of just checking each other against the answer sheet.

- When students have questions, have them *ask a teammate* before asking you.

- While students are working in teams, *circulate through the class*, praising teams that are working well, sitting in with each team to hear how they are doing, and so on.

Test

Time: $\frac{1}{2}$ to 1 class period

Main idea: Individual quiz

Materials: One quiz per student

- Distribute the quiz and give students adequate time to complete it. *Do not let students work together on the quiz*; at this point students must show what they have learned as individuals. Have students move their desks apart if this is possible.

- After students have finished the quiz, either allow them to exchange papers with members of other teams or collect the quizzes to score after class. Be sure to have the quizzes scored and team scores figured in time for the next class if possible.

Team Recognition

Main idea: Figure individual improvement scores and team scores, and award certificates or other team rewards.

Figuring Individual and Team Scores. As soon as possible after each quiz, you should figure individual improvement scores and team scores and award certificates or other rewards to high-scoring teams. If possible, the announcement of team scores should be made in the first period after the quiz. This makes the connection between doing well and receiving recognition clear to students, which increases their motivation to do their best.

Improvement Points. Students earn points for their teams based on the degree to which their quiz scores (percent correct) exceed their base scores, as follows:

QUIZ SCORE	IMPROVEMENT POINTS
More than 10 points below base score	0
10 points below to 1 point below base score	10
Base score to 10 points above base score	20
More than 10 points above base score	30
Perfect paper (regardless of base score)	30

Figuring improvement points is not at all difficult, and when you get used to it, it will take only a few minutes. The purpose of base scores and improvement points is to make it possible for all students to bring maximum points to their teams, whatever their level of past performance. Students understand that it is fair that each student should be compared to his or her own level of past performance, as all students enter class with different levels of skills and experience in mathematics.

Put the points you have calculated on each student's quiz as follows (for example): base score = 83; quiz score = 90; improvement points = 20. Put the improvement points on students' team summary sheets (see Figure 3-3).

Team Scores. To figure team scores, add the students' improvement points and divide the total by the number of team members who were present, rounding off any fractions (.5 is rounded up). See Figure 3-3. Note that team scores depend on improvement scores rather than on raw scores on the quiz.

Figure 3-3 *Example of Team Scoring*

Team Name _____

Team Members	Weeks							
	1	2	3	4	5	6	7	8
Frank	30							
Otis	10							
Ursula	20							
Rebecca	30							
Total Team Score_____	90							
÷ Number of Members____	4							
Average Team Score_____	23							

Criteria for awards. There are two levels of awards given based on average team scores. These are as follows:

CRITERION (TEAM AVERAGE)	AWARD
18	Greatteam
23	Superteam

Note that all teams can achieve the awards; teams are not in competition with one another.

You should provide some sort of recognition or reward for achieving at the "Greatteam" or "Superteam" level. Attractive certificates for each team member may be used, with a large, fancy certificate ($8\frac{1}{2}$ inches by 11 inches) for Superteams and a smaller one for Greatteams. Many teachers make bulletin board displays listing the week's Superteams and Greatteams or displaying photographs of the successful teams. Others prepare one-page newsletters, give students special buttons to wear, or let Superteams and Greatteams line up first for recess or receive other special privileges. Use your imagination and creativity, and vary rewards from time to time; it is more important that *you* are excited about students' accomplishments than that you give large rewards.

Returning the First Set of Quizzes

When you return the first set of quizzes (with the base scores, quiz scores, and improvement points) to the students, you will need to explain the improvement point system. In your explanation, emphasize the following:

1. The main purpose of the improvement point system is to give everyone a minimum score to try to beat and to set that minimum score based on past performance so that all students will have an equal chance to be successful if they do their best academically.

2. The second purpose of the improvement point system is to make students realize that the scores of all the people on their team are important—that all members of the team can earn maximum improvement points if they do their best.

3. The improvement point system is fair because everyone is competing only with himself or herself—trying to improve his or her own performance—regardless of what the rest of the class does.

Recomputing Base Scores

Every marking period (or more frequently, if you like), recompute students' average quiz scores on all quizzes and assign students new base scores.

Changing Teams

After five or six weeks of STAD, reassign students to new teams. This gives students on low-scoring teams a new chance, allows students to work with other classmates, and keeps the program fresh.

Grading

When it comes time to give students report-card grades, the grades should be based on the students' actual quiz scores, not on their improvement points or team scores. If you wish, you might make the students' team scores a part of their grades; up to 20 percent of their grades might be determined by team scores. If your school gives separate grades for effort, you might use team and/or improvement scores to determine the effort grades.

STAD: One Teacher's Response

John Strebe, a mathematics teacher at Mount Hebron High School in Ellicott City, Maryland, uses STAD with his low-achieving algebra 1, part A, classes and his honors geometry classes. He has made many adaptations of STAD, including occasionally teaching individual team members (not necessarily high achievers) and having them teach their teammates. He has also added team homework checking and team review for exams to the basic STAD model. Following are some of his comments on what it is like to use STAD as a basic organizational plan for secondary mathematics:

"I have used STAD for two years in algebra 1, part A, and honors geometry with 9th and 10th grade students. For me, the use of cooperative-learning techniques has resulted in a low-stress, highly exciting environment for learning and teaching. The emphasis has shifted from me, the teacher, struggling with them, the students, to one where all of us work together to accomplish the goal of learning. Everyone in class is enjoying the learning process and none of us would choose 'traditional' teaching and learning methods over STAD. Last year the students enthusiastically voted in favor of cooperative-learning methods over others they had experienced, with 70 of 71 students choosing STAD. This year the students are just as enthusiastic, expressing disappointment when we do not meet in 'our teams' during the class period. When both students and the teacher enjoy a learning method and as much or more material is covered in the course of a year, then you have a learning style that should be shared with all those who desire to teach. Teaching is fun, and cooperative learning helps me to continue to let it be fun.

"My classes are run with STAD as the underlying structure. On a given day, the students will either sit in pairs or in their teams. I will teach from the board in both setups. In the middle of a class I may decide that it is now time to change from one arrangement to the other. The kids have learned to do that in about 30 seconds. Throughout the course the students maintain a constant team consciousness. Once the students have selected their own team name and that name is posed on the sideboard standings sheet, a group identity rapidly develops. This identity becomes a dynamic for learning in the classroom, a dynamic that has become an essential tool in my teaching. New groups are formed after 6 to 8 weeks, enabling students to interact meaningfully with most of the students in the class.

"One of the exciting results of using STAD is that I know my students better, since I interact with them individually. As a result, I am able to have more of an impact on them in the nonmath areas of their lives. This closer relationship seems to improve our communication and definitely increases the effectiveness of my teaching."

STUDENT TEAM LEARNING*
Subject: Algebra 1
Worksheet: 19. Direct and Inverse Variation
Topics:
- Direct variation
- Inverse variation
- Word problems involving direct or inverse variation

Directions: In the following problems, y varies directly as x.

1. x is 8 when y is 2. If x is 4, what is y?

2. x is 12 when y is 4. If x is 24, what is y?

3. x is 9 when y is 3. If x is 12, what is y?

---

* Reprinted with permission from the Center for Research on Elementary and Middle Schools, The Johns Hopkins University.

4. x is -4 when y is 36. If x is 4, what is y?

5. x is 20 when y is 5. If x is 5, what is y?

6. y varies directly as the square of x. x is 3 when y is 2. If x is 6, what is y?

7. x varies directly as the square of y.
   x is 10 when y is 4. When x is 5, what is y?

8. Peaches are sold by weight. If 12 pounds of peaches cost $2.00, how much would 18 pounds cost?

9. Five kilometers are represented on a map by 3 centimeters. If you measure on the map and find Upton 12 centimeters from Downville, how far apart are the cities?

10. A population of amoebas varies as the square of the surface area it occupies. In a dish with 100 square centimeters there are 20,000 amoebas. How many would there be in a dish with 200 square centimeters?

Directions: In the following problems, y varies inversely as x.

11. y is 12 when x is 4. If x is 2, what is y?

12. y is 18 when x is 18. If x is 6, what is y?

13. y is 3 when x is 9. If x is 27, what is y?

14. y is 7 when x is 21. If x is 7, what is y?

15. y is 2 when x is 24. If x is 8, what is y?

16. y varies inversely as the square of x.
    y is 4 when x is 2. If x is 4, what is y?

17. y varies inversely as the square of x.
    y is 9 when x is 9. If x is 3, what is y?

18. Two rectangles have the same area. The *width* of rectangle A is twice the width of rectangle B. If the *length* of rectangle A is 12 inches, what is the *length* of rectangle B?

19. If a team of 5 workers can make 24 yo-yos per hour, how

long would it take 15 workers to make 24 yo-yos?

20. The loudness of a sound (in decibels) varies inversely as the square of the distance from the source. Ten meters away, the sound of a trombone is measured at 100 decibels. What would it be at 100 meters?

Directions: The following problems may involve direct or inverse variation. Decide which is involved and solve the problem.

21. If you double the length of a rectangle but leave the width the same, what happens to the area?

22. If you double the length of a rectangle but the area stays the same, what happens to the width?

23. If each side of a square is multiplied by x how is the area increased?

24. It takes 8 librarians 6 hours to shelve 1000 books. How much time would it take 12 librarians to do the job?

25. It takes 8 librarians 6 hours to shelve 1000 books. How long would it take them to shelve 1500 books?

26. It takes 8 librarians 6 hours to shelve 1000 books. How many books could 2 librarians shelve in the same time?

27. $E = mc^2$. If E remains the same and c doubles, what happens to m?

28. Milton has enough money to buy 24 gumballs at 4¢ each, but he decides to buy some 6¢ jawbreakers instead. How many jawbreakers can he afford?

29. On a map, 8 miles are represented by 6 inches. It is 52 miles from Hereford to Thereville. How many inches would be shown on the map to represent this distance?

30. The brightness of a light diminishes as the square of the distance from its source. If a light is measured at 12 brightness units 6 meters from the source, how far from the source would it be if it measured 3 brightness units?

Answers to Worksheet 19: Direct and Inverse Variation

1. $y = 1$
2. $y = 8$
3. $y = 4$
4. $y = -36$
5. $y = \frac{5}{4}$
6. $y = 8$
7. $y = 1$
8. $3.00
9. 20 kilometers
10. 80,000 amoebas
11. $y = 24$
12. $y = 54$
13. $y = 1$
14. $y = 21$
15. $y = 6$
16. $y = 1$
17. $y = 81$
18. 24 inches
19. $\frac{1}{3}$ hour (20 min.)
20. 1 decibel
21. It doubles.
22. It is halved.
23. It is multiplied by x^2.
24. 4 hours
25. 9 hours
26. 250 books
27. m is quartered
28. 16 jawbreakers
29. 39 inches
30. 12 meters

Student Team Learning*
Subject: Algebra 1
Game/Quiz: 19. Direct and Inverse Variation

Directions: In the following problem, *y* varies directly as *x*.

1. *x* is 12 when *y* is 3. If *x* is 24, what is *y*?

2. *x* is 15 when *y* is 5. If *x* is 30, what is *y*?

3. *x* is 16 when *y* is 2. If *x* is 32, what is *y*?

4. *x* is –5 when *y* is 45. If *x* is 5, what is *y*?

5. *x* is 18 when *y* is 3. If *x* is 3, what is *y*?

6. *y* varies directly as the square of *x*.
    x is 4 when *y* is 3. If *x* is 8, what is *y*?

7. *x* varies directly as the square of *y*.
    x is 20 when *y* is 16. When *x* is 10, what is *y*?

8. Grapes from the market are sold by the pound.
    If 4 pounds cost $6.00, how much would 9 pounds cost?

9. Fifteen miles are represented on a map by 2 inches. If
    you measure on the map from point *A* to point *F* and
    find them to be 6 inches apart, how many miles are
    represented?

10. A certain kind of fish will vary directly in length
    according to the fish tank's volume squared. If the fish
    reached a maximum length of 15 centimeters in a 10-
    gallon tank, what length will it reach if transferred to a
    20-gallon tank?

Directions: In the following problems, *y* varies inversely as *x*.

11. *y* is 27 when *x* is 9. If *x* is 3, what is *y*?

12. *y* is 24 when *x* is 24. If *x* is 4, what is *y*?

* Reprinted with permission from the Center for Research on Elementary and Middle
Schools, The Johns Hopkins University.

13. y is 5 when x is 25. If x is 125, what is y?

14. y is 9 when x is 36. If x is 9, what is y?

15. y is 3 when x is 15. If x is 5, what is y?

16. y varies inversely as the square of x.
    y is 16 when x is 8. If x is 16, what is y?

17. y varies inversely as the square of x.
    y is 4 when x is 4. If x is 2, what is y?

18. Two table tops have the same area. The width of the first table top is twice that of the second table top. If the length of the first table top is 5 feet, what is the length of the second table top?

19. If an assembly line of 14 workers can manufacture 150 pens in an hour, how long would it take 21 workers to make the same number of pens?

20. The amount of material that a mechanized weaving loom can weave varies directly as the square of the amount that a human can weave. In an hour, a human can weave 2 yards and a machine can weave 6 yards. How much will the machine weave in 3 hours if the human wove 5 yards?

Directions: The following problems may involve direct or inverse variation. Decide which is involved and solve the problem.

21. The area of a right triangle is $A = \frac{1}{2}bh$, where A is the area, b is the base, and h is the height.
    If you double the base of a right triangle but leave the height the same, what happens to the area?

22. If you triple the height of a right triangle but keep the area the same, what happens to the base?

23. The area of a circle is $A = \pi r^2$, where A is the area and r is the radius. If you double the radius of a circle, what happens to the area?

24. It takes 6 painters 20 hours to paint 25 rooms. How much time would it take 4 painters to do the job?

25. It takes 6 painters 20 hours to paint 25 rooms. How many rooms can they paint in 60 hours?

26. It takes 6 painters 20 hours to paint 25 rooms. How many rooms could 3 painters paint in the same amount of time?

27. $P=I^2R$. If I is doubled and R is halved, what happens to P?

28. The shopper had only enough money to buy eight items at $4.00 each. How many items could the shopper buy at $.50 each?

29. A map has a scale of 6 centimeters for every 16 miles. If a road on the map is 45 centimeters long, how long is the actual road?

30. The force of gravity between two objects varies inversely as the square of the distance between the two objects. If a force from earth of 30 units acts upon the moon in its present position, how many units of force would act upon it if it were twice as far away?

Answers to Game/Quiz 19: Direct and Inverse Variation

1. $y=6$

2. $y=10$

3. $y=4$

4. $y=-45$

5. $y=\frac{1}{2}$

6. $y=12$

7. 2

8. $13.50

9. 90 miles

10. 60 centimeters

11. $y=81$

12. $y=144$

13. $y=1$

14. $y=36$

15. $y=9$

16. $y=4$

17. $y=16$

18. 10 feet

19. 40 minutes ($\frac{2}{3}$ hours)

20. $37\frac{1}{2}$ yards

21. It doubles.

22. It is divided by 3.

23. It is quadrupled.

24. 30 hours

25. 75 rooms

26. $12\frac{1}{2}$

27. It doubles.

28. 64 items

29. 120 miles

30. 7.5 units

Resources

Teacher's Manuals, Materials, and Training

1. For Student Team Learning (STAD, TGT), teacher's manuals and curriculum materials for mathematics, grades 2–8, plus metric education, consumer mathematics, algebra 1, and geometry, are available from:

    > The Johns Hopkins Team Learning Project
    > Center for Research on Elementary and Middle Schools
    > Johns Hopkins University
    > 3505 North Charles Street
    > Baltimore, Maryland 21218
    > 301-338-8249

    Training (usually 1- to 2-day workshops) is also provided by the Johns Hopkins Team Learning Project. For information on training, call 301-338-8249 or write to the preceding address.

2. For Team Assisted Individualization (TAI) curriculum materials and training, contact:

    > Charlesbridge Publishing
    > 85 Main Street
    > Watertown, Massachusetts 02172
    > 800-225-3214

    TAI is distributed by Charlesbridge Publishing under the name Team Accelerated Instruction. They provide training in this method as well as teacher's manuals, implementation guides, and curriculum materials. For information on training in TAI, call 301-363-1948.

Research Reviews

1. For Student Team Learning:

Slavin, R.E. 1983. *Cooperative learning.* New York: Longman.

———. 1983. When does cooperative learning increase student achievement? *Psychological Bulletin* 94: 429–445.

————. 1982. *Cooperative learning in student teams: What research says to the teacher.* Washington, D.C.: National Education Association.

2. For Team Assisted Individualization:

Slavin, R.E. 1985. Team assisted individualization. In *Learning to cooperate, cooperating to learn,* edited by R.E. Slavin et al., 177–209. New York: Plenum.

————. 1987. Cooperative learning and individualized instruction team up to improve elementary mathematics achievement. *Arithmetic Teacher* 35: 14–16.

3. For cooperative learning in mathematics:

Davidson, N. 1985. Small-group learning and teaching in mathematics: A selective review of the research. In *Learning to cooperate, cooperating to learn,* edited by R.E. Slavin et al., 211–30. New York: Plenum.

References

Coleman, J. 1961. *Adolescent Society.* New York: Free Press.

Davidson, N. 1985. Small-group learning and teaching in mathematics: A selective review of the research. In *Learning to cooperate, cooperating to learn,* edited by R.E. Slavin et al., 211–230. New York: Plenum.

Edwards, K.J., and D.L. DeVries. 1972. Learning games and student teams: Their effects on student attitudes and achievement. Report No. 147, Center for Social Organization of Schools, The Johns Hopkins University.

————. 1974. The effects of Teams-Games-Tournaments and two structural variations on classroom process, student attitudes, and student achievement. Report No. 172, Center for Social Organization of Schools, The Johns Hopkins University.

Edwards, K.J., D.L. DeVries, and J.P. Snyder, 1972. Games and teams: A winning combination. *Simulation and Games* 3, 247–69.

Good, T.L., D. Grouws, and H. Ebmeier, 1983. *Active mathematics teaching.* New York: Longman.

Huber, G.L., W. Bogatzki, and M. Winter. 1982. Kooperation als Ziel schulischen Lehrens und Lernens. Tubingen, West Germany: Arbeitsbereich Padagogische Psychologie der Universitat Tubingen.

Hulten, B.H., and D.L. DeVries. 1976. Team competition and group practice: Effects on student achievement and attitudes. Report No. 212, Center for Social Organization of Schools, The Johns Hopkins University.

Madden, N.A., and R.E. Slavin. 1983. Effects of cooperative learning on the social acceptance of mainstreamed academically handicapped students. *Journal of Special Education* 17: 171–82.

Miller, R.L. 1976. Individualized instruction in mathematics: A review of research. *Mathematics Teacher* 69: 345–351.

Oishi, S., R.E. Slavin, and N.A. Madden. 1983. Effects of student teams and individualized instruction on cross-race and cross-sex friendships. Paper presented at the annual meeting of the American Educational Research Association, April, Montreal.

Schoen, H.L. 1986. Research report: Individualizing mathematics instruction. *Arithmetic Teacher* 33: 44–45.

Slavin, R.E. 1983a. *Cooperative learning.* New York: Longman.

———. 1983b. When does cooperative learning increase student achievement? *Psychological Bulletin* 94, 429–45.

Slavin, R.E., and N.L. Karweit. 1984. Mastery learning and student teams: A factorial experiment in urban general mathematics classes. *American Educational Research Journal* 21: 725–36.

———. 1985. Effects of whole-class, ability grouped, and individualized instruction on mathematics achievement. *American Educational Research Journal* 22: 351–67.

Slavin, R.E., M. Leavey, and N.A. Madden. 1984. Combining cooperative learning and individualized instruction: Effects of student mathematics achievement, attitudes, and behaviors. *Elementary School Journal* 84: 409–22.

Slavin, R.E., N.A. Madden, and M. Leavey. 1984a. Effects of Team Assisted Individualization on the mathematics achievement of academically handicapped and nonhandicapped students. *Journal of Educational Psychology* 76, 813–19.

———. 1984b. Effects of cooperative learning and individualized instruction on mainstreamed students. *Exceptional Children* 84: 434–43.

Robert E. Slavin *is the Director of the Elementary School Program at the Center for Research on Elementary and Middle Schools, The Johns Hopkins University. Dr. Slavin has done extensive research on such topics as cooperative learning, ability grouping, school and classroom organization, desegregation, and mainstreaming. He is the author or coauthor of ten books, including* Cooperative Learning; Educational Psychology: Theory into Practice; School and Classroom Organization; *and* Effective Programs for Students at Risk. *Dr. Slavin is currently the president of the International Association for the Study of Cooperation in Education (IASCE).*

4.

Using Cooperative Learning in Math

DAVID W. JOHNSON AND ROGER T. JOHNSON

The Nature of Cooperative Learning

In a third grade classroom, the teacher assigns his students a set of math story problems to solve. He assigns his students to groups of three, ensuring that there is a high-, medium-, and low-performing math student and both male and female students in each group. The instructional task is to solve each story problem correctly and to understand the optimal strategies for doing so. Each group is given a set of story problems (one copy for each student) and a set of three "role" cards. Each group member is assigned one of the roles. The *reader* reads the problem aloud to the group. The *checker* makes sure that all members can explain how to solve each problem correctly. The *encourager* encourages all members of the group in a friendly way to participate in the discussion, sharing their ideas and feelings.

Within this lesson, *positive interdependence* is structured by the group agreeing on (1) the answer and (2) the strategy for solving each problem. Since the group certifies that each member (1) has the correct answer written on his or her answer sheet and (2) can correctly explain how to solve each problem, *individual accountability* is structured by having the teacher pick one member's answer sheet at random to score and to select group members randomly to explain how to solve the problems. The *collaborative skills* emphasized in the lesson are checking and encouraging. Finally, at the end of the period the groups *process* their functioning by answering two questions: (1) What is something each member did that was helpful for the group? (2) What is something each member could do to make the group even better tomorrow?

The preceding math teacher is using cooperative learning so that students work together to accomplish shared goals. Having students work cooperatively, competitively, or individualistically has important implications for the success of math instruction. In a *cooperative* learning situation, students' goal achievements are positively correlated; students perceive that they can reach their learning goals if and only if the other students in the learning group also reach their goals. Thus, students seek outcomes that are beneficial to all those with whom they are cooperatively linked. While students work on math assignments, they discuss the material with the other members of their group, explain how to complete the work, listen to each other's explanations, encourage each other to try to understand the solutions, and provide academic help and assistance. When all the students in the group have mastered the material, they look for another group to help until everyone in the class understands how to complete the assignments.

Cooperative learning may be contrasted with competitive and individualistic learning. When math lessons are structured competitively, students work against each other to determine who is best. Students are graded on a curve, which requires them to work faster and more accurately than their peers. In an individualistic lesson, students work by themselves to accomplish learning goals unrelated to those of their classmates. Individual goals are assigned each day, students' efforts are evaluated on a fixed set of standards, and rewards are given accordingly. Each student has a set of materials and works at his or her own speed, ignoring the other students in the class. While it is possible to give a lecture and conduct a whole-class discussion in a cooperative manner, traditionally most whole-class instruction has underlying competitive elements where students try to give the "best" answer and then are expected to work individualistically on worksheets and textbook assignments.

Basic Elements of Cooperative Learning

Simply placing students in groups and telling them to work together does not in and of itself promote greater understanding of mathematical principles and ability to communicate one's mathematical reasoning to others. There are many ways in which group efforts may go wrong. Less-able members may "leave it to George" to complete the group's tasks (the *free-rider effect*), and more-able group members may expend less effort to avoid the *sucker effect* or may engage in all the explanations and elaborations (the *rich-get-richer effect*) (Johnson and Johnson, n.d.). Group efforts can be characterized by self-induced helplessness, diffusion of responsibility and social loafing, ganging up against a task, reactance, dysfunctional divisions of labor, inappropriate dependence on authority, destructive conflict, and other patterns of behavior that debilitate group performance (Johnson and Johnson, n.d.). It is only under certain conditions that group efforts may be expected to be more productive than individual efforts. Those conditions are:

1. *Teachers must clearly structure positive interdependence within each student learning group.* Positive interdependence is the perception that one is linked with others in a way that one cannot succeed unless the others do (and vice versa) and, therefore, that their work benefits one and one's work benefits them. All cooperative efforts begin with the realization that "we sink or swim together" and that the efforts of each group member to learn math must be coordinated. Positive interdependence may be structured through common goals or rewards, being dependent on each other's resources, assigning specific roles to each member, or a division of labor.

2. *Students must engage in promotive (face-to-face) interaction while completing math assignments.* Promotive interaction includes assisting, helping, supporting, and encouraging each other's efforts to achieve. There are cognitive processes and interpersonal dynamics that occur only when students get involved in explaining their mathematical reasoning to each other. This includes orally explaining how to solve problems, discussing the nature of the concepts being learned, teaching one's knowledge to classmates, and connecting present learning with past learning.

3. *Teachers must ensure that all students are individually accountable to complete math assignments and promote the learning of their*

groupmates. Students must know that they cannot "hitchhike" on the work of others. Common ways to structure individual accountability include giving individual tests to each student and randomly selecting one group member's product to represent the entire group.

4. *Students must learn and frequently use required interpersonal and small-group skills.* Learning groups are not productive unless members are skilled in cooperating with each other. Many students have never been required to collaborate in learning situations and, therefore, lack the needed social skills for doing so. Cooperative skills include leadership, decision-making, trust-building, communication, and conflict-management skills. These skills have to be taught just as purposefully and precisely as academic skills. Procedures and strategies for teaching students social skills may be found in Johnson (1986, 1987), Johnson and F. Johnson (1987), and Johnson, Johnson, and Holubec (1986).

5. *Teachers must ensure that the learning groups engage in periodic and regular group processing.* Group processing is the discussion of how well group members are learning math and maintaining effective working relationships among members. Group members need to reflect on how well the group is functioning, describe what member actions are helpful and unhelpful, and make decisions about what behaviors to continue or change. In essence, group processing is metacognitive thought about the functioning of the group. Group processing enables learning groups to focus on group maintenance, facilitates the practice and learning of social skills, and ensures that students receive feedback on their participation in the group. Some of the keys to successful processing are allowing sufficient time for it to take place, making it specific rather than vague, and reminding students to use their social skills while they process (Johnson, Johnson, and Holubec, 1986, 1988).

Traditionally structured student learning groups often do not function effectively. There are many ways that groups can become dysfunctional. Structuring productive learning groups takes some understanding of the five basic elements just discussed and some understanding of the teacher's role in structuring learning situations cooperatively.

Cooperative Learning and Learning Mathematics

If mathematics instruction is to help students think mathematically, understand the connections among various math facts and procedures, and be able to apply formal mathematical knowledge flexibly and meaningfully, cooperative learning must be employed in math classes for at least six reasons (Johnson and Johnson, 1983, n.d.; Johnson, Johnson, and Maruyama, 1983; Johnson et al., 1981).

1. *There can be little doubt that cooperation promotes higher achievement in math class than do competitive and individualistic efforts.* In our meta-analyses (Johnson and Johnson, n.d.; Johnson et al., 1981), we found a number of studies comparing cooperative, competitive, and individualistic learning experiences on achievement in math classes. Seventeen studies comparing cooperative and competitive math learning contained enough data to compute effect sizes (average effect size = 0.55) and 31 studies contained enough data to compute effect sizes to compare cooperative and individualistic math learning (average effect size = 0.68). These results indicated that students at the 50th percentile in the cooperative condition would perform at the 71st percentile in the competitive condition and at the 75th percentile of the individualistic condition. In addition to the successful solution of math problems and the mastery and retention of math facts and principles, cooperative learning, compared with competitive and individualistic learning, promotes more frequent discovery and use of higher-quality reasoning strategies, the generation of new ideas and solutions (that is, process gain), and the transferring of the math strategies and facts learned within the group to subsequent problems considered individually (that is, group-to-individual transfer).

2. *Mathematical concepts and skills are best learned as part of a dynamic process with active engagement on the part of students.* Math learning needs to be active rather than passive.

Traditional math instruction has been based on the assumption that students were passive absorbers of information, who stored what they knew in easily retrievable fragments, as a result of repeated practice and reinforcement. Active learning requires intellectual challenge and curiosity, which are best aroused in discussions with other students.

3. *Mathematical problem solving is an interpersonal enterprise.* The method of instruction is inseparable from curriculum content. Talking through math problems with classmates helps students understand how to solve the problems correctly. Explaining reasoning strategies and analyses of problems to classmates often results in discovering insights, using higher-level reasoning strategies, and engaging in metacognitive thought. Furthermore, such discussion requires students to use the language of mathematics and demonstrate their mathematical reasoning to others. The meanings of technical words are best grasped as one uses them in discussions with classmates. Overt statement of one's reasoning allows classmates (and the teacher) to check assumptions, clarify misconceptions, and correct errors in understanding and application of mathematical principles. Silent students are deprived of such monitoring and feedback. To internalize mathematical concepts and apply them to new situations, students must express their thoughts and discuss alternative strategies, approaches, and explanations. Students have more chances to explain their reasoning in small groups than in whole-class discussions. Furthermore, most students are more comfortable speculating, questioning, and explaining concepts in order to clarify their thinking in small groups.

4. *Math learning groups have to be structured cooperatively.* Students will not engage in the intellectual interchange required for learning mathematics within competitive and individualistic structures. Students competing with each other or learning individualistically tend to cut off communication, avoid sharing analyses and strategies with each other, and even deliberately communicate false information to each other. When students are asked to work together and discuss math assignments, a carefully implemented cooperative structure

must be used. Structuring math lessons cooperatively ensures that students have to explain to each other what they are learning, learn each other's points of view, give and receive support from classmates, and help each other dig below the superficial level of understanding of the math they are studying. Cooperative learning increases the likelihood that all students will engage in the components of problem solving (such as formulating problems, analyzing problems and selecting strategies to solve them, finding solutions, and verifying and interpreting solutions), explore different approaches and strategies to solving any one problem, and observe peers modeling how various problems may be solved.

5. *By working cooperatively within math classes, students gain confidence in their individual math abilities.* Within cooperative groups, students receive considerable encouragement and support in their efforts to learn mathematical processes, strategies, and concepts. The promotive interaction and experience of actively working through math problems with others helps students gain confidence in their individual math abilities. When students work together in cooperative groups, furthermore, they tend to like each other, support and encourage each other's efforts to solve math problems successfully, provide help and assistance in doing so, value each other, and see each other as able in solving math problems. The positive peer relationships and perceptions of each other as being competent in math situations result in higher levels of math self-esteem and a sense of self-efficacy in approaching math problems.

6. *The choice of what math courses to take and what careers to consider is heavily influenced by peers.* If one's peers perceive certain classes as being inappropriate (such as home economics for males), then there is considerable resistance to taking them. Within cooperative learning situations (compared with competitive and individualistic ones) students tend to like and enjoy math more and be more intrinsically motivated to learn more about it continually. Students are more apt to like and enjoy math and want to take advanced math courses when math is taught cooperatively than when it is taught competitively or individualistically. This is especially important for

female and minority students. If large numbers of female and minority students are going to take advanced math courses and enter math-related careers, classmates must encourage and support their doing so.

The data on cooperative learning indicate that in order to work on math projects and become confident and successful mathematical problem solvers, students need to work cooperatively with others. Not only is problem-solving success and individual achievement higher in cooperative groups than in competitive or individualistic situations, but the more conceptual the learning and the more analysis required, the greater the necessity to discuss, explain, and elaborate what is being learned, all of which increases students' ability to communicate mathematically. The support, encouragement, assistance, and liking from classmates found within cooperative groups, furthermore, results in more positive attitudes toward mathematics and greater self-confidence in one's ability to solve problems mathematically.

Approaches to Cooperative Learning

There are two approaches to cooperative learning: conceptual and direct. Based on our theorizing and research, we have formulated a *conceptual application* that provides teachers with a conceptual framework consisting of general procedures and principles as to the nature of cooperative learning and how it may be used. Teachers then take their existing math lessons, materials, and curricula and adapt them to include cooperative learning. Lessons are uniquely tailored by teachers to their instructional needs, circumstances, subject areas, and students. Cooperative learning can thus be used with any math lesson with any age student. A *direct application* involves providing teachers with specific curriculum packages or specific strategies for use in detailed and structured ways. The curriculum packages from Johns Hopkins University and the procedures developed by Marilyn Burns (Groups of Four), Spencer Kagan (Co-Op, Co-Op), and Shlomo Sharan (Group Investigation Method) are examples of the direct approach. This chapter describes our conceptual application of cooperative learning.

The Teacher's Role in Implementing Cooperative Learning

A fifth-grade teacher is concerned with the higher-level problem-solving skills of her students. She randomly assigns her students to groups of three, ensuring that a high-, medium-, and low-achieving student is in each group. She informs students that they are an engineering team being asked to submit a proposal for the development of some land into an environmental park. The instructional task is to plan a city park that includes a playground. Students are to (1) plan the design of the park, specifying what materials and equipment will be needed (the total cost of these materials and equipment must be $5000 or less), (2) draw a picture of how the park will look (including a stream, several trees, and two hills), and (3) write a report describing their design and proposing that it be implemented. The groups are to make the park suitable for all age levels, usable in both day and night, usable in all seasons, safe, beautiful, cost-effective, and innovative. Each group is given a description of the task and a copy of a worksheet listing a variety of materials and equipment and their cost and some basic information about their city. Each student is assigned one of three roles: *accountant* (who makes sure that all group members can do the math computations), *architect* (who ensures that all members help lay out the park on a piece of tagboard), and *elaborator* (who relates the group work to previous math problems solved in class).

Students have three class periods to complete the tasks. While the groups work, the teacher quietly moves from group to group, observing the strategies the groups are adopting and assessing how well they are working together. At the end of each class session, the teacher announces the results of her observations and then asks the student groups to process how effectively they worked and how they can improve in the future.

Positive interdependence is structured by requiring one park plan from the group and structuring a division of labor through the assigned roles. All decisions must be made by consensus. Individual accountability is assured by picking one member at random to present each part of the group's plan to the class and by assigning each group member a role that is essential to the group's work. The processing of how well the group is functioning increases individual accountability as it provides a procedure for students to give each other feedback as to how effectively they are working within the group. The social skills taught were checking (ensuring that everyone can explain), encouraging participation, and elaborating. The processing of how well the group was functioning ensured that students would increase their social skills as a result of participating in the unit.

When using cooperative learning in math class, you, the teacher, function as both an academic expert *and* a classroom manager to promote effective group functioning (Johnson, Johnson, and Holubec, 1986, 1988). First, you specify the objectives for the lesson. Second, you make a number of preinstructional decisions. Third, after the lesson is planned, you explain to students the learning task, the positive interdependence, and the related instructions for working with each other. It is at this point that you teach the academic concepts, principles, and strategies that students are to master and apply. Fourth, while students work in groups, you monitor students' effectiveness in completing the assignment and in working together cooperatively. You provide task assistance (such as answering questions and teaching math skills and strategies) and assist students in increasing their interpersonal and small-group skills. You instruct students to look to their peers for assistance, feedback, reinforcement, and support. You expect students to interact with each other, share ideas and materials, support and encourage each other's academic achievement, orally explain and elaborate the concepts and strategies being learned, and hold each other accountable for learning. Finally, you evaluate students' achievement and help students process how well they cooperated with each other. A criteria-referenced evaluation system is used. Sounds simple? It is not. Here are some details.

Objectives

When you begin to plan a cooperative lesson, you need to specify two types of objectives: (1) an *academic objective* specified at the correct level for the students and matched to the right level of instruction, and (2) a *social skills objective* detailing what interpersonal and small-group skills are going to be emphasized during the lesson. A common error made by many teachers is to specify only academic objectives and to ignore the social skills objectives needed to train students to cooperate with each other.

In addition to these immediate objectives for the lesson, there are a number of long-range academic and attitudinal objectives. The *long-term academic objectives* include becoming a mathematical problem solver, learning to communicate mathematically, and learning to reason mathematically. The *attitudinal objectives* include:

1. Positive attitudes toward math

2. Confidence in one's ability to reason mathematically

3. Willingness to try various strategies and risk being wrong

4. Ability to accept frustrations that come from not knowing and willingness to persevere when solutions are not immediate

5. Attributing failure to not using the right strategy yet, rather than to not being competent

Confidence in one's ability to reason mathematically is considered a prerequisite for learning. Once lost, it is difficult to restore.

Decisions

Once you are clear about your long- and short-term objectives, some decisions have to be made. The first decision is *deciding on the size of learning groups.* Teachers experienced in using cooperative learning groups keep them small. Learning groups in math should be made up of two, three, or sometimes four students. The more inexperienced the students are in working cooperatively and the shorter the class period, the smaller the group should be. We prefer groups of three.

The second decision involves *assigning students to groups.* You may wish to assign students to learning groups that are heterogeneous or homogeneous in ability. When working on a specific skill, procedure, or set of facts, homogeneous groups may be useful. When working on problem-solving tasks and learning how to communicate mathematically, heterogeneous groups are most appropriate. When in doubt, assign one high-, medium-, and low-achieving student to each learning group. In addition, try to maximize heterogeneity in terms of ethnic membership, sex, and social class. Take special care in building a group where students who have special learning problems in math or who are isolated from their peers will be accepted and encouraged to achieve.

You will next need to *plan how long groups will work together.* Usually it is preferable to keep groups together for at least two or three weeks, so that eventually every math student works with every other classmate. Some teachers, however, assign students to groups that last a whole semester or even a whole academic year. In some schools, student attendance is so unpredictable that teachers form new groups each day.

Your next decision involves *how to arrange the room.* Move the furniture to the sides of the room and arrange each triad in a circle. You want students to sit close enough to each other that they can share materials and talk to each other quietly and maintain eye contact with all group members. Circles are usually best. You should have clear access lanes to every group. Common mistakes that teachers make in arranging a room are (1) to place students at rectangular tables where they cannot have eye contact with all other members or (2) to move several desks together, which may place students too far apart to communicate quietly with each other and share materials.

You need to decide *how instructional materials will be distributed among group members* so that all students participate and achieve. Especially when students are inexperienced in cooperating, you will want to distribute materials in ways that indicate the assignment requires a joint (not an individual) effort and that students are in a "sink or swim together" learning situation. Materials can be arranged like a jigsaw puzzle so that each student has part of the materials needed to complete the task or one copy of the materials may be given to each group to ensure that the students will have to work together.

Finally, you plan *whether or not to assign students specific role responsibilities.* To gain confidence and proficiency in math problem solving, students must experience the reward of arriving at solutions through their own efforts. Students must take an active role in solving math problems and not simply observe the teacher or other students leading the way. In order to ensure the active involvement of each student, teachers assign students specific roles and then rotate the roles daily so that all students play all the roles over a period of days. When students are young and not all the students can read well enough to comprehend the assigned problems, assigning the roles of *reader, explainer,* and *praiser* may be advisable. When all group members can read well, our favorite roles for math groups are *checker* (who ensures that all group members can explain how to arrive at an answer or conclusion), *accuracy coach* (who corrects any mistakes in another member's explanations or summaries), and *relater/elaborator* (who asks other members to relate current concepts and strategies to material studied previously). Assigning students such complementary and interconnected roles is an effective method of teaching cooperative skills and fostering positive interdependence.

Explaining the Academic Task and Cooperative Goal Structure

Once students have been assigned to triads, are seated close together, have the materials needed to complete the assignment, and understand their roles, you, the teacher, explain the assignment. First, you *explain the academic task* so that students are clear about the assignment and understand the objectives of the lesson. An assignment might be, for example, to identify all the ways to write the numbers from 3 to 15 as the sums of (consecutive) numbers. Then, with the whole class, present or review the concepts, facts, principles, and strategies they are expected to learn or apply. Direct teaching may take place at this point. Modeling problem-solving behavior for students to imitate in their cooperative groups is always a good idea, especially if it includes demonstrating that being temporarily perplexed is a natural state in problem solving. Pose a problem similar to (but smaller than) the ones they are expected to solve, explain the steps for solving the problem, and check students' understanding of your explanation. Make sure that students comprehend that (1) understanding the strategies required for solving the problems is more important than having the right answer and (2) problem solving is a process with solutions coming as a result of exploring situations, stating and restating questions, and devising and testing strategies over a period of time. Answer any questions students have about the concepts, facts, strategies, or procedures they are to learn or apply in the lesson.

Second, you *explain the positive goal interdependence.* Cooperative learning begins with a group goal. In a cooperative learning group, students are responsible for learning the assigned material, making sure that all other group members learn the assigned material, and making sure that all other class members learn the assigned material, in that order. You may ask the group to produce a single answer to a problem and arrive at consensus concerning the optimal strategy to be used. For example, you may ask students how many ways they can represent 28 with 10-rods and 1-units and ask them to do it twice, once with physical materials and once symbolically. In addition to group goals, positive interdependence may be strengthened by providing group rewards (such as giving bonus points if all members of a group reach a preset criterion of excellence), assigning complementary and interlocking roles, and jigsawing materials among group members.

Third, you *ensure that students understand that they are individually accountable for completing the assignment.* The purpose of the learning group is to maximize the learning of each member. Lessons need to be structured so that the level of each student's learning is assessed and groups provide members with the encouragement and assistance needed to maximize performance. Individual accountability may be structured by individually testing students, choosing a student at random to explain the group's answers and strategies to the class, or having each student teach what he or she knows to another student.

Next, you *explain the criteria for success,* ensuring that all students realize that a criterion-referenced evaluation system is being used, *structure intergroup cooperation* by giving additional bonus points if all members of the class reach a preset criterion for excellence, and *specify the behaviors you expect to see* while you observe the learning groups. Beginning behaviors are "stay with your group," "use quiet voices," and "take turns." Some general roles include *summarizer* (who restates the group's major conclusions or answers), *checker* (who ensures that all members can explain how to arrive at an answer or conclusion), *accuracy coach* (who corrects any mistakes in another member's explanations or summaries), and *relater/elaborator* (who asks other members to relate current concepts and strategies to material studied previously). Other roles or expected behaviors specifically relevant for math may include:

1. *Problem restater*: Tells students to get to know the problem by restating it in their own words. Students are to state the information provided and the information they seek.

2. *Elaborator*: Asks, "Does this problem remind us of any problem previously solved by the class?"

3. *Strategy suggester/seeker*: Suggests possible alternative strategies to use in solving the problem and/or asks others to do so. Asks, "What's another strategy we could use?"

4. *Approximator*: Asks, "What range of answer would be reasonable?" so that group members estimate and approximate the answer before solving it exactly.

5. *Review/Mistake Manager*: If the group missed the problem, asks, "What can we learn from this mistake?" If the group solved the problem correctly, asks, "How may our solution be improved?"

6. *Confidence builder*: Says, "We can do it!"

Monitoring and Intervening

After the lesson has been structured and students have been given their initial instructions, students begin exploring the problems and working cooperatively toward solutions. While students do so, you (the teacher) should observe each group to keep track of the successes and difficulties students are having in solving the problems and working together effectively. Carefully and systematically observing students working allows you to see how they are failing and, therefore, what they do not understand. You will be able to observe what strategies they have selected to solve the problems and why.

When it is needed, you provide students with assistance in (1) understanding the process and strategies of solving the math problems and (2) being effective in working cooperatively. When giving assistance, your objective is to get the groups working productively and independently. In essence, you become an intellectual and social skills coach who works with students as they engage in the process of thinking through math problems cooperatively. You will wish to ensure that members of each learning group understand the components of problem solving (that is, formulating the problem, analyzing the problem and selecting strategies for solving it, finding the solution, and verifying and interpreting the solution). Follow the rules that (1) you will not respond to a student's question unless all group members have their hands in the air and wish to ask the same question and (2) you will not give correct answers but rather will help students understand where they have made mistakes. Frequently, students embark on a single poor strategy to solve a problem without questioning its effectiveness. This practice guarantees that they will fail. You will need a set of questions to ask students to break their fixation on the strategy they are using and to help them consider other strategies. Three possible questions are:

1. *What are you doing?* This requires students to discuss the nature of the problem and the strategy they are using to solve it.

2. *Why are you doing it?* This requires students to explain why the strategy they are using is the most desirable one.

3. *How will it help?* This requires students to consider whether the strategy they are using is proving effective.

When helping a group, join the group at their eye level by pulling up a chair or kneeling, question the group members or provide a missing role function, and leave when the group members can function independently. You will also need to have some extensions of the problems to give to groups who finish before the rest of the class.

While monitoring the learning groups, teachers often find students who do not have the necessary cooperative skills and groups where members are having problems in working together. In these cases, the teacher should intervene to suggest more effective procedures and more effective student behaviors. Basic interpersonal and small-group skills may be directly taught (Johnson, 1986, 1987; Johnson and F. Johnson, 1987).

You will also wish to provide closure to the lesson. At the end of the lesson, ask students to face the front of the room and conduct a whole-class discussion in which you randomly pick students to (1) summarize how they solved the problems with the emphasis being on strategy chosen and why, rather than answers, and (2) elaborate by relating the problem solved to previous ones worked on or by giving students similar but slightly different problems to solve. Ask, "What strategy did your group use?" and "Did you consider other strategies and how did you decide on using this one?" Also ask, "Can you think of another problem you have solved that this one reminds you of?" At the end of the whole-class discussion, you may wish to summarize the major points in the lesson, answer any final questions students have, and pose additional challenges that extend the problems for the more interested and able students. Asking students to consider the strategies they used to solve the assigned problems and justify their selection of the strategy ensures that they engage in metacognitive consideration of the way they worked to discover which strategies are appropriate for solving a problem.

Evaluation and Processing

At the end of the lesson you will evaluate students' learning and give feedback as to how their work compares with the preset criterion of excellence. Qualitative as well as quantitative aspects of performance should be addressed. The learning groups then process, or assess, how well they worked together and plan how to improve their effectiveness in the future. Our two favorite questions for doing so are: "What actions helped the group work productively? What actions could be added to make the group even more productive tomorrow?" A common error of many teachers is to provide too brief a time for students to process the quality of their collaboration.

Inside Cooperative Learning Groups

In order for cooperative groups to function, students must interact with each other. Many teachers wonder, therefore, what student behaviors they should be looking for when they monitor cooperative learning groups in math class. Over the past ten years we have gathered hundreds of hours worth of data concerning what students say to each other while they learn cooperatively (Johnson and Johnson, 1983). These studies have included both elementary and secondary classrooms and have occurred in science, math, social studies, English, language arts, engineering, and physical education classes. Through these studies, combined with the work of other researchers, we now know a great deal about the nature of interaction that takes place within cooperative learning groups and what differentiates effective from ineffective cooperative learning groups.

The types of statements students make in cooperative learning groups generally fall into the following categories. First, students discuss the procedures by which they are to learn: "We're only supposed to do the odd-numbered problems." "Wait, it's my turn. I'll go next." Students reexplain instructions, give suggestions as to how the work should be approached, and clarify what order should be used in approaching the work. Teachers will find that they have to repeat instructions less frequently when students work in cooperative learning groups.

Second, students share their knowledge and reasoning. They give their ideas, argue for their conclusions, and provide their factual knowledge for others to benefit from. Examples are, "Here is how I got 37." "There are three reasons why I think this conclusion is best." "Here is why I choose *a*." Students compare, defend, and evaluate arguments in reaching a consensus as to what an answer should be. Students give explanations as to how math problems are worked.

Third, students ask each other questions that encourage oral rehearsal and rethinking of what they are learning. Examples are, "How did you get 14?" "Tell me how you did that." "Didn't we learn something related to this last week?" Asking such questions is helpful, since when students explain answers and relate what is being learned to previous learning, new insights are often achieved and new perspectives are frequently gained.

Fourth, students confirm each other's answers and reasoning when they are correct and disagree when they are not. Examples are, "That's a good idea." "I disagree." "I get a different answer." Continuous feedback concerning the accuracy of one's knowledge, the soundness of one's conclusions, and the soundness of one's reasoning is provided to each group member. Through such feedback and challenge, students' learning grows continuously.

Finally, students encourage each other to work harder and be more responsible. "You can do it!" "Just try!" "We'll help!" "Has everyone done their homework?"

Surprisingly, within well-structured cooperative learning groups, students rarely make negative comments to each other or discuss topics unrelated to their task.

While such oral interaction is going on, students can observe, imitate, and build on each other's reasoning strategies and processes; experience the encouragement, support, warmth, and approval of a number of classmates; have peers evaluate, diagnose, correct, and give feedback on their conceptual understanding; teach material to peers; be exposed to a diversity of ideas and strategies, more critical thinking, and creative responses while completing assignments; and have classmates encourage them to stay with the task and exert concentrated effort to achieve. It is no wonder that teachers frequently hear members of cooperative groups say, "This is fun!"

Getting Started

Implementing cooperative learning involves a structured, but complex, process. It is not easy. It can take years to become an expert. You are encouraged to start small by taking one math class or math unit and using cooperative learning procedures until you are comfortable and then expanding cooperative learning into other classes or units. There are simple ways, however, to start using cooperative learning procedures in math classes. You are using cooperative learning whenever you ask the class a math question such as, "Which is greater, $\frac{3}{4}$ or $\frac{2}{3}$? Why?" and tell students to turn to a partner and decide in two minutes on an answer that either partner can explain. Learning partners may be used to check each other's homework, prepare each other for a test, contribute different parts to solving a math problem, and think up alternative strategies to use in solving a math problem.

Teacher Professional Support Groups

To gain and maintain expertise in using cooperative learning within math class takes assistance and support from colleagues. You do not become proficient in using cooperative learning procedures by reading this chapter or even by attending a workshop. You become proficient and competent from using cooperative learning in your math classes. Sustained use of cooperative learning is ensured by a collegial support system within which you give and receive continuous and immediate in-class assistance in utilizing cooperative learning. You and your colleagues can have frequent discussions about the use of cooperative learning in math classes, model the use of cooperative learning for each other, coteach lessons with each other, help each other solve implementation problems, and provide help when it is needed and wanted.

Summary

Cooperative learning is essential if math teachers are to promote the goals of problem-solving competency, ability to communicate mathematically, ability to reason mathematically, valuing of mathematics, and self-confidence in one's ability to apply mathematical knowledge to new problem situations in one's world. Although competitive and individualistic assignments should at times be given (even though they place students in the role of being passive recipients of information), the dominant goal structure in math should be cooperative.

There are a number of fairly simply ways teachers may begin to use cooperative learning in math classes, including having students turn to their partners to decide on an answer to a question or having students work in pairs to check each other's homework and prepare each other for a test. Cooperative learning, however, involves far more than simply assigning students to groups and telling them to work together. There are many ways that groups can be nonproductive. In order to be cooperative, a lesson must include positive interdependence, face-to-face interaction among students, individual accountability, the use of collaborative skills, and the processing of how well the learning groups functioned. Any math lesson with students of any age may be taught cooperatively. All it takes is a teacher who is skilled in translating the old competitive and individualistic lessons into cooperative ones. When done correctly, cooperative learning tends to promote higher achievement, greater motivation, more positive relationships among students, more positive attitudes toward the subject area and the teacher, greater self-esteem and psychological health, greater social skills, and many other important instructional outcomes.

The teacher's role in structuring learning situations cooperatively involves clearly specifying the objectives for the lesson, placing students in learning groups and providing appropriate materials, clearly explaining the cooperative goal structure and learning task, monitoring students as they work, and evaluating students' performance. For cooperative learning groups to be productive, students must be able to engage in the needed leadership, communication, trust-building, and conflict-resolution skills. Teaching students the required interpersonal and small-group skills can be done simultaneously with teaching academic material. In order to sustain the long-term implementation and in-classroom help and assistance needed to gain expertise in cooperative learning, teachers need support groups made up of colleagues who are also committed to mastering cooperative learning. Good relationships among colleagues take as careful structuring and monitoring as do cooperative learning groups.

References

Cohen, E. 1985. *Designing groupwork*. New York: Teachers College Press.

Deutsch, M. 1962. Cooperation and trust: Some theoretical notes. In *Nebraska symposium on motivation*, edited by M. Jones. Lincoln, Nebr.: University of Nebraska Press.

Johnson, D.W. 1986. *Reaching out*, 3d ed.. Englewood Cliffs, N.J.: Prentice Hall.

———. 1987. *Human relations and your career*, 2d ed. Englewood Cliffs, N.J.: Prentice Hall.

Johnson, D.W., and F. Johnson. 1987. *Joining together: Group theory and group skills*. Englewood Cliffs, N.J.: Prentice Hall.

Johnson, D.W., and R. Johnson, 1974. Instructional goal structure: Cooperative, competitive, or individualistic. *Review of Educational Research*, 44: 213-40.

————. 1975. *Learning together and alone: Cooperation, competition, and individualization.* Englewood Cliffs, N.J.: Prentice Hall.

————. 1983. The socialization and achievement crisis: Are cooperative learning experiences the solution? In *Applied social psychology, annual 4,* edited by L. Bickman. Beverly Hills, Calif.: Sage Publications.

————. n.d. *Cooperation and competition: Theory and meta-analysis.* New York: Lawrence Erlbaum.

Johnson, D.W., R. Johnson, and E. Holubec. 1986. *Circles of learning,* rev. ed. Edina, Minn.: Interaction Book Company.

————, ed. 1987. *Structuring cooperative learning: Lesson plans for teachers.* Edina, Minn.: Interaction Book Company.

————, ed. 1988. *Cooperation in the classroom.* Edina, Minn.: Interaction Book Company.

Johnson, D.W., R. Johnson, and G. Maruyama, 1983. Interdependence and interpersonal attraction among heterogeneous and homogeneous individuals: A theoretical formulation and a meta-analysis of the research. *Review of Educational Research,* 52: 5–54.

Johnson, D.W., et al. 1981. Effects of cooperative, competitive, and individualistic goal structures on achievement: A meta-analysis. *Psychological Bulletin,* 89: 47–62.

Sharan, S., and Y. Sharan. 1976. *Small-group teaching.* Englewood Cliffs, N.J.: Educational Technology Publications.

Slavin, R. 1983. *Cooperative learning.* New York: Longman.

David W. Johnson is Professor of Educational Psychology with an emphasis in Social Psychology at the University of Minnesota. He is also a practicing psychotherapist. For the past 20 years Dr. Johnson has served as an organizational consultant to schools and businesses in such areas as cooperative learning, management training, team building, ethnic relations, and interpersonal and group skills training. He is the author of numerous articles and books, including The Social Psychology of Education; Learning Together and Alone: Cooperation, Competition, and Individualization; and Circles of Learning: Cooperation in the Classroom.

Roger T. Johnson is a professor in the Department of Curriculum and Instruction with an emphasis in Science Education at the University of Minnesota. Dr. Johnson has taught in kindergarten through eighth grade in self-contained classrooms, open schools, nongraded situations, cottage schools, and departmentalized (science) schools. He is also a well-known consultant in cooperative learning and ethnic relations. Dr. Johnson is the author of numerous articles and is coauthor with David Johnson of Learning Together and Alone: Cooperation, Competition, and Individualization and Circles of Learning: Cooperation in the Classroom.

5.

Cooperative Learning and Computers in the Elementary and Middle School Math Classroom

MARY MALE

Introduction

John Naisbitt's *Megatrends* (Naisbitt, 1982) describes the impact of high technology on the need for human interaction. With the move from an industrial society to an information age, many teachers feel an accompanying pressure to improve and increase communication skills of listening and sharing, decision making, and networking. The computer has the potential to provide an opportunity to provide both "high tech" and "high touch" experiences for students in math classrooms.

In this chapter, you will:

1. Review the essential ingredients that will make your cooperative computer groups successful both in accomplishing the math task you set for them with the computer and in discovering effective ways to work in a group.

2. Select the type of math activity for which you will be using the computer.

3. Design lessons or implement the sample lessons contained in the chapter.

Three cooperative learning strategies will be applied to the use of computers in the math classroom: *Learning Together*, developed by

Drs. David and Roger Johnson at the University of Minnesota (Johnson and Johnson, 1986) and described in Chapter 4; *Jigsaw*, developed by Dr. Elliot Aronson at the University of California, Santa Cruz (Aronson, 1978); and *Teams-Games-Tournaments*, developed by Dr. David DeVries at the Johns Hopkins University (Slavin, 1986) and described in Chapter 3. Although relatively little research has been done that has documented the effects of cooperative learning in computer-using classrooms, initial studies have documented the positive impact of cooperative learning in drill-and-practice computer use as well as in higher-order thinking skills (Johnson, Johnson, and Stanne, 1986; Webb, Ender, and Lewis, 1986).

Essential Ingredients of Cooperative Computer Lessons

The three cooperative learning strategies featured in this chapter are by no means the only cooperative learning strategies that can be applied to the instructional use of computers; in fact, you will want to invent your own, as other teachers have. In selecting or designing computer lessons in the math classroom, however, your success will be enhanced if you are sure to include the following five ingredients, considered essential by teachers who have used cooperative learning in other subject areas.

Assignment to Teams and Team Preparation

The purpose of team assignment is to assure a good heterogeneous mix of students, taking into account sex, race, cultural and language differences, problematic behaviors, and past performance (academic achievement in the subject area to be addressed). In the past, schools have made every effort to group students homogeneously—by chronological age, ability, and so on—with limited success. Cooperative learning offers teachers an opportunity to capitalize on the benefits of heterogeneity and to abandon the near-impossible task of finding homogeneous groups.

Some teachers prefer to use random assignment of students to teams, in order to keep team assignment simple and to demonstrate to students that they are expected to work together in groups, no matter where they are assigned. Assignment to teams can be as simple as having students count off or dealing a deck of cards.

Other teachers prefer a more structured approach, to take personality variables into account. Some teachers allow students to request one or two people to work with as team assignments are made, so that students have some choice and so does the teacher.

If students have not worked together before, some structured team-building activities will result in fewer problems later on (Anderson, 1988). A getting-acquainted activity—such as having students complete a computer-made crossword puzzle, designed by the teacher with clues about each person on the team—models the teacher's philosophy that how well students work together is as important as how much they learn. Two other examples of team-building activities include a team data base of personal characteristics about each team member or a team-designed poster or motto printed out by the computer. Many teachers, particularly in the upper grades, feel that team-building activities are awkward or take up too much time. These same teachers, however, later wish they had taken time in the beginning to establish good starting points for group work, rather than having to back up and solve problems.

Establishing Positive Interdependence

Positive interdependence is the feeling among team members that no one is successful unless everyone is successful. In the very beginning of the lesson, you must be able to answer the questions, "Why is it important for students to work together? Is there a group grade? Is there a bonus for superior group performance? Is it important for students to come up with a wide variety of ideas or possible solutions to a problem?" Your answers to these questions will communicate the level of interdependence and will shape the ways students interact with each other. If this group goal is *not* communicated directly, you may find that students begin to operate in traditional, individualistic or competitive ways out of habit.

Some techniques to communicate this feeling to students include:

- *Goal interdependence:* "You're not finished until everyone in the group can explain how to teach the turtle to polygon."

- *Task interdependence:* "Each of you will be an expert on a different subprocedure. Your team must agree on how to assemble the procedures into a finished Logo design."

- *Resource interdependence:* "I will give only one worksheet to the group. You must record your group's predictions of what the turtle will do on the worksheet."

- *Role interdependence:* "Each of you will have a job; one of you will be a checker, for example, to make sure that everyone can explain how they came up with that answer. I will be giving your group credit for how well each of you does your job."

- *Reward interdependence:* "If everyone on the team scores at least 10, then you can earn bonus points for your own grade."

Because students have had so much practice with the competitive and individualistic structures, this positive interdependence must be communicated clearly, concretely, and in advance of the group work. Otherwise, students may use their usual ways of working to get the job done, and this will result in problems for the group. For example, before you start the groups, establish why it is important to work in the groups; what is the payoff? "You will want to work closely with each other, so that your group grade will go up." "You will receive bonus points for your grade for every student who makes 100 percent in your group." "If your group does all of its work correctly, you can earn up to 15 minutes of free computer time."

Direct Teaching of Social Skills

Teachers who use cooperative learning make no assumptions about the social skills of their students; they may choose to teach these skills just as they would teach any other area of the curriculum or just as they would teach students how to use a computer. The direct teaching of social skills involves selecting the skills to be practiced in a cooperative computer lesson, defining the skills, discussing with students why the target skill is important, providing practice in using the skill by role-playing or brainstorming words or phrases that could be used, and monitoring to make sure that students continue to use the skill.

Each of the sample lesson plans includes different social or group skill roles. Some examples of these roles are:

Keyboarder: The person who enters text at the keyboard.

Recorder: The person who writes the group's ideas on paper.

Reporter: The person who reports to the whole class what the group has done.

Praiser: The person who makes his or her teammates feel good about contributing their ideas. This person says things like: "That was a good idea." "Thank you." "You did a good job on that."

Checker: The person who checks to make sure each person on the team can perform the skill, answer the questions, and so on. This person says things like: "How did you do that?" "Do you agree with that answer?" "Can you explain the steps you followed?"

Summarizer: The person who reviews all the group's ideas before the recorder writes them down or before the keyboarder enters them at the computer. This person says things like: "The ideas our group has come up with are...." "What I heard the group say was...." "We think that...."

Encourager: The person who encourages each person to participate. This person says things like: "What do you think about that answer, Fred?" "Do you agree with Fred's answer, Alice?" "We haven't heard your ideas yet, Juan."

Teachers select the social/group skill roles they want to teach and emphasize based on the skills they have observed or that they see are needed for particular kinds of tasks. As students master particular skills, those roles may be replaced with new ones. Logistical roles such as the following are also useful in some activities.

Mover: The person who puts the desks together.

Organizer: The person who makes sure the group has the materials it needs and turns in the group work to the teacher.

Timekeeper: The person who makes sure the group stays on task and uses its time wisely. This person also lets the group know how much time is left.

Networker: The person who checks with other groups to find more information or share ideas and resources.

Ensuring Individual Accountability

Once the teams have completed their work, how can you make sure that each group member participated? How do you make sure that no one group member dominated the group? What about hitchhikers? Structuring individual accountability is the surest way to guarantee ongoing group participation and satisfaction with the cooperative learning activities. Some examples of ways to build in individual accountability include:

- Individual quizzes

- Calling on students at random from each team to demonstrate a particular skill at the computer

- Collecting one student's paper at random from each team

In a cooperative computer activity, for example, each student must be able to explain, produce a printout, or score at a certain level on a quiz on his or her own. Each student must know, *in advance*, that he or she will be responsible individually for demonstrating mastery.

Each of the lesson plans includes a different technique to ensure individual accountability. The type of technique you select is less important than making sure you have provided some way of guaranteeing individual accountability. Most teachers use a variety of techniques to keep group members on their toes and motivated to participate.

Processing

The teacher's role in observing and assisting not only with the curriculum content questions, but also with issues about how well groups are functioning, emphasizes the importance the teacher places on group skills. The time for students and the teacher to process what they observed, what they learned, and how they want to improve is essential if the teacher wants students to behave as though, in the classroom, "we are all in this together, sink or swim." Along with team-building and preparation for teamwork, processing frequently gets shortchanged, which results in the need to take extra time as problems come up for the groups that they are unable to solve for themselves. Giving the class an opportunity to generate solutions for problems and to become aware of the behaviors and social skills that make the group work well frees the teacher from dealing with problems group by group.

How Do I Get Started?—General Design Principles for Cooperative Learning Computer Lessons in the Math Classroom

As you become familiar with the essential ingredients of cooperative learning and how they can be incorporated into your lessons, you will want to begin selecting software and applying the essential ingredients to the specific programs you will be using.

Selecting Software

Virtually any software program can be adapted for use in a cooperative learning lesson. In cooperative computer lessons, the same principles of software selection apply as in traditional, individualistic lessons. To get maximum results from the use of the computer as well as to benefit from the diversity of skills, interests, and abilities of the cooperative team, the following software selection criteria may be helpful.

Does the program make the user more powerful and productive than he or she would be without using the program? For example, a user can experiment with creating various mathematical outcomes using a spreadsheet program, performing instantly calculations that are time-consuming for a calculator (and a nightmare done with pencil and paper). With drill-and-practice programs in math, students can track their progress in mastering basic mathematical skills. Instant feedback, cues for correct solutions, and game formats make practice appealing.

Is the program adaptable? Can the user add his or her own math problems? Can the user change the rate of presentation, use of sound, or number of tries before cues are presented? The best way to ensure that software will be of enduring value and interest to students is if it is infinitely changeable to respond to new skills and situations. Many programs offer "miniauthoring" capability, so that the teacher (or even better, the students themselves) can create their own formats and content of the lessons. *Tic-Tac-Show*, for example, allows the user to put in his or her own questions and format the responses for fill-in-the-blank, true-false, or multiple-choice options. *Square Pairs* lets the user design his or her own "Concentration"-type game with varying complexity (up to five rows of four boxes each). *Math Blaster* can use the math problems of the user's choice in any of its four presentation formats.

Is the program easy to use for both teacher and student? No matter how valuable the purpose of the program may be, if the manual is long and incomprehensible, the chances are the program will remain on the shelf. Most teachers find it helpful to provide a simple, one-page reference guide to the commands needed to operate the program successfully, in order to refresh their own memories easily without needing to refer to the manual and to enable students to work independently.

Is the print clear and easy to read? When students are working in a group around the monitor, visibility and clarity of the print are particularly important, so that each student can participate. Examples of programs with large, easy-to-read print include *Math Blaster*, *Math Machine*, and *Milliken Math Sequences*.

Does the program provide cues to obtain the correct response if an incorrect answer is entered, and is the reinforcement for correct responses more powerful than the feedback for wrong answers? In trying out programs, be sure to test out the computer's reaction to wrong answers as well as the reinforcement for getting the correct ones. Many times students find the explosion for a wrong answer more entertaining than the "Way to go" for a correct answer. Some programs will not move on until the student has entered the correct answer, and no additional cues are provided. If the student knows all the correct answers already, what is the point of the drill? And if the student does not know the answers and gets no cues, how can this type of program be of any use?

These software criteria apply most directly to the use of drill-and-practice programs. Other types of software that are used with even more impressive results in a cooperative learning and math situation are *productivity tools* (such as spreadsheets), *simulations*, *problem-solving*, and *Logo*. Samples of lessons using these types of software are included in this chapter.

Preparing Materials

Regardless of the cooperative learning strategy (Learning Together, Jigsaw, or Teams-Games-Tournaments) you select, you will want to assemble some or all of the following in your computer lessons:

- The software program

- A simple one-page summary of the commands

- A blank data disk for each team, if the the team's work cannot be stored on the software program disk (for example, spreadsheet programs)

- The team's task sheet with clear instructions

- An observation sheet to use in monitoring the group skills for each team and/or for the whole class

- An individual quiz or way of measuring each student's contribution to the team effort

Sample Lessons

The five essential ingredients will be illustrated specifically within each of the cooperative learning strategies (Learning Together, Jigsaw, and Teams-Games-Tournaments) we have selected for computers in the math classroom (Male, Johnson, Johnson, and Anderson, 1986). As you begin to adapt and invent your own cooperative learning strategy, keep the essential ingredients in mind. They absolutely work, and they will reduce the number of problems you might have as you get started!

Learning Together Strategy

*Electronic Money**

This program has two modules. The first module explores some forms of money used over time and involves students in using the computer to simulate electronic money transactions. The second module simulates a family budget-management system. A quiz is included to evaluate student progress upon completion of the program.

Subject areas: Math or Social Studies

Grade Level: 6 and up

    I. Objectives:

        A. Students will be able to define terms related to money management.

        B. Students will be able to use knowledge of money systems to participate successfully in a money-management simulation.

    II. Materials needed: *Electronic Money* program disk, handouts, overheads (included with program), pencils.

    III. Time required: 1–3 hours.

---

* Minnesota Educational Computing Corporation, 3490 Lexington Ave., St. Paul, MN 55126.

IV. Procedures:

A. Preparation

1. Assemble and duplicate needed materials.

2. Make sure you know how to use *Electronic Money*. Try out the simulation. Review the teacher preparation section of the *Electronic Money* manual, page 16.

B. Set

1. Ask students how much money the people in the room have as a total. Generate a discussion on money—where it comes from and how it is used.

2. Tell students the objectives of the lesson and explain that they will be working in teams to practice money management and using the computer—just as many adults use computers at a bank or at home.

C. Input

1. Review the key vocabulary with students (pages 2–3 in the *Electronic Money* manual).

2. Follow the outline in the *Electronic Money* manual (pages 6–9) as you explain the key money management concepts using transparencies.

3. Demonstrate the *Electronic Money* program.

4. Assign students to heterogeneous "families" (teams).

5. Set the group goal. "You will be working together to master money management skills. It will be important to make sure each person in the "family" understands and can do the problems, because I will be giving an individual test at the end, and everyone in your family will receive the same grade."

6. Assign group roles (keyboarder, recorder, praiser, checker).

7. Distribute the task sheets.

D. Guided practice

1. Teams work through the activity sheet. The recorder lists the group's responses to turn in.

2. Teacher monitors performance of group roles and assists as appropriate if problems or questions arise.

3. Checker makes sure each person on the team agrees and understands how the group came up with the answer.

E. Closure

1. Teacher collects the task sheets and reviews them with students.

2. Teacher gives an individual quiz to check mastery of students.

3. Teacher leads a discussion on how well the groups worked, awards special recognition points, or provides other recognition or rewards for good teamwork and performance. The teacher asks questions such as: "What did your group do well?" "Were there any problems in your group?" "What could your group improve on next time?"

F. Independent practice

1. Students develop their own money management problems. Problems may be shared for future "family" activities.

2. Students take a field trip to a bank to learn more about money management, electronic funds transfers, loans and interest, and so forth.

ELECTRONIC MONEY
LESSON 2
HANDOUT #4*

Ordinary Family

Your group represents an ordinary American family. As a group, your job is to make sound decisions about how to spend your money during one pay period. After you have written down your choices on these sheets, you will have the opportunity to enter your choices into the computer using the program *Electronic Money*. The program will give you ending balances. The following chart reflects the status of your accounts before you start using the program.

Checking account balance:	$ 24.36
Savings account balance:	862.12
Bank card charge:	245.46 (min. pay. 30.00)
Sterling's charge:	126.45 (min. pay. 20.00)
North Slope Oil charge:	36.15 (min. pay. 10.00)
Disco Den charge:	23.50 (min. pay. 10.00)
Cash on Hand	22.31

Monthly Expenses	Decision	Amount
1. Your paycheck is electronically deposited to your checking account—$1410.50 after deductions. You normally try to save 10% (about $150) of every check.	1. a. transfer to savings: b. withdraw cash:	_____ _____

---

* Reprinted with permission from Minnesota Educational Computing Corporation.

2. You have a payment on a loan of $156.25 per month, which you may pay by automatic transfer or by check.

2. Make payment
   a. by check: _____
   b. by automatic transfer: _____
   c. make payment later: _____

3. You have purchased a personal computer; payment including tax is $354.29.

3. Make payment by check: _____

4. Your utility bills are paid by automatic transfer each month.
   Water and
   electricity: $48.83
   Heat: 62.50
   Telephone: 18.70
   Cable T.V.:   10.95
   Total Bill $140.98

4. Make payment
   a. by automatic transfer: _____
   b. make payment later: _____

5. Better get to the store for groceries. Two weeks' worth comes to $154.23.

5. Make a purchase
   a. cash: _____
   b. check: _____

6. Your gas tank nears empty and it costs $23.19 to fill it.

6. Make a purchase
   a. cash: _____
   b. check: _____
   c. North Slope charge: _____

7. You stop by the Disco Den to pick up three new record albums. They cost $23.50.

7. Make a purchase
   a. cash: _____
   b. Disco Den charge: _____

8. Your car payment comes due and you pay your car dealer by check in the amount of $108.50.

8. Make payment
   a. check: _____
   b. pay later: _____

9. You start thinking about school clothes and visit Sterling's Department Store. You spend $79.50 on jeans and shirts.

9. Make a purchase
   a. cash: _____
   b. check: _____
   c. bank card: _____
   d. Sterling's charge: _____

10. Monthly bills have arrived and you must decide what to do with them.

10. Make payment

Bank Card
charge: $245.46
min. pay: 30.00

   a. check: _____
   b. pay later: _____
   c. automatic transfer: _____

Sterling
charge: $126.45
min. pay: 20.00

   a. check: _____
   b. cash: _____
   c. automatic transfer: _____

11. You buy the rest of the month's groceries for $175.13.

11. Make a purchase
    a. check: _____
    b. cash: _____

12. Your car needs gas again—$25.17.

12. Make a purchase
    a. check: _____
    b. cash: _____
    c. North Slope charge: _____

13. A bad filling means a sudden trip to the dentist and a $22.50 bill.

13. Make a purchase
    a. check: _____
    b. cash: _____

14. If you are short of cash or if your checking account is low, you might want to do something about it.

14. Transfer funds
    a. savings to checking: _____
    b. checking to savings: _____
    c. draw on bank card: _____

15. Company arrives unexpectedly and a quick trip to the grocery store costs you $23.50.

15. Make a purchase
    a. cash: _____
    b. check: _____

16. Another tank of gas—hopefully the last one this month. $19.30—ouch!

16. Make a purchase
    a. cash: _____
    b. check: _____
    c. North Slope charge: _____

17. Are there any bills you didn't pay that need paying now?

17. Check back and decide what to do about them.

18. Aren't you glad payday is tomorrow?

Learning Together Strategy

Gertrude's Secrets*

Students learn skills of order and planning ahead while solving problems according to given rules or by guessing a secret rule. They play with sets of shapes or create their own with Gertrude the Go-Getter Goose.

Subject areas: Critical thinking and problem solving

Grade level: 2 and up

    I. Objectives:

        A. Students will be able to solve one- and two-difference puzzles, using attributes of color and shape.

        B. Students will be able to design their own games using the "Shape Edit" feature of the program.

    II. Materials needed: *Gertrude's Secrets* program disk, manual and/or simplified reference card.

    III. Time required: One class period per activity.

    IV. Procedures:

        A. Preparation

            1. Assemble needed materials.

            2. Practice using *Gertrude's Secrets;* become familiar with the commands to move around the screen and pick up and drop objects; visit each of the rooms. Try designing your own shapes.

        B. Set

            1. Ask students if they would like to try a different sort of guessing game. Using a basket of blocks of different shapes and colors, ask students which block should come next after you hold up a blue circle. When a student gets an answer

* The Learning Company, 6493 Kaiser Drive, Fremont, CA 94555.

correct (any blue shape or any colored circle), ask how he or she figured it out.

2. Tell students that they will be playing with Gertrude the Goose on the computer to solve similar kinds of puzzles. Tell students they will be working in teams to solve the puzzles.

C. Input

1. Using attribute blocks, demonstrate for students the concepts of color and shape and rule making.

2. As students suggest or solve attribute problems, ask them to do their thinking out loud.

3. Call on students to demonstrate.

4. Introduce Gertrude the Go-Getting Goose and show how the program works.

5. Assign students to heterogeneous teams.

6. Set the group goal. "You will need to agree among your group on what the next puzzle piece should be and where it should go, and you will need to work together to decide on the best strategy for solving the puzzles. Every team that wins six prizes from the Treasure Room will have their team banner flown on the bulletin board right next to Gertrude!"

7. Assign group roles (keyboarder, checker, praiser, reporter).

D. Guided practice

1. Students work in their teams to solve Gertrude's Secrets.

2. Teacher monitors each group to see how well the students are doing on the problems and how well the groups are working together.

E. Closure

1. Teacher calls on the reporter from each group to determine if their team banner is flown next to Gertrude.

2. Teacher leads a processing/debriefing discussion on observations made as teams worked. "What did you like best about the way your team worked together? Which secrets were the most fun to solve? Why? Did you have any disagreements in your team? How did you solve them?"

F. Independent practice

1. Teams decide on new shapes to add to the puzzles and challenge other teams to solve their puzzles.

2. Teacher extends difficulty level of attribute activities in team situations using manipulatives and worksheets.

Learning Together Strategy

Layer Cake*

Layer Cake is a variation of the old "Towers of Hanoi" puzzle, in which the object is to move a stack of blocks ranging in size from small on the top to large on the bottom from one post to another without placing a large block on a smaller one. The problem illustrates the concept of recursion, important in defining and understanding many mathematical processes.

Subject areas: Critical thinking and problem solving

Grade Level: 3 and up

I. Objectives:

A. Students will use concepts such as "bigger than" and "smaller than" to sequence steps in a problem solving activity.

* Apple Computer, Inc., 20525 Mariani Ave., Cupertino, CA 95014.

B. Students will be able to develop a strategy to move a set of rectangles (layers, increasing in size) from one place to another without putting a big rectangle on a small one.

II. Materials needed: *Mix and Match* disk, platter, and rectangles (optional), role sheet.

III. Time required: 1 hour.

IV. Procedure:

A. Preparation

1. Assemble needed materials.

2. Practice loading *Layer Cake* from the *Mix and Match* disk and become familiar with the program.

B. Set

1. Ask how many students like to solve mysteries. Explain that the program they will be working on is a version of an ancient mystery, the "Towers of Hanoi," and that with the help of their team, they will learn the quickest way to solve the mystery.

2. Tell students that developing practical solutions to brain-teasing problems is a skill that will be helpful all their lives.

C. Input

1. Model the process of moving layers (or rectangles) either with manipulatives or on the computer.

2. Ask a student to demonstrate on the computer.

3. Assign students to teams.

4. Assign group roles (keyboarder, recorder, praiser, and data summarizer). Model, explain, and/or

role-play the behaviors for each role. Distribute role sheet.

5. Set the group goal. "Each group that can come up with the strategy that can solve the Layer Cake problem in the fewest number of moves will get to eat a piece of a *real* layer cake. I may call on anyone in your group to share and explain your strategy, so it will be important that each team member understands."

D. Guided practice

1. Teams try a strategy first, noting how many moves it takes to get the layer cake from one platter to another. The recorder writes down the number of moves.

2. Teams experiment with different strategies, noting the results and keeping track.

3. Teacher circulates among the groups to help them test their hypotheses and observes for group skills.

E. Closure

1. Teacher asks the recorders to raise their hands as soon as they can explain how their team figured out the mystery.

2. Teacher comments on the number of different strategies tried.

3. Teacher summarizes the results of his or her observation of group skills and then asks the class what they learned by solving the mystery. "Did you do it faster in your group than you would have on your own?" "Are you ready for a harder problem next time, with the help of your group?"

F. Independent practice

1. Teacher gives each student 7 blocks and asks what are the least number of moves it would take to move the stack from one platter to another, without putting a big block on a little one. The teacher asks students to record their thought processes or what they say to themselves as they are solving the mystery.

2. Teacher leads a discussion of the types of problems to which this mystery could relate in other subjects or aspects of life.

Group Roles for *Layer Cake*

Keyboarder: enters the sequence of moves suggested by the team (all team members must agree before the move is entered).

Recorder: writes down the number of moves it takes to solve the mystery for each round.

Data Summarizer: writes down a formula that would describe the steps the group completed to solve the mystery in the shortest number of moves ("First, move the top layer to the middle platter. Then move the next layer to the third platter. Then take the next layer from the left platter and move it to the middle platter....").

Praiser: makes each person in the group feel good about suggesting a strategy to try. If there is disagreement, the praiser helps to resolve the differences.

Learning Together Strategy

Puzzle Tanks* (formerly Amazing Think Tanks)

Two tanks, each with a specific capacity, are filled and emptied as liquid is transferred to produce the requested amount of liquid in a storage tank. Lively graphics and animation are seen as problem-solving skills are developed. The number of tries to reach a solution are recorded. Four levels of difficulty.

Subject areas: Critical thinking and problem solving

Grade level: 3–8

I. Objectives:

A. Students will be able to solve problems related to storage capacity and combinations of amounts.

B. Students will be able to develop a problem-solving strategy for problems of this type, rather than trial and error.

II. Materials Needed: one copy of *Puzzle Tanks* disk for each computer, one worksheet per group, one role sheet for each student, pencils.

III. Time Required: 1 hour.

IV. Procedure:

A. Preparation

1. Assemble needed materials.

2. Practice several problems by filling tanks, moving liquids, and emptying tanks. Try out problems on different levels. How many moves does it take you to solve a problem?

B. Set

1. We've got a problem. We need 17 gallons of liquid. Our storage tanks hold 8 gallons and 9

* Sunburst, 39 Washington, Pleasantville, NY 10570.

gallons. How can we get 17 gallons into
the truck?

2. Now we need 41 gallons of liquid. Our storage
tanks hold 7 and 9 gallons. How can we get 41
gallons into the truck?

3. Today we'll work on solutions to problems. This
is a skill that will be helpful to you all your life.

C. Input

1. Demonstrate the process of filling, moving, and
emptying tanks to solve a problem with *Puzzle
Tanks*.

2. Ask students for ideas on how to solve a problem
in *Puzzle Tanks*. Develop a solution with the
whole class participating.

3. Assign students to teams.

4. Distribute worksheets and role sheets.

5. Discuss group roles of keyboarder, solution
seeker, summarizer, and encourager. Once in
their group, students each take one of the roles.
After a problem is solved, they are to rotate the
roles in their group.

6. Set the group goal. "Today your group is to solve
as many problems as possible. Each time I hear
the success music I will verify your solution by
initialing your worksheet. We will see how
many problems we can solve as a class. If we
solve ten problems today, all of you will get an
extra ten minutes of time at the computers."

D. Guided practice

1. Groups work on solving a problem.

2. Teacher observes effective strategies in groups
and group skills.

E. Closure

1. Groups report on the number of problems they solved. These are added together for a total for the class and recorded on a chart.

2. "What helped your group solve problems?" Group members discuss effective strategies.

3. Teacher reports on observations of good problem solving and good group skills.

4. Arrangements are made for extra computer time if the class total of solutions was ten or more.

F. Independent practice

1. Next week the class tries to outdo itself and solve more problems than it did the first session.

2. Extra points can be added next for solutions that are achieved with five or fewer tries.

(Lesson designed by Mary Anderson, Sterne School, San Francisco, CA.)

Worksheet for *Puzzle Tanks*

Amount of liquid needed _____

Number of tries _____

Did you solve the problem? _____ _____
                          Yes   No

Amount of liquid needed _____

Number of tries _____

Did you solve the problem? _____ _____
                          Yes   No

Group Roles for *Puzzle Tanks*

Keyboarder: enters the solutions suggested by the team (all team members must agree before the solution is typed).

Solution Seeker: asks each group member for his or her ideas about how to solve the problem.

Summarizer: explores ways to combine ideas, add one to another, or modify ideas.

Encourager: uses encouraging comments following members' contributions.

Jigsaw Strategy

Logo*

A computer language with no ceiling and no floor; appropriate for all ages of students. Students begin to learn programming through graphics with a "turtle." The sophisticated language progresses through the most advanced programming concepts.

Subject areas: Thinking and problem solving

Grade level: 3 and up

  I. Objectives:

    A. Students will be able to enter Logo commands to make a spider.

    B. Students will be able to teach the turtle a procedure called "spider."

    C. Students will be able to teach the turtle other procedures based on "spider."

* Apple Computer, Inc., 20525 Mariani Ave., Cupertino, CA 95014.

II. Materials needed: Logo program disk, file disks expert sheet, procedure sheet, Logo reference card (one per team).

III. Time required: 1 to 2 hours, depending on age and experience with Logo.

IV. Procedure:

A. Preparation

1. Assemble needed materials.

2. Make sure you know the basics of Logo (review the reference card) and can make a spider following the commands on the procedure sheet.

B. Set

1. Ask how many students think turtles are smart. Ask how many students think they are smarter than a turtle.

2. Tell students they will be working in teams to teach the turtle first to make a spider and then to make different versions of spiders. Tell students that teaching the turtle is one way of programming the computer, only it's more fun.

C. Input

1. Review the basic turtle commands and editing commands with students as a large group.

2. Call on students to demonstrate the commands to check for understanding of general Logo vocabulary.

3. Assign students to teams.

4. Distribute expert sheets and procedure sheets.

5. Give instructions: "First, you will be teaching the turtle the procedures that make up the spider. You will each have a role—keyboarder, checker, or praiser. Second, you will each become

an expert on one of the spider designs on the expert sheet. Decide who will be an expert on which design. Third, you will go to a meeting of experts with the same design as yours. You will be working with that group to decide on the best way to do the design as well as the best way to teach your teammates how to do the design."

6. Set the group goal. "Each team that can construct all three of the designs, no matter whom I call on, will get a "Turtle Tutor" button and will have 15 extra minutes of computer time. I will also be observing how well you are working together in both the expert groups and your team groups, and you can earn extra points for your team by doing your job well. Remember, you won't know whom I will call on to demonstrate the three designs, and I may call on all of you, so your group is not finished until each of you can do all the designs."

D. Guided practice

1. Students work in their teams to enter the basic spider design. Teacher observes for demonstration of group roles.

2. Students move to their assigned expert groups. Teacher moves from group to group assisting with the design and with ideas to teach the team as necessary.

3. Students return to their teams. Each student takes a turn demonstrating the design that they completed in the expert group and teaches the other teammates how to make the design. Students practice all three designs.

4. Teacher moves from team to team monitoring group roles and task mastery.

E. Closure

1. Teacher enters spider procedure with several bugs in it and calls on students to help debug the design.

2. Teacher calls on students to demonstrate the designs, making sure to call on at least one student from each group.

3. Teacher checks to make sure students remember the turtle commands and reviews the day's activities.

F. Independent practice

1. Teacher distributes the next Logo activity sheet for students to work on to review procedures mastered so far.

2. Teacher goes from group to group to make sure each student can do the three spider designs.

3. Teacher leads a discussion of how he or she saw the groups working, awards Turtle Tutor buttons, special recognition points, and extra computer time. Teacher asks questions such as "What did your group do well? Were there any problems in your group? What will your group do differently next time?"

Note: The MECC Activity Guide for Logo has excellent materials that lend themselves naturally to cooperative learning, either in the Jigsaw or Learning Together format. The guide is available from Minnesota Educational Computing Corporation, 3490 Lexington Ave., St. Paul, MN 55126.

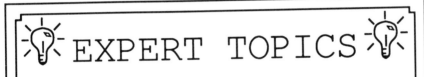

EXPERT TOPICS

1. MAKE A SMALLER SPIDER.
2. MAKE 2 SPIDERS STAND NEXT TO EACH OTHER.
3. MAKE A SPIDER STAND UPSIDE DOWN.

```
TO LEFTLEG            TO RIGHTLEG
FD 30                 FD 30
LT 90                 RT 90
FD 30                 FD 30
BK 30                 BK 30
RT 90                 LT 90
BK 30                 BK 30
END                   END
```

```
TO LEFTSIDE           TO RIGHTSIDE
LT 90                 RT 90
REPEAT 4              REPEAT 4
  [LEFTLEG RT 20]       [RIGHTLEG LT 20]
RT 10                 LT 10
END                   END
```

```
TO SPIDER
LEFTSIDE
RIGHTSIDE
FD 10 BK 10
END
```

Teams-Games-Tournaments Strategy

Math Blaster*

Math Blaster contains over 600 problems in addition, subtraction, multiplication, division, fractions, and decimals. Problems are grouped in families of facts and can be used with four different learning activities, including a fast-action arcade game. The program also has an easy-to-use editor to add more problems.

Subject area: Mathematics

Grade level: 2 and up

    I. Objectives:

        A. Students will be able to add, subtract, multiply, and divide (basic math facts).

        B. Students will be able to change decimals into fractions and vice versa.

        C. (If you have made up a data disk with your own problems, you can use any mathematic objective related to basic skill acquisition, for example, adding fractions.)

    II. Materials needed: *Math Blaster* program disk, data disk, worksheets, flashcards (optional), pencils.

    III. Time required: 1–3 hours, depending on the students' existing skill levels.

    IV. Procedure:

        A. Preparation

            1. Assemble needed materials.

            2. Make sure you know how to use *Math Blaster* (selecting the presentation mode you and/or the students want to use, time limits, and so on).

---

* Davidson & Associates, 3135 Kashiwa St., Torrance, CA 90505.

B. Set

   1. Tell students the objectives of the lesson.

   2. Tell students that they will be learning by playing games.

C. Input

   1. Model different strategies for mastering math facts (flashcards, worksheets, visualizing, and so on).

   2. Show how *Math Blaster* works, including the arcade game.

   3. Call on students to demonsrate.

   4. Assign students to teams.

   5. Assign group roles (praiser, checker, encourager, timekeeper).

   6. Set the group goal. "It will be important for you to work well together and speed up your recall on math facts, because the top-scoring teams will have an opportunity to win a "no homework" pass. On tomorrow's test, if everyone scores 100 percent, we will have a class celebration."

   7. Assign students to three-person (homogeneous) computer tournament tables.

   8. Rehearse moving from team to computer tournament table.

D. Guided practice

   1. Teams use worksheets, flashcards, or computers (as available) with *Math Blaster*'s Look and Learn, Build Your Skill, or Challenge Yourself.

   2. Teacher monitors performance of group roles.

   3. Teacher announces start of tournament.

4. Students move to computer tournament tables (can be on a staggered schedule if only a small number of computers are available).

5. Students take turns completing three rounds of *Math Blaster* arcade game (at appropriate skill levels and speed, if teacher is individualizing for high- and low-ranking tournament tables). Total scores are added to determine the winner at each table.

6. High-scoring student takes 6 points back to his or her team; medium-ranking student takes 4; low-scoring student takes 2. If there is a tie, students split the difference (tie for high score = 5 points; low score = 3 points).

E. Closure

1. Teacher reviews tournament results.

2. Teacher leads processing/debriefing discussion. "How did it feel to bring points back to your team? Do you know what facts you still need to work on? How did your team help you get ready for the tournament? Would you want to do another tournament for the next skill level?"

3. Teacher provides recognition/rewards for team performance and discusses observations of group skills.

F. Independent practice

1. Teacher gives an individual test to check mastery; plans class celebration.

2. Teacher gives homework assignment.

References

Anderson, M. 1988. *Partnerships: Developing teamwork at the computer.* San Francisco: MAJO Press.

Aronson, E. 1978. *The jigsaw classroom.* Beverly Hills, CA: Sage Publications.

Johnson, D., and R. Johnson. 1986. *Circles of learning.* Edina, MN: Interaction Book Company.

Johnson, R., D. Johnson, and M. Stanne. 1986. Comparison of computer-assisted, cooperative, competitive, and individualistic learning. *American Educational Research Journal.* 23(3), 382–392.

Male, M., R. Johnson, D. Johnson, and M. Anderson. 1986. *Cooperative learning and computers: An activity guide for teachers.* Santa Cruz, CA: Educational Apple-cations.

Naisbitt, J. 1982. *Megatrends: Ten new directions transforming our lives.* New York: Warner Books.

Slavin, R. 1986. *Using student team learning.* Third Edition. Baltimore: The Johns Hopkins University.

Webb, N., P. Ender, and S. Lewis. 1986. Problem solving strategies and group processes in small groups learning computer programming. *American Educational Research Journal.* 23(2), 243–262.

Mary Male is a professor of Special Education at San Jose State University. She has taught a variety of courses, including computers and special education, mainstreaming, cooperative learning, and methods and assessment. She is the author of Special Magic: Computers, Classroom Strategies, and Exceptional Students *and coauthor of* Cooperative Learning and Computers: An Activity Guide for Teachers. *Dr. Male has also served as a consultant to a number of schools and school districts throughout the country.*

6.

Cooperation in the Mathematics Classroom: A User's Manual

ROBERTA L. DEES

I never intended to teach. When I backed into teaching, I had had no teacher training at all. Consequently I began by teaching as I had been taught. I basically used a lecture-recitation method—but a more lively one, I hoped, than what I remembered from my own high school days.

From the beginning, I believed that students should be actively involved; the question was how this could be made to happen. Usually it was accomplished by my determination: the first day, if all the students went to the back of the room to take their seats, then I went to the back of the room to lecture. I often started, on the first day, with a diagnostic test to ensure that the students were participants, rather than spectators, and began calling on students immediately. In these ways I was often able to get students involved.

Still, I was always intrigued with students who had trouble learning mathematics. Early in my teaching, I recognized that one cause was the lack of manipulatives, or concrete embodiments of mathematical concepts, in the students' previous experiences. Therefore, I used hands-on models in my classes and helped to develop a mathematics laboratory at our college.

When the "individualized instruction" movement came, I was quick to implement the idea and was pleased to see a larger percentage of my students beginning to be successful in mathematics. In one of my teaching situations, I had, through a grant, even more equipment and materials than I could realistically use. In this individualized lab, secondary students in remedial classes could routinely raise their math scores one or two grade levels in a semester. This pleased them greatly, but something was still lacking. Students would often ask me questions to which they already knew the answers. Apparently they just wanted to interact with another human being. Our lab furniture consisted mostly of carrels that had high sides, like blinders, to keep students from distracting each other. I found myself rewarding the students on Fridays, for keeping their noses to the grindstone all week, by having the class meet together as a group!

Despite my master's degree in mathematics, I had many questions about teaching and learning; I decided to enter graduate school in mathematics education. One of my class reading lists included *Learning Together and Alone* (Johnson and Johnson, 1975). When I now talk to teacher groups about this, I sometimes hold up my battered yellow paperback copy and say, "This book changed my life." That is not an exaggeration, because I was then approaching burnout, which was prevented largely by my adapting and using the ideas in the book.

One more statement will complete my personal frame of reference: I have no patience with schemes, no matter how elegant, that cannot be implemented by a regular classroom teacher in a regular class. This chapter will describe cooperative methods I have used in a wide variety of settings, from middle school to university level and adult school, with gifted students, disadvantaged students, and "ordinary" students.

I do not recommend that teachers change their teaching styles or their programs of instruction drastically or overnight. One primary advantage of cooperative learning for me has been its extreme flexibility; it was easy to try it. Teachers who use either a lecture-recitation method or an individualized teaching program may elect to try a cooperative activity once every week or two. They can then decide when to try others, at a pace that is comfortable for them.

Students are not in danger! I have often seen great gains from the expert use of a cooperative method. But even when a novice teacher uses a cooperative method, I have not seen evidence of harm. (The Introduction and Chapters 2, 3, and 4 contain reviews of research on this issue.) It is not suggested that all lecture, whole-group work, and individual seatwork be abandoned. However, the mathematics classroom is traditionally a place where very little cooperative learning is seen and much more can be done.

Therefore, this chapter is a how-to manual containing practical ways to use cooperative teaching methods. One particular concern is the special problems encountered in working with older students. Young children are flexible and usually cooperate readily if encouraged to do so. At the secondary level and above, implementation of cooperation in the classroom is not always simple.

Methods

There are two major terms I use in talking about cooperative learning: *cooperative classroom management* and *cooperative learning*.

Cooperative Classroom Management

First, students *have a cooperative attitude* or *work cooperatively* when they help each other and value each other's successes. Students may lend each other pencils, act as tutors to each other, check each other's papers, and share materials. However, each student hands in an individual paper or project and is graded individually. Many teachers have these friendly, cooperative classrooms.

In one highly organized approach, called Team Assisted Individualization, or TAI (Slavin, Chapter 3), students work in teams to master certain mathematics content, sometimes competing with other similar groups. Within the groups, students work individually on their own learning goals but assist each other by checking answers, drilling each other, and tutoring when they can. Each group is rewarded according to the progress of all its members. Thus in TAI the students are cooperating to help manage their individualized learning system. I refer to methods like this as *cooperative classroom management*.

In general, cooperative classrooms have been linked positively to achievement of the following ends:

1. Learning of specific facts or concepts

2. Learning of specific skills or algorithms

3. Managing the classroom

4. Planning and implementing class activities

5. Reducing difficulties in interpersonal relationships (both peer/peer and teacher/student), including improved interracial relationships

6. Improved student self-concept

Achievement of these ends makes the classroom more pleasant and more efficient.

Cooperative Learning

In another major approach (Johnson and Johnson, Chapter 4), students are considered to be using *cooperative learning* when they work together on the same learning goal and produce one end product or solution. In this method, which the Johnsons call "using cooperation as a learning mode," students perceive that they can attain their goals if and only if the other team members also attain their goals. Thus each group hands in only one paper or project, which carries the names of all group members. Examples might be a scale drawing, the proof of a theorem, a budget for a field trip, or simply the solution to a problem. The method requires that each member is committed to the group's end result. This is what I will usually mean by the term *cooperative learning*—a method that uses cooperation as a mode of learning.

In practice we have seen that this method has the potential to yield rich rewards. Some studies of cooperative learning in mathematics seem to indicate that the greatest advantage of the cooperative method may be seen when students engage in complex tasks, such as concept learning and problem solving (Cohen, 1982; Dees, 1983; Webb, 1978). Besides the benefits that accrue when students work cooperatively (see the preceding list), we have come to expect additional results when we use cooperation as a learning mode. They include:

7. Understanding of mathematics concepts (as distinguished from skills)

8. Increases in both individual and group problem-solving ability

9. Greater success for slow learners

10. No loss of achievement for fast learners

11. Increased commitment to peers and reduced prejudices

In practice, these two methods—cooperative classroom management and cooperative learning—reinforce each other; the extent to which a teacher encourages a cooperative attitude increases chances for the success of cooperation as a mode of learning and vice versa.

After the initial attitude adjustment, when students experience the benefits of working together, they often react by asking why they were not exposed to a cooperative method before. Some students tell me that they feel they have been cheated by their previous mathematics instruction.

Guiding Principles

It is important to note that a teacher interested in increasing the students' cooperation and/or cooperative attitude can begin with small increments. Some of the activities that are suggested are especially designed to be nonthreatening to both students and their teachers. In their commitment to increasing the use of cooperative strategies, teachers will still need to be guided by certain principles. Here are two that I propose:

Principle I. Each cooperative activity should support the intended curriculum and should not be an aside or a diversion. This is simpler if the textbooks, teacher's manual, and supplementary manual have been prepared to be used cooperatively. Such materials do exist at some levels (See the resource materials in the appendix). If cooperative materials are not available, the teacher must do some preparation in organizing for instruction.

Principle II. The teacher is the leader and has the primary responsibility for providing an environment conducive to learning; that is, a cooperative classroom is not a permissive or chaotic classroom. Students can understand the guidelines related to a cooperative environment; they can learn when they are supposed to talk to each other and when they are to work alone, such as when taking tests. It is the teacher's duty to explain the guidelines that are appropriate for each type of activity.

Getting Started

A climate conducive to cooperation can be established from the first day of class. The teacher sets the ground rules. This is especially important if students have not previously had experience working in a cooperative setting. The teacher might begin with a statement of philosophy consistent with the teacher's own views and including such positive statements as: "We are going to have a pleasant, constructive learning environment."

The cooperative process is given proper status and respect by the teacher. The teacher can explain (at the students' level of understanding) that research shows the method to be effective; that in a tutor-tutee relationship, the tutor usually learns at least as much as the tutee and often more. Thus cooperation is not being used simply because it is more fun and more pleasant but because it makes learning more efficient.

The teacher makes an active effort to model cooperation. Ways to do this include team teaching, joining the class next door for a film, sharing an aide or student assistant with another teacher, sharing laboratory materials with other classes, and starting a paperback library or game collection with the other teachers in the wing. Cooperation with another teacher is especially appropriate when that teacher has many of the same students; a joint project with the industrial arts teacher, for example, could involve students making scale drawings during mathematics class and building the objects in the shop.

The teacher describes the different learning modes and what is expected of the students in each of them. During a lecture, for example, the teacher can expect the students to listen, to refrain from talking among themselves, and to raise their hands when they want to ask questions. The teacher should try not to exceed the students' attention spans in this mode.

When working cooperatively, students are expected to talk to each other and contribute to the work of their groups. Limits can be placed on the volume in keeping with general classroom rules; even small children can learn to talk quietly.

It should not be assumed that students know how to cooperate; instruction must be provided. For example, if two students are given a set of mathematics problems to solve together, they may attempt to divide the problems up, each doing one half of them. The teacher will need to explain that *both* students are to be committed to *each* solution and that the paper should not be handed in until both agree on all the answers. They can be directed to use a single sheet of paper and take turns writing; at the end, both students should sign their own names.

Besides forming the groups, the instructor will need to give guidelines for the particular activity at hand. These might include specific ways of working together as well as the method in which the results are to be presented. As in all instruction, there will have to be materials provided that are appropriate for the level and background of the students and the nature of the task. These may include texts, worksheets, manipulatives, tools such as measuring devices, or other materials. Often materials intended for use by a single student can be adapted for a cooperative activity.

Getting to Know Each Other

Students should get to know each other quickly. Here are some ways to speed up the process.

Activity 1: Names Test

The teacher says: "To work together effectively, you will need to know the name of every student in the class. Your first test will be on Friday. At that time you will number your paper from 1 to 27 and as I point to each student, you will write that student's name. Right now, you should write down the students' names as they introduce themselves. Will each of you please tell us, along with your name, enough about yourself (your hobbies, goals, and so on) to help us remember who you are. I'll begin by introducing myself."

The teacher identifies his or her preferred form of address and gives one or two personal facts, perhaps about hobbies or number of children. The teacher then asks a student to continue. When I do this activity, I usually make some notes, such as, "red hair" or "softball." I also stop students periodically to see how many students I can name. (Learning names quickly often averts potential discipline problems. I practice naming students often; before I hand out papers, I separate them into two stacks. If I already know the students, I give their papers to another student to hand out. Then I personally hand the papers to those students whose names I am still trying to learn.)

The students will ask if the test "counts." The teacher says "Yes," and means it. The students will ask what score is passing. The teacher says "100 percent." To say otherwise would indicate that some students' names are not as important as others.

There are details to be worked out. For students who fail the test or for missing students, makeup days will have to be provided. Questions about whether the spelling must be correct and whether first names only, or both first and last names, must be known, can be refereed by the teacher with regard to the age and abilities of the students.

During the week, students must take the first few minutes or the last few minutes of the class period to practice naming their classmates. Those students who need extra practice can be asked to hand out papers or call roll.

In recent years I have asked my college students to write down their names, addresses, and telephone numbers on the first day of class. I collate these and, at the second class meeting, I distribute the list. Students then have someone to contact for information if they miss a class. Occasionally they also use the list to form car pools or study groups.

Activity 2: Three-Minute Teams

Students can be getting to know each other while learning mathematics. Suppose that the teacher has just presented a new concept; it is time to give an example. The teacher presents the question or problem (on the chalkboard or screen, or on paper, handed out). Then the teacher says, "It is important that we all understand the problem. Please turn to the person next to you (if there are an odd number of students, there can be one group of three) and take three minutes to discuss it to make sure you agree on what the problem means. After three minutes you will give me your attention again."

After the three-minute discussion, the teacher may ask a student to explain or paraphrase the problem for the whole class before going on to demonstrate the solution. This minigroup work can be used several times during a single class period. Students are involved and attention spans are not severely taxed. The teacher can be specific about the amount of time allowed (three minutes, five minutes, or ten minutes, depending on the task) or, instead, watch the progress of the groups to decide when to "call time." Some teachers like to have a preestablished student signal, saying: "When you are finished, put your pencil down and look up at me."

This three-minute method is easier to use if students have been asked at the beginning of the class period to sit next to a partner. I often write instructions such as the following on the chalkboard:

> Please sit next to a partner you have not worked with before.
> Or:
> Please sit next to a student who has a calculator.
> Or:
> Please sit next to a partner who has a textbook.

The students can then rearrange their chairs as needed before I begin the lecture.

(I have also used one- or two-minute buzz sessions in presentations at conferences, where the audience consisted of teachers. The shared experience gives a different feeling than just listening to a speaker does; even if they do not profit from what I say, they sometimes make new friends.)

Activity 3: Peer Feedback

Here is another getting-to-know-you activity. Sometimes there are some interesting papers to return, and I feel that students could learn from seeing each other's work. I may put the flow chart shown in Figure 6–1 on the chalkboard or screen.

Figure 6-1

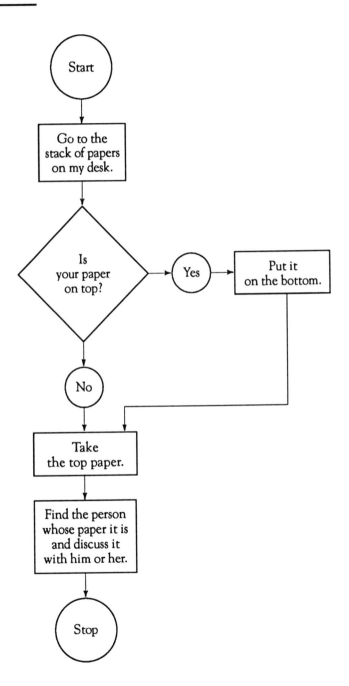

Notes on Activity 3. Each student gets acquainted with at least one and usually two other students, giving comments on another student's paper and receiving comments on his or her own paper.

Structuring Cooperative Activities

Some of the methods I will mention can be adapted to several different levels; other methods are more content-specific and have definite prerequisites.

A simple way to induce students to work together is to ensure that there are *not* enough materials to go around (scissors, protractors, or whatever is being used) and to explain that students will need to share. The best physical arrangement consists of tables and chairs. The materials being used can then be placed centrally on the table, with students arranging their chairs conveniently for the task. If desks are used, partners can be asked to push their desks next to each other, or groups of three or more can make circles, with all group members facing each other. To encourage cooperation, the teacher can give each team or group only one reporting sheet, with spaces for the names of all group members. Students should be directed to make sure that they agree with everything on the reporting sheet before they hand it in, since their signatures represent their commitment to the answers.

For many sharing activities, the teacher needs a prearranged quiet signal for attention. When I have an overhead projector available, I may turn on its light. If students are very involved in their discussions with each other, it is considerate to give them some advance notice when time is nearly up. I sometimes circulate among the groups and say, "You will need to finish up in about one more minute."

After the activities are planned and guidelines prepared, an evaluation procedure will have to be chosen and explained to the students. Will they be given an individual grade or a group grade? On what basis? The teacher will also have to evaluate the activity itself in terms of how well it met the objectives for which it was designed. How did the students work together? If there were problems, could they have been avoided? Did the activity take the amount of time expected? More? Less?

There may also be special problems that have to be addressed. Physical facilities may inhibit working cooperatively (when students' desks are bolted to the floor, for example). There often are several issues of classroom management to consider. There may be students mainstreamed from special education or developmentally disabled classes. Some students may have physical handicaps, such as difficulties in seeing or hearing, which make it difficult for them to work with others. The constraints of time and the urgency of the need to "finish the book" also cannot be ignored. Many of these concerns are addressed in the context of certain activities; some are discussed in Chapter 12.

When Students Are Not Used to Cooperating

The teacher who works with older students (middle-school age through adults) faces the additional task of changing attitudes that have been well ingrained through the years. These may include:

"In math class, we sit in straight rows, and no talking is allowed."

"There is only one right answer and only one right way to do a math problem."

"We must keep our eyes on our own paper; otherwise it looks like we are cheating."

In a clinical study at the college level, I was trying to find out why and how the cooperative method helped (Dees, 1985). I noticed that several of the older students, having been independent for many years, did not understand the difference between working individually in a group and "really working together," as I put it.

For example, if three students were given a set of mathematics problems to solve together, they often attempted to divide the problems up into three parts, each doing one third of the problems. I made the guidelines more specific: "*All* students are to be committed to *all* answers, and the paper should not be handed in until all three agree on every one."

In spite of this, they were still not talking. Students, though sitting next to each other, were working individually until they either thought they had an answer or were stumped. Only then did they turn to speak to their partners.

I conducted individual interviews with each student. At some point in the interviews, the students helped me arrive at the models in Figure 6–2 to describe what they had been doing and what I was trying to get them to do.

Figure 6–2

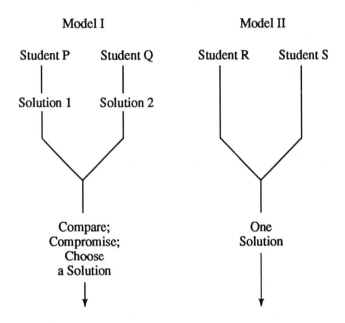

Thus, Model I shows working individually and having a cooperative attitude. Students may sit next to each other, share erasers, and so on, but still work individually. When at least one has found a solution, that student shares the solution. The other student may accept or reject it. If both students have solutions or ideas of how to go about solving the problem, they may then compare and compromise by choosing one of the solutions. Such behavior often occurs when teachers assign seatwork and allow student interaction.

Model II, on the other hand, shows the results of *using cooperation as a learning mode*, or "really" working together, as I call it for students' benefit. From the beginning, both students share their understanding of the problem and then begin to attempt together to find a solution. Each individual student still offers suggestions or even solutions, but the effort is a joint one. It was observed that in this class of adults (set in their ways?), Model II was used only when I required it. During the interviews we discussed the reasons for this; students often cited their previous training to "keep your eyes on your own paper," especially in mathematics classes. In this class, when I wanted them to work together, I was careful to give teams only one copy of the problem and one answer sheet and to remind them frequently of the guidelines for the activity.

The teacher must consistently encourage and reinforce instances of cooperation. Teacher comments to the students might include the following:

"You three worked very well together."

"Ann, will you please help Jim?"

"You were very effective in helping your group today."

"I need help with this. Who can help me?"

"How does your group feel about this?"

"What does your partner say?"

The students may try to cast the teacher in the role of referee. The teacher should not be too quick to settle differences, saying instead, "Can you convince her that your answer is correct?" Enthusiastic arguments about mathematics concepts may result.

Discipline

In some junior high and secondary schools, teachers are forced to spend considerable energy on control of the classroom. Having spent several years working with grades 7 through 12, often with less than enthusiastic students of mathematics, I will give some suggestions about discipline.

The classroom should be governed by as few rules as possible. One who tries to make specific rules to cover every eventuality is doomed to failure. Instead, one initial all-purpose rule, made by the teacher, might be: *No one is allowed to interfere with another student's learning.*

For me, this rule seems to take care of most situations. If students subsequently participate in making any further needed rules, discipline problems are greatly reduced. Therefore, time taken from mathematics for class meetings to solve problems or make plans is time saved from conflicts that detract from the educational process.

Discussions in our class meetings have often concerned racial prejudices or other interpersonal problems. During these meetings we sit in a circle. My sitting at the same level with the students signifies that, during these meetings, my opinions have the same weight as theirs and that all of us are free to express our opinions. Three rules I insist on for class meetings are:

- One person talks at a time.

- No name calling.

- You cannot say, "Shut up."

One class of disadvantaged students I taught in secondary school spent an inordinate amount of class discussion time, I thought, on the washroom issue. My position was that for the 50 minutes when they were supposed to be in mathematics class, they should leave the room only in the most extreme emergency. On the other hand, I had to agree that it was difficult for me to tell which was a real emergency for someone else. Our compromise: Every student was allowed one emergency washroom trip during the semester. They could use it whenever they wanted it, just by telling me that it was an emergency. I think it was the freedom to make the choice that made the rule work; in fact, students guarded that one trip so carefully that when the end of the semester came, very few students had actually used their trip!

In class meetings, when students tried to list other rules that were needed, they usually found that our all-purpose rule (don't keep someone else from learning) covered most situations. It turned out there was no need to make a rule about not hitting or not whistling out loud, as those acts would certainly interfere with someone else's learning.

Forming Groups

The size and composition of groups will vary. I will mention some activities that can be done by two partners and others that can be done by groups of three to six students. In some cases, the entire class might be thought of as a group, with smaller subgroups responsible for different portions of a project.

Some teachers use teams that work together for long periods of time, even an entire semester. Groups may organize themselves on the basis of friendship or common interests or they may be carefully composed by the teacher to be heterogeneous with respect to abilities, sex, personality types, race, or other variables. The teacher must somehow initiate the formation of the groups, consistent with the particular objective of the activity. I have often taught disadvantaged students; I was never able to count on perfect attendance in those classes. Therefore, I felt that I needed to have a flexible grouping system, or at least plan activities that could be finished in one class period. Otherwise, students could get very annoyed with partners who were absent and thus left them in the lurch in the middle of a project.

When groups are being formed, the students can be allowed to choose sometimes, and sometimes the teacher can make the choice. I like to use both methods. Since my students have some opportunities to choose their own group members, I can be stubborn when I choose. When a student says, "I can't work with him; may I change groups?" I often say, "Certainly, just as soon as you have learned to work with him." Even very prejudiced students have learned to value and respect other students to whom they had formerly been hostile, after having positive experiences working together.

When new groups are formed, it may be necessary to have short group "warm-ups." Before beginning a group project or activity, each student in the group can be asked in turn to share something with the other group members. Some examples of questions that the teachers can ask are:

- Tell about any game you have enjoyed playing that involved mathematics.

- See if you can remember how old you were when you first realized that four quarters were worth the same as a dollar.

- Tell about the first time you ever heard of negative numbers and what you thought about them.

- Discuss the following quotation: "Give me a place to stand on and I will move the earth" —Archimedes.

- Name something that is symmetrical and identify its axis or axes of symmetry.

- Give your reaction to this picture (or poster or print) or other geometric design (such as one of Escher's tesselations).

These are intended as nonthreatening openers to conversations about mathematics.

Sample Cooperative Learning Activities

It is easier to make cooperation seem necessary or at least reasonable if you assign projects like the following.

Things not easily done by one person alone:

- Measuring one's own head size

- Measuring a soccer field

- Building a play store

- Projects for which there are not enough tools to go around (I have even put some away to make sure that this was true.)

- Putting up streamers

- Painting a geometric wall mural

Things that one student might hesitate to do alone:

- Finding out about school finances

- Making a survey

- Asking a business to donate a computer

Things that are more fun when you do them together:

- Planning a field trip

- Going on a field trip

- Making holiday decorations (such as paper polyhedra with glue and glitter on the sides)

- Planning a party

- Having a party

There is a lot of mathematics involved in selecting a party menu, computing the cost, and figuring out how much each student should contribute. There are also some ethical decisions to be made: What happens if someone cannot afford the contribution?

One of my college-level remedial classes redecorated a vacant room for a student lounge. In the process they learned how to figure the amount of carpet needed, how to ask vendors for bids for the furnishings, how to stay within a budget, and how to calculate the amount of paint needed for the walls.

Teachers whose schools do not have the flexibility for outside projects can nevertheless use the cooperative mode in teaching mathematics. An entire wall of the classroom can be used to put up a Venn diagram that illustrates the relationships of the whole numbers, integers, rational numbers, real numbers, and so on. It should be large enough that several students will have to help.

Measurement Activities

In learning about measurement, students need to be actively involved in measuring. Some things are easier to measure when you have help—one partner can hold each end of the measuring tape, for example. Students might have difficulty measuring their own heights, but it is easy to measure each other's in turn.

Activity 4: Our Size

Following is an example of a laboratory sheet designed to help elementary school children learn to measure. It is designed for two students; the teacher should also have a version to accommodate a third name if the class contains an odd number of students.

OUR SIZE

Name _____   Name _____

How tall? _____   How tall? _____

Head size? _____   Head size? _____

Waist size? _____   Waist size? _____

Wrist size? _____   Wrist size? _____

Length of foot? _____   Length of foot? _____

Width of
thumbnail? _____   Width of
thumbnail? _____

Notes for Activity 4. This activity does not specify the unit of length; it could be used one day with inches, another day with centimeters. (It is assumed that these units of measurement have already been introduced.) Students should not be allowed to write a number without the appropriate measurement units. They may, of course, use abbreviations or symbols when writing measurements, such as 5 in. or 5 cm.

Essentially the same exercise can be used at any grade level, once students have learned to read. A version with pictures and oral directions can even be used for nonreaders, if they know how to read and write numerals. The measuring tools vary: Beginning measurers can use the primary version of a centimeter measuring tape, for example. This contains only whole centimeters (no halves or tenths marks), and the children measure to the nearest whole centimeter. Older students and adults can be given measuring tapes with centimeters divided into halves or tenths, with instructions to measure to the nearest half-centimeter or to the nearest tenth, as appropriate. Students should be asked to compare their measurements with those of their partners and to decide whether the results seem reasonable.

A small child's thumbnail is about 1 centimeter wide. In adults or older children, a fingernail is usually about 1 centimeter wide. In the exercise, use the one that would probably yield an answer of 1 centimeter for most students. For an approximate model for an inch, use the distance between the first two joints of an adult's index finger.

The teacher might want to prepare a list of partners in advance to make sure that in each team there is at least one student who knows how to begin measuring.

The teacher should be aware of special problems that may occur with measuring body parts—as when a student is physically handicapped or obese or for some other reason might be embarrassed. The worksheet can be adapted to avoid such difficulties; in junior high school, the teacher may choose to omit the waist measurement and substitute the biceps, for example.

The guidelines the teacher gives aloud might include something like this: "You and your partner should help each other. I will help you, but only if you and your partner can not figure it out together. When you have all the blanks filled in and you both agree, please let me look at your answers." The teacher can then scan the papers before accepting them, asking a question if the figures look unreasonable or if the students have forgotten to write the units for each measurement.

Even when the guidelines have been given, students may have to be reminded of them often. They may expect the teacher to settle disagreements by saying which student is correct. Instead, the teacher should encourage their dialogue with each other by saying such things as, "What does your partner say?" and then following with, "Well, did that convince you?" or "Can you convince your partner that your answer is correct?"

As I circulate around the room, if I need to help a team, the students are at the same place, and I am able to talk to the two partners at once. This effectively doubles my availability. With half as many papers, I find that I am able to glance at them and, with a few words, give the feedback the students need to continue their work.

Activity 5: Spans and Cubits

In another exercise for middle school or junior high, students measure their own hand spans and cubits (the length of the arm from the elbow to the tip of the longest finger). In learning to use these archaic units of measure, some students can come to realize why they are not used any more and to appreciate the need for standard units of measure. Students are then asked to compare the cubits to spans to see whether it seems to be a constant ratio. Such activities relate mathematics to biology and the other sciences.

SPANS AND CUBITS

← span →

Span: the width of your outstretched hand, from tip of thumb to tip of little finger.

← cubit →

Cubit: Length from elbow to tip of longest finger.

Name _____	Name _____
My span? _____	My span? _____
My cubit? _____	My cubit? _____
Ratio of cubit to span _____	Ratio of cubit to span _____

Are the ratios the same for both of you?_____

Close? _____   Discuss. _____

_____

Activity 6: Sizes in the Classroom

The next example is not as personal but is nonthreatening at any level. Materials needed are:

- Centimeter rulers

- Meter sticks

- A reference chart that gives the relationships of centimeters and millimeters to meters

Students can again work in pairs (with one three-person team, if necessary) to complete the laboratory sheet shown on page 182. Here are some suggested guidelines: "When you and your partner have agreed on all the answers, find another team that is finished and compare your measurements. If they are different, see if the four of you can figure out why. If you have made errors, correct them. When both teams are done, show me your work."

SIZES IN THE CLASSROOM

Name _____   Name _____

Part I.	In centimeters	In millimeters
Length of your mathematics book?	_____	_____
Width of your mathematics book?	_____	_____
Thickness of your mathematics book?	_____	_____
Length of your longest pencil?	_____	_____

Part II.	In centimeters	In meters
Length of chalkboard?	_____	_____
Width of chalkboard?	_____	_____
Width of classroom door?	_____	_____
Height of doorknob from floor?	_____	_____

Part III.	In meters	In decimeters
Length of classroom?	_____	_____
Width of classroom?	_____	_____

Notes for Activity 6. In this activity, the entire class must cooperate. Not all teams can measure the door at the same time, so the guidelines should make clear that objects do not have to be measured in the order listed. If there are not enough meter sticks for each team to have one, some teams can be using the shorter rulers to measure the smaller objects as others use the meter sticks.

When the students show their work, if it is still not correct, the teacher has four students with the same misundertandings and can help them all at once. Alternatively, another group whose work was finished correctly can be asked to come and help the group members, one-to-one, with their difficulties.

The teacher here must often conquer the students' notion that correcting their errors in this situation is cheating. It helps to emphasize that this is a laboratory exercise for learning how to measure, not a test.

This exercise involves more than the act of measuring; since students have to record each answer in two different units, they may discover the relationships between units. Other important ideas are reinforced: that small units are used for lengths of smaller things, such as pencils and textbooks; that all measurement is approximate. Most doorknobs are about one meter from the floor; students who notice this fact can then use this distance as their personal estimate of a meter.

More advanced students could also be asked for the area of the chalkboard and the volume of the mathematics book.

Activity 7: Scale Drawings

A group of three or four can make a scale drawing of the classroom. They should first make a rough sketch, estimating and labeling the various lengths. Then they should measure each dimension and record it on the sketch. Next they must decide on an appropriate scale and make a proportional drawing. I often include such questions as, "How good were your estimates? Were you better at estimating short distances or long distances?"

Again, the sophistication required will depend on the students' levels. Some students may include doors and windows; others may even locate the electric outlets and furniture. After they have mastered the process together, students can be given a homework assignment to make a scale drawing of a room or rooms at home.

Activity 8: City Map

Students can make a giant wall map of their city or neighborhood and use colored tacks to represent their homes. This teaching aid can then be used as a concrete reference for such concepts as horizontal and vertical, parallel, rectangular, diagonal, and so on. It can also be the basis of questions such as, "What is the shortest distance from your house to Amy's house?" "How many paths are there?"

Different Kinds of Mathematics Learning

In learning elementary mathematics, we distinguish between learning:

1. *Facts*, such as the multiplication tables;

2. *Skills*, such as how to multiply two three-digit numbers;

3. *Concepts*, such as the commutative property of multiplication; and

4. *Applications*, such as when multiplication is used.

In a calculus course, to give another example, there are differences in complexity between learning:

1. *Facts*, such as integration formulas;

2. *Skills*, such as how to integrate, using a trigonometric substitution;

3. *Concepts*, such as the meaning of the integral as the limit of a sum; and

4. *Applications*, such as how to set up the integral that is needed to find a particular area.

In these two illustrations, the types of learning are arranged (roughly) in order of lower-level to higher-level cognitive processes (or in order of increasing difficulty). When I teach algebra I notice that nearly 100 percent of my students can learn to solve simple equations; far less than 100 percent are able to set up the equations needed to solve problems.

In an oversimplification, we might say that the learning of facts, as in part 1, requires only memorization. Learning of skills, such as in part 2, may also need memory work, but there is more; in an algorithm there are usually several steps, including some decision points. Since students cannot memorize all the steps of every single computation they will ever encounter, they must organize the information in some manner so that they will be able to simulate a procedure. This is a cognitive process of a higher level than the simple recall of facts.

Learning of concepts, as in part 3, may or may not be more complex but still may be of a high cognitive level. Understanding of a concept does seem to require the ability to relate specific instances to a generalization, and then again, from the generalization to apply the concept to other specific cases.

Some would argue that the ability to apply knowledge, such as to the situations in part 4, should be our goal for students in the teaching of all mathematics. Certainly this ability to make applications is of a higher cognitive level than those in 1, 2, and 3, since it may involve the use of any or all of the first three levels.

Perhaps the highest level cognitive process is problem solving. By problem solving, mathematics educators mean figuring out something new. If students are only practicing skills that have already been learned, we say they are doing exercises. Thus what may be a "problem" for one student may be only an "exercise" for another student who has seen that problem or a similar one before and has already acquired strategies for attacking it.

For mathematical problems requiring cognitive processes more advanced than simple computation, I find that students do better when they can discuss the problems. Groups of two to four students can work together very efficiently on word problems, on writing geometry proofs, or on finding a general term for a sequence.

In multistep problems, such as verifying trigonometric identities, graphing polynomials, or solving differential equations, an incorrect sign or an arithmetic error may prevent a student working alone from reaching a correct result. When two students work together, one is not apt to make the same minor error as another, and the two are more likely to complete the problem correctly. In communications with a computer, a misplaced comma or misspelled word may result in maddening error messages; again, when two students work together, one can often spot the other's typo. Many programming tasks can be assigned to teams of two.

Students in mathematics classes may be inexperienced in working with others to solve problems. An excellent method for getting them started is to have them work together at the chalkboard. If students stay at their seats, I cannot see what they are doing; students may tend to work alone on their own papers (using Model I behavior). The guidelines for this work might be: "Take turns writing; each student has a duty to watch everything that is being written. You must either agree with it (and understand why) or question it."

Observing students as they work at the chalkboard is very instructive; as I walk around the room I can quickly see what progress is being made and which group needs help.

The examples given illustrate the fact that cooperative activities can be designed at any level of mathematics. The method seems to be particularly beneficial for students who have not previously been successful in mathematics. These students may be in remedial classes at the college level or adult school or in "overcoming math anxiety" classes in continuing education programs. In such classes, students often report that being able to talk to other students about their fears and difficulties makes learning mathematics easier. They say that realizing they are not alone is very valuable to them; they also find, by working in a group, that they have something to contribute to the problem-solving process.

Here is a common event that often happens early in the term: A group, formed by me to be heterogeneous, is working on a problem. Jim, who the others seem to think is the smartest, makes an invalid assumption and quickly proceeds to a (wrong) solution. Sometimes there is a student in the group who had secretly thought Jim was wrong but who did not have the confidence to raise a question. Now the group asks me to check their work. With a few questions, I expose their poor reasoning. It is hard to say which group member is more shocked: Jim, who thought himself incapable of making an error, or the others, to whom it never occurred to question Jim. I use the occasion to point out to the students that there should be no spectators in the group: "There are four pairs of eyes here; how can you let such a mistake get by?"

After an experience like this, students begin to realize that they all have something to contribute to the group's end product.

In my experience, women seem to profit even more than men from a cooperative method. For example, in the algebra-geometry study (Dees, 1983), university women were at a disadvantage at the beginning of the course, compared with the men, on entering algebra knowledge and on the confidence variable. At the end of the course, only 30 percent of the males and 32 percent of the females in the control labs had made grades of C or better; in the cooperative labs, 48 percent of the males and 72 percent of the females had made grades of C or better. Why cooperation seemed to help women more than men is not totally clear; one important variable may be the lack of confidence women often exhibit in their ability in mathematics. They tell me that working together and sharing their fears seems to increase their confidence.

Solving Word Problems

Teachers have a hard time teaching students how to do "word problems" or "story problems" or "real-life problems"; often those pages gets skipped! Sometimes teachers think, "If I can at least give them the skills, then maybe next year they can learn how to apply them." In fact, the cooperative method can be an effective strategy for this very difficult topic. This section has some specific suggestions. But first, here are some general comments on problem solving, whether word problems or anything else that students do not know how to do.

Suppose students have been asked to work together on problem solving. I often observe the following behavior, which I have referred to earlier as Model I: Students all attempt to solve the problem individually and then, when they think they have the solution, they will share their solutions or ask for approval by the other group members. This may not be productive, in that each student may have a totally different understanding (or misunderstanding) of the problem, and they could therefore each be going off in a different direction. Alternatively, those students who do not have any beginning strategy may be forced to simply wait until another group member comes up with something.

I want the students to begin working together immediately on acquiring an understanding of what the problem is about. This requires discussing it together in the earliest stage of the problem-solving process. After all are agreed on what the problem is about or what is being asked, they should try out ideas together: evaluating, discarding, and finally arriving at a group solution together.

To encourage this process, start the group out with activities that force each person to participate and contribute to the solution. The SPACES project (1982) has produced some cooperative logic problems that achieve this. The various facts necessary for solving the problem are divided up and put on individual pieces of paper, and one piece is given to each group member. The group is instructed as follows: "You may talk and share the information on your piece of paper with your group. You may *not* give the piece of paper to someone else to read."

No one person has enough information to solve the problem alone. Furthermore, if one person does not contribute his or her piece of information, the group will not be able to solve the problem. One of my middle school groups took 20 minutes before they figured out what the question was! There also exists the possibility that, once the information is all out in the open, the stronger group members will arrive at the solution without the complete involvement of the weaker members. To reduce this possibility and ensure full group participation, I include the following statement in the guidelines: "When you have all agreed on a solution and all understand it, let me know. When I come to your group, I will select the student who will be the spokesperson for the group. That person will then present the solution to me and explain how you found it." The group is informed that they are responsible for making sure that each member thoroughly understands the solution and can explain it.

Activity 9. How Much Candy?

Following is an example of a cooperative logic problem, divided up for group solution, with a group of four. (Each student receives only one piece of the problem.) I am not specifying the grade level for this activity; however, a prerequisite is the ability to work with fractions.

It would help if the students have also had some previous experience with logical reasoning. This problem is probably appropriate for students about 13 years old or for bright students at a younger age.

Your group has a problem to solve: Mary, Eddy, Sammy, and Lionel purchased a bag of candy, which they divided as follows: First, Sammy took one candy plus one third of the candy remaining. (Note: Each person should end up with a whole number of pieces of candy.)	Your group has a problem to solve: Mary, Eddy, Sammy, and Lionel purchased a bag of candy, which they divided as follows: After Sammy took his, Mary took one candy plus one third of the candy then remaining. (Note: Each person should end up with a whole number of pieces of candy.)
Your group has a problem to solve: Mary, Eddy, Sammy, and Lionel purchased a bag of candy, which they divided as follows: After Mary and Sammy took their candy, Eddy took one candy plus one third of the candy remaining. (Note: Each person should end up with a whole number of pieces of candy.)	Your group has a problem to solve: Mary, Eddy, Sammy, and Lionel purchased a bag of candy, which they divided as follows: Lionel was the last one. If he received all the remaining pieces of the candy, how many pieces did he get? (Note: Each person should end up with a whole number of pieces of candy.)

Notes for Activity 9. At first glance it may appear that there is not enough information. Actually, students who experiment with different multiples of three will readily find a solution: Lionel gets 6 pieces of candy.

When a group is given this type of assignment for the first time, the teacher must make it clear what is expected: group consensus. Often a group will inform me that they have the solution, saying something like, "At least, we *think* we do." I often respond, "Well, call me back when you're sure." The teacher can, while observing the group interaction, note which student seems least active and can then later ask that student to be the presenter. If the student is unable to present the solution and explain it, the teacher can give the group another chance to help the student understand the solution, saying, "I'll come back when you're ready." This does not connote failure but an acknowledgment that more time is needed.

In this activity, participation is induced by the teacher. Once students have had some experience in working together and reaching group consensus, it may not be necessary to induce participation artificially. Helping one's group to reach its goal seems to be highly motivating; after students realize that they all are needed, they seem willing to make the effort. Often even the weaker student has some productive insights to offer in addition to sharing information. The stronger students learn patience and better ways to express themselves in order to make sure that each group member understands the solution. The teacher can help by pointing out that asking the right questions is more effective than telling.

Getting Meaning from Word Problems

There seem to be many reasons why students have difficulty with word problems, but the most prominent one may be that they simply do not read and understand the problems. They want to start calculating right away; they attempt to find two numbers and then do something to them. How they decide what to do to them has been the subject of teachers' humor and despair. Sample student rule: "If the two numbers are about the same size you add them—unless it says 'less,' then you subtract. If one number is a lot bigger than the other, you divide the little one into the big one—unless it says 'times,' then you multiply."

The teacher must give some instruction on how to tackle word problems. As a first step, the student should learn to read the problem and then paraphrase it. This sounds simple, but it is not. Here is an example. If I asked a student to read the textbook problem and tell me "what the problem is about," here is how I would like him or her to respond:

Problem: Mr. Brown has $120 to buy maple trees, which cost $14 each at Smith's Nursery. How many trees can he buy?

Jill: Well, this man has a certain amount of money, and it wants to know how many trees he can buy.

And now, here is a more typical, undesirable student response:

Jack: You divide.

Jack's response is not desired for several reasons. First, it shows that the student was not following the guideline ("Tell what the problem is about"). Second, experience has shown that this type of response sometimes leads to answers such as "8.57," whereas responses such as Jill's should eventually lead to the answer "8 trees." Third, division is not the only correct operation. This problem could actually be solved in several ways. For example, we could simply keep subtracting 14 from 120 until the difference was less than 14. Then we could count how many 14s were subtracted. This number would also be the number of trees we could buy.

The next activities are provided to ensure that students at least make an effort to read and understand the problems.

Activity 10: What Is the Problem About?

For this activity, assign students to teams of two, attempting to have at least one strong reader in each pair. If there is an odd number of students, there will have to be one group of three.

Do not allow students to have pencils and paper or calculators; the goal here is to prevent them from succumbing to the temptation to plunge into computation immediately.

Materials: a set of word problems. (Take from any textbook at your grade level.)

Directions: "You will take turns. First, one person will silently read the first problem and then look up and, without looking again, tell his or her partner *what the problem is about*. The reader should *not* try to memorize the numbers in the question. The reader should *not* say how the problem should be worked.

"Next, the second partner will read the same problem and decide whether he or she reaches the same understanding that was received from the first reader. If not, please discuss it and attempt to agree on what the problem is about. After you agree, the second partner will become the reader and the process will then be reversed on the next problem."

Notes on Activity 10. At first, the students will think this activity is very strange. The teacher must make it clear, through the guidelines, that "getting the answer" is not desired in this activity. Instead, the students will be using each other as helpers to improve their understanding of what they are reading.

Even with the guidelines, the teacher will have to monitor the process carefully at first. In extreme cases, where students seem determined to *work* the problem rather than discuss what it is about, it may be necessary for the teacher to remove the questions. The problems then become stories or situations.

Here is a textbook-type problem:

> *John got a new bicycle for his birthday. It is 3.2 miles to Grandmother's house and 1.6 miles farther to Uncle Bill's house. If John rides his bike to visit both his grandmother and his uncle, how many miles will he ride in the trip?*

Students who see this will often begin by adding 3.2 and 1.6. Many will then leave John stranded at Uncle Bill's house, not adding the miles for the return trip home. But then, perhaps John is going to spend the night at Uncle Bill's. If the teacher removes the question, students can concentrate on the meaning of the situation. Alternatively, the teacher can give a nontraditional question such as: "What factors should John consider in deciding where to try out his new bike?"

Answers might include:

"Are Grandmother and Uncle Bill both at home?"

"How long before dinner?"

"What is the weather like?"

Another activity might be to give the situation, without a question, and have the students make up a list of questions that could be asked about it.

After students have had similar practice, perhaps once a week for two or three weeks, they may be ready to begin working together actually to *solve* problems. Emphasis should still be on first agreeing *what the problem is about* before attempting to solve it. The activity can be open-ended, even after a solution is reached; for example, the students can be asked whether there is another way to solve the problem and whether it will yield the same answer. If the groups find different solutions, they can be asked to present their solutions, and how they found them, to another group or to the whole class.

Activity 11. Newspaper Problems

Here is an activity designed to help students in problem solving. Assume that instruction has been given in a particular mathematical concept or skill; for example, a fifth grade class has been learning how to find one third of 24, or a third grade class has been adding money values together and making change. Or a ninth grade general mathematics class has been learning about percentages or about reading graphs.

The materials needed are pencils, paper, and the stimuli—pages taken from a daily newspaper. Pages that contain advertisements are especially appropriate, but the front page or sports pages often work just as well.

The teacher forms groups of four (with some groups of five if necessary) so that they are heterogeneous with regard to mathematical skills. There should be at least one strong (leader-type) student in each group.

Here are sample guidelines:

"Your task is to work together to make up a few (specify two, three, or four) problems from things you find in the paper. You must all agree that they are reasonable problems for the class, given what we have been studying. Take turns writing the problems, as neatly as you can, all on one sheet. Then work the problems together; when you all agree on the solutions, make an answer key on a separate sheet.

"When you have finished, you will exchange problem sets with one of the other groups. Your group will work together on the problem set you receive. Take turns writing the solutions; when you are all agreed, hand your solution sheet back to the group that wrote the problems. You will then get the other group's solution sheet to *your* problems, so that you can check them. Again, you must all agree on whether the other group's solution is correct, *even if they did it in a way different from your answer key.*"

Notes for Activity 11. The teacher should monitor the time and call for an exchange so that each group will be able to work on another group's problem set. It is important that the class gets an opportunity to go through the entire sequence with at least one problem, rather than making up a large selection of problems which no one has time to solve.

This type of activity has been used at all grade levels. It could be adapted for more advanced levels by using, for example, blueprints or pages from professional journals as the stimuli.

Grading

Before I began to use a cooperative method, my experiences in teaching, especially the use of individualized instruction, had already forced me to examine the philosophy of grades. Suppose one student comes from far behind, is working hard, and is making excellent progress but still is not up to "grade level" (whatever that is). Another student has more natural ability but is lazy and is not making any effort. What grades should each receive? Each teacher has to come to grips with this issue.

One opinion I will give firmly: Whatever else it does, the grading system should never reward a student for other students doing poorly. This is the basis of grading "on the curve," where the highest scorer gets an A and the lowest scorer gets an F. This highly competitive method is destructive of interpersonal relationships among students and should never be used. Instead, students should be graded on how well they have achieved the stated criteria, whatever they are.

Basically any grading system, except the curve, can be used in a cooperative classroom. When students are cooperative and help each other, they may still be tested individually and receive a grade based on their individual mastery of the material. Students can understand that at test time they are expected to do individual work. When students work together in a small group or in teams of two, the group's product can be evaluated, and each member of the group can be given that grade. Tests can even be given to pairs or groups and the same score assigned to each group member. When I have done this, I have usually assigned the students to teams, rather than letting them choose, so that they do not always work with the same team members.

Such group grading procedures can be used occasionally with no loss of integrity in the mathematics program. I believe that many different forms of evaluation are appropriate: oral as well as written, group as well as individual, essay questions as well as short-answer questions.

Keeping Records

One responsibility that often seems to detract from the educational process is the voluminous paperwork teachers must do. Since I believe that students should experience working with as many other students as possible, I have experimented with various record-keeping methods. I was trying to minimize the hassle and still keep up with which students have worked together.

I will describe one satisfactory method in the context of a course I taught recently. There were 20 students in a five-hour class of second-semester calculus. The class met every day. I often asked the students to work for short periods with a partner (as in Activity 2) during the lectures. I did not bother to record this.

However, once I gave a homework assignment to partners, I graded it jointly, giving both students the grade assigned to the paper. But I used an additional record, separate from the gradebook, to record the fact that these two students had worked together.

I made an array with students' names down the left side and across the top. I shaded in the diagonals, and the chart was ready (see Figure 6–3).

Now, for example, if Mark and Joe L. were partners, I would make two marks in the chart to indicate this.

Figure 6–3 *Working Together Record*

	Joe B.	Ann	Mark	Joe L.	Stef.	Abd.	Li
Joe B.	▨						
Ann		▨					
Mark			▨	✓			
Joe L.			✓	▨			
Stef.					▨		
Abd.						▨	
Li							▨

Often I had the students work at the chalkboard in groups. I could make five groups of four, or, with six groups, there would be two groups of four, the rest with only three. Here is how I organized this.

I gave a quiz the first day of class to see how much the students remembered after the vacation. Before the end of the first week, I had presented some new concepts and worked some examples, and they had done homework. I decided to make five groups, which I formed (in advance) as follows:

I found the students with the five highest grades on the quiz and put one of those names in each group. Next I took the names with the five lowest grades on the quiz and put one name in each group. Then I distributed the rest of the students so that each group would be as heterogeneous as possible.

After the groups were listed, I made a copy of the list and cut the second copy into five pieces. Now I had one complete copy and five slips of paper; on each slip were the names of four students.

At the beginning of class, it was necessary to see if anyone was missing. If so, there might need to be a slight rearrangement. If only one person was missing from a group, I would let the group go ahead (unless it was the high scorer who was absent). If the high scorer was missing or if two people were absent from a group, then I would redistribute the remainder of the students from that group into other groups. This planning was done quickly, without the students noticing it.

I gave the guidelines and instructions ("Please do problems $4n + 5$, $n = 0$ to 6," for example), and handed the slip of paper to one person in each group. That person was to locate the rest of the group members; the group would then go to the chalkboard to work.

One of the guidelines was, "Before you begin, make sure you know the names of everyone in your group. Write all your names at the top of your board space." (That was so that I could learn their names.) "Take turns writing, but everyone must agree with and understand each line before you go on."

That first time, I divided the board up myself, by drawing vertical lines, and assigned the spaces of board (Group 1, Group 2, and so on). Later, the groups chose their own work spaces.

As I walked around the room, going from group to group, it was easy for students to stop me and ask for help if they didn't know how to get started. Also, I could stop near each group and ask questions: "Where did this come from? How did you know to use this?"

I was careful to ask a different person each time, rather than let one do all the talking. Sometimes an error would be due to the writer having made a mistake, perhaps copying the problem wrong. When I saw this, I chastised the rest of the group: "You are supposed to be doing this together. You are supposed to be helping!"

Another guideline was "No spectators." Thus one of my functions was to help with the mathematics; another was to help the students learn to work as a team.

After class, I recorded check marks on the array to indicate which student had worked with which other students. After this session, all students who were present would have two, three, or four check marks in their rows, representing the other members of their groups.

The second time I arranged groups, then, I might begin with the same five highest scorers. But when I started to assign the low scorers, I would check the array and put them with a high-scoring person with whom they had not worked before. After I gave a second test, I might have a different group of high scorers.

There were other considerations:

- I tried to separate students who were "buddies," putting each one in a different group.

- In this particular class, there were only five girls, so I sometimes distributed one in each group, and sometimes I ignored the sex in assigning groups.

- As soon as the leaders (or the more outgoing, more talkative students) began to make themselves known, I often tried to distribute one of them in each group.

- Sometimes I let the students form their own groups; when they did this, I would try to note who worked with whom, so that I could later record that information on the array.

As the semester came to a close, only eight weeks later, the array had a check in almost every box. This meant that almost every student had worked with every other student at least once. When students commented on working in groups at the chalkboard, they said they had never done that before in any class. They uniformly liked it; one said: "In some classes we don't even know the other students; in this class we do, and we are all very friendly."

Student Reactions to Working Together

Children enjoy each other, either working or playing, so it is not surprising that most of them have favorable reactions to working together. But when I left high school teaching and returned to a university position, I was not sure how college students would react to a cooperative learning mode. However, I saw the need for cooperative learning immediately.

One of my first assignments was a technical mathematics class. Designed for high-risk students, it had a laboratory time scheduled, in which they were to do their homework under supervision. Previously this lab time had been poorly used by students. When I organized the lab time cooperatively, the students made constructive use of it and began working together outside the lab as well. They were successful in learning mathematics. At the end of the term, I asked not only for a course/instructor evaluation but also for an anonymous evaluation of the method used in the lab. Their evaluation of the cooperative method was uniformly favorable. Some of their comments were:

"I have only worked cooperatively here in college. In high school, math was my lowest subject. Now math is my best subject."

"I like this way. It builds confidence and you're not afraid to ask questions."

"Getting involved helps you learn faster and better."

This comment from a student can serve as a summary for that class: "Working in groups not only helps the group in itself, but it also helps the individual to understand exactly what's going on with the equation and why—especially when you have to explain to someone else what you're doing. Then you know how to solve the equations and why they're solved that way. I think this is one of the best methods of learning mathematics."

And in the algebra-geometry review class, one mature student puzzled for some time over how the cooperative model helped her to learn mathematics. We were well into the next semester and she was no longer in my class, when she passed by the room where I was lecturing to my new class. She asked me to come to the door and told me excitedly what she had figured out. "It's the ears," she said. So I asked her to write it down:

"When you work with someone else and you have to explain a process or definition to them, simply by saying the words aloud you not only help the other student, you tremendously help yourself. It seems that by saying the words aloud, your ears hear what your brain knows, and this very fact helps you immeasurably."

The remainder of her statement shows us, I think, a painless way to help provide an opportunity for our students to achieve synthesis: "Things you were unsure of or things you thought you understood, but didn't, seem to come clearer when two or more work together."

References

Cohen, E.G. 1982. Sex as a status characteristic in a cooperative math-science curriculum. Paper presented at the Conference of the International Association for the Study of Cooperation in Education, July, Provo, Utah.

Dees, R.L. 1983. The role of co-operation in increasing mathematics problem-solving ability. Paper presented at the annual meeting of the American Educational Research Association, April, Montreal.

———. 1985. How does working co-operatively help students in increasing problem-solving ability? Paper presented at the meeting of the American Educational Research Association's Special Interest Group for Research in Mathematics Education, April, San Antonio, Texas.

Johnson, D.W., and R.T. Johnson, 1975. *Learning together and alone: Cooperation, competition, and individualization.* Englewood Cliffs, N.J.: Prentice Hall.

SPACES. 1982. Lawrence Hall of Science, University of California, Berkeley, Calif.

Webb, N.M. *Learning in individual and small group settings.* Ph.D. diss., Stanford University, 1978.

Roberta L. Dees is Assistant Professor of Mathematics at Purdue University Calumet in Hammond, Indiana. She is on loan to the ITM/MUCIA Cooperative Program in Malaysia, where she is the Area Coordinator for Mathematics. Her primary professional ambition has been to understand and assist students who have difficulty in learning mathematics; her search for help for these students led her to a cooperative approach. She is now applying these ideas with her Malaysian students.

7.

Small-Group Learning in the Secondary Mathematics Classroom

CALVIN D. CRABILL

In the summer of 1968 I was working alone in my high school classroom on a secondary mathematics curriculum that emphasized content and minimized technical symbols and jargon. The school, located in the central valley of California, was not air-conditioned and the temperature was more than 100 degrees that afternoon; I was exhausted and also a little angry. I was chairman of salary negotiations, and the prospects were poor that the teachers would get the salary raises they wanted.

In the heat and frustration of the moment I had a mischievous thought: What if I were paid according to the number of students I had in the classroom—how many students could I crowd into the room? That's how I would increase my salary! Many times while making lesson plans in the classroom, I had pretended school was in session. This was one of those times that I acted out my fantasy. There was a convenient door opening to an unused adjacent classroom. I started pulling desks from that other room into mine. I kept this up until I had over 60 desks in my room. Amazing! I noticed that if I placed desks touching each other in groups of four, two by two facing each other, the room would easily hold 60 students, and I would still have ample aisle space for getting to each student. But reality set in and I was quickly overcome by guilt feelings, for our annual negotiations always included pleas for reduced class size. My colleagues would never allow me to accept such a giant class. So I took back the extra desks to the other room, leaving the original 36. Staring at them I suddenly realized that if I left the 36 desks in groups of four, the room would have much more open floor space than it had with the same desks in rows!

I pranced about the room pretending what class would be like in such an arrangement. It felt terrific! I could see that I had access to any student desk by moving just a few steps. Isn't that what I always wanted? But would it work? Wouldn't they just talk about last night's game? Could I interest them in talking mathematics?

That fall I began teaching in groups of four, brave enough to experiment with only one class. At the end of the first week, I could contain myself no longer. That first Friday I made an announcement, "Class, please forgive me for being carried away, but I want to congratulate you. This is the most mature class I have ever experienced in all my years of teaching. Now, please don't make me a liar by the end of the year!"

They did not make me a liar. On the contrary, I have taught many other secondary classes since then and they, too, have exemplified the same mature learning behavior habits that first class did. Moreover, teaching in small groups saved me from burnout! My students learned that teaching and learning are inseparable: You can't teach what you don't understand, but when you teach you reinforce what you have learned. They discovered that learning and teaching are mutually fulfilling roles. Since that fall of 1968, I have observed scores of other teachers having the same success in small-group learning, for the method frees the teacher for options far beyond the singular lecture method.

It was not clear to me at first why small-group learning was so refreshing and successful. All I knew was that the method worked. Gradually I came to believe that groups present a solution to the classroom dilemma that has arisen historically.

The Classroom Dilemma

Traditionally, school has been a place where students accumulate facts. There has been a hidden assumption that one who masters facts can also *think*; that if one masters enough facts one can master anything. Today we believe differently. Our world, our society, our needs have changed so dramatically that students will be ill-prepared for economic survival if they have only a memorized assortment of facts, if they have not also mastered the *processes* of learning. Today there is a growing agreement that the most important role of the school is to provide a place where students learn how to think. Much of the information that students will need in their future has not yet been discovered. They, themselves, will need to be capable of generating new information and new ways of using information. Facts just aren't enough.

For a generation, schools have been severely criticized for poor teaching, partly because students' scores on recognized tests are less than the scores of their parents. One of the major obstacles that teachers have not been able to bypass is the control or discipline problem. For many reasons, students today are not as obedient, respectful, polite, and placid as they were in previous generations. They have been bred in a fast-paced but lonely society—the world of the flashing TV screen, where ideas are not completed, but only briefly blinked on and off. Stories are often violent, comical, or ridiculous; they are seldom informational, rarely requiring a thoughtful response.

Shouldn't we expect that the lecture method will bore students raised on bits and pieces of entertainment? These students are bored and cause teaching difficulties in the classroom. Not always is there overt rebellion, but there is resistance to learning, which leads to loss of classroom control.

The teacher may be using only the lecture method of teaching, a method that was feasible in the past, but one that has often not worked in recent times, as evidenced by the prevailing criticism of schools. The major question for today's teacher is: What must I do to provide an environment where students learn and where there is a minimum of discipline problems?

The small-group method is an excellent way for students to explore the process of learning. Small groups provide natural control of the classroom for many reasons. These reasons are discussed throughout this chapter.

What Is Small-Group Learning?

To use the small-group method in the secondary classroom, the teacher should consider the following suggestions.

1. Have a successful plan for establishing and monitoring the small groups, including student knowledge of teacher and student roles.

2. Select problems that invite discussion, both for the small groups and the total class.

3. Believe in and encourage *process* in learning, as opposed to the emphasis of finding the answer to the problem.

For the student to be active in the learning process, he or she needs a great deal of dialogue to assist in separating that which is understood from that which is not understood. If the student is allowed to discuss his or her confusions, then much self-help can occur. A major stumbling block for students is that of not having a clear definition of the problem to be solved. More specifically, the student needs to define what the problem is asking and is handicapped if he or she is unable to express any logical difficulties. When the student can define the problem in his or her own mind, the human computers (students working in small groups) can solve the problem, if that problem is not beyond their abilities.

Learning flows naturally when the proper curriculum is available and the teacher knows how to guide the students in helping each other to learn. This method of learning needs a teacher who can rejoice in students finding ideas on their own, who does not need to control students for ego gratification. The text or materials are crucial because a conventional text often does not work well in small-group learning, as the spirit of discovery is smothered by excessive explanations, symbols and jargon, and by exercises that are not designed to invite dialogue among students. Quite the opposite, the text often presents deliberate, repetitious drill exercises, so that a student may remember how to solve a particular type of problem but not know how to think through the process. Of what value is knowledge if one does not know how to use it?

The best way to learn a subject is to teach it, and small-group learning allows students to experience the other side of the learning process—teaching. By his or her own trial and error, by hearing peers make mistakes and recover, the student begins to understand the process of learning.

Composing Groups

Using the small-group method of teaching and learning is markedly different from using traditional methods. It is imperative that the role and function of class members and teacher be clearly understood by all.

The seating arrangement of the groups is important. Groups may be formed in a variety of ways, depending on the students, the environment, the subject, and the teacher. However, one highly successful grouping consists of four students arranged with their desks close together. This seating arrangement permits six different dialogue patterns; each student can easily converse with any other student in the group.

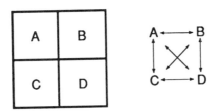

It is especially important that no one feels left out of a discussion. For example, if any two students have a spirited discussion, the remaining two students may start their own discussion or, at least, there is no single one left out of the conversation; they may even listen and learn, for students in small groups generally listen very attentively to each other because of the physical closeness. This is not true for an odd number of students in a small group, since students tend to pair off and a solitary student may be left out of many of the discussions:

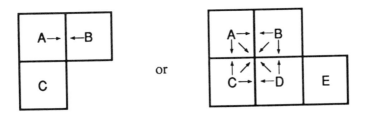

or

Admittedly, we are speaking of ideal arrangements. The teacher may adapt these suggestions to the actual classroom situation on any given day. If it is not possible to form all students of the class in groups of four, a group of five students is generally preferable to a group of three. Three may resemble the "three is a crowd" syndrome in everyday life, for the third person must make a strong effort to break into the relationship of the other two. The odd member in the group of five can break into any one of the six possible dialogue pairings of the others.

Some teachers prefer that students in a group of four face each other in opposing pairs,

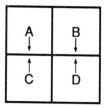

whereas others prefer that each person in a group of four face the side of another person:

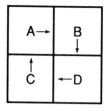

For less mature students, this second method may alleviate discipline problems, since they do not face each other directly, as mature students prefer.

In a grouping of six or more students, some students become rather passive, whereas others may see an opportunity to dominate and hence become "permanent teachers," thus stifling the creativity of the less aggressive students.

Five Key Roles

There are certain key roles in each group. Apart from appropriate course materials, most failures with group learning may be attributed to the absence of one or more of five essential roles. It is important that everyone in the classroom understand these roles and the flexibility in learning that is possible because of them:

1. The *assured leader*, or *initiator*, is a person who is not afraid to speak up and will do so almost immediately. The person in this role is simply the icebreaker and may not even state a mathematical idea. (However, it is more efficient if he or she does.) For example, a student may start talking about something outside the classroom. If the group does not soon pull the discussion back to the mathematical problem to be solved, the teacher as a roving coach must be prepared to do so with a positive, gentle effort.

2. The *idea person* must offer a mathematical idea, a possible method for solution of the problem. Everyone seems to be aware of this person, especially in the traditional classroom, where the teacher often absorbs this role. (It may or may not be the most important role in the ideal learning situation.) The idea person may state a fantastic mathematical idea that no one understands or possibly an idea that all the others agree is completely false. In any case, an idea has been presented for the reaction of the others. Without this person the group won't get started.

3. The *challenger*, or *rebel*, questions ideas. This is the role that often annoys the traditional teacher because the student does not passively accept ideas from others. (However, this role is the mover and shaper of the process in small-group learning.) This student may irk the teacher and fellow students alike; yet, the secret of success in small-group learning is to appreciate and utilize the challenger, who exuberantly comes up with counterarguments that may or may not lead to greater generalities. The group will not achieve its purpose without the rebel; he or she ensures discussion.

4. The *synthesizer* reconciles opposing ideas. The timing for this role of peacemaker varies with the degree of difficulty of the problem. Some problems may make it easy to synthesize opposing views. Synthesis for other problems may require a high mathematical intuition. (The teacher will have to be most alert to know when to assume or not to assume this role.) One of the serendipitous byproducts of using small groups is that a low-ability student may assume this role to the astonishment of everyone in the room. In the traditional classroom, synthesis is often assumed too quickly by the teacher.

5. The *ego-builder* praises others in the group and promotes the members' pride in achievement. Without this role, team spirit does not exist, for there is only competition between individuals. (In most cases observed, the role of the ego-builder is present in a classroom to the same extent that it is present in the teacher.) Cooperative learning becomes more effective and caring when everyone involved learns to become an ego-builder. This praise may be subtle, perhaps just a look or a smile; or, it may involve a complimentary remark directed to one or more other persons in the group. Or, better yet, when everyone in the group becomes ego-builders, they may compliment themselves as a winning team!

Our observations are that any other role that occurs will probably turn out to be a variation of one of these five basic roles. For optimum learning, the roles must not be assigned or remain static but need to be played by any or all of the members of the group from time to time during the class period.

The most successful group is one that has students of varying abilities. A heterogeneous group encourages shared leadership of the various roles, allowing even the less able student to assume one or more of the key roles. Again, the natural group dynamics must be allowed to occur; roles must not be assigned.* If roles are assigned, students resemble actors striving to recite a memorized script; thinking suffers.

---

* *Note to the Reader: This viewpoint on roles is quite different from the ones expressed in several other chapters. (N. Davidson, ed.)*

The Teacher's Role

The teacher must be the observant and diagnostic coach ready to fill a role that is missing in a group. This teaching role may be very subtle, or it may be very directive, such as giving a lecture or asking a question of the entire class. The work of the teacher with groups varies from moment to moment and requires great concentration to know when to keep silent or when to speak out. Fortunately, this system of learning is self-corrective, so that within moments the alert teacher may correct a poor teaching decision without much penalty.

For the bored teacher who is eager for a new life in the classroom, small-group teaching is a different job description. Teaching is stimulating again! The teacher may exercise more options in observation, diagnosis, and intervention.

It is an exciting experience to observe a group of students debating mathematics for an entire class period. When the group approach is operative, a class of 36 students working in groups of 4 can be monitored by a teacher almost as easily as a class of 9—and in some cases more easily, since the teacher has 36 assistants if everyone is involved in the teaching-learning process. The so-called slower student may originate ideas, and all students quickly realize that playing teacher is not only fun but an efficient way of learning. The teacher can spend time with an individual student in a counseling or teaching role during the regular class period at no expense to the rest of the class, because they are occupied with mathematics discussions.

Note: *Although the teacher is seemingly on the sidelines, he or she cannot afford to retire to his or her desk or withdraw from the students.* When the method is working optimally, it may seem that there is nothing for the teacher to do—what a marvelous time to catch up on the paper work. Not so! Only the best of classes will continue learning smoothly. The teacher is as needed as ever; only the function has changed. Instant feedback is available when the teacher moves about the room, is alert to the needs and progress of each group, and is a catalyst for any group that lacks leadership. The teacher can sense when one or more of the groups are stymied and consider steps to identify and remove obstacles to learning. The formal lecture is still useful and necessary at times when many students will benefit, such as when the teacher is introducing new material or summarizing or when the students are meeting a common difficulty. To adhere rigidly to the one method of small-group learning is as stifling and nonproductive as to insist on the lecture as the sole method of instruction.

Classroom control is imperative, but the control emanates from students through their discussion of mathematics as well as from personal control by the teacher. It should be made clear that students as well as the teacher may initiate a "lecture" or general discussion. This demands a teacher who practices sharing the teaching process. We suggest the following "golden rule": *If anyone wishes to speak to the entire class, he or she should be given courteous attention.*

This rule is most crucial, for a teacher may wish to initiate several short lectures in a class period, and this must be done quickly and efficiently. More importantly, however, it is a subtle method of crowd control, since most students have a ghastly fear of making a speech before the entire class. Extroverts who are not afraid to speak before the class quickly perceive from their classmates that they must have something worthwhile to say, or else they should remain silent. In teaching with small groups in secondary classrooms since 1968, I have witnessed only two instances where a student made an overt attempt to take advantage of this rule. In one case it was a tongue-in-cheek humorous joke for the teacher's benefit, a parody of teaching style. In the other case, the student could filibuster less than five minutes. The class laughed at him and he never attempted it again. (It was, of course, vital that the teacher assist the student in regaining self-esteem.)

Many teachers, especially some who work with elementary students, recommend the following rule for small-group learning: No one in a group may ask a question of the teacher until each member of the group has the same question. Quite frankly, this writer does not accept that rule for older students; they may feel abandoned and insulted by it. Moreover, they may have accumulated phobias that can be exacerbated. Indeed, there may be times when waiting to answer a question is the best choice for the teacher to make, but only the specific situation determines when that is. One doesn't need a rule, one needs sensitivity.

Trouble-shooting

Trouble-shooting when the small-group method is not working well provides a challenge for the teacher, ensures a lively classroom environment, and convinces students that they are getting help. To clear up a difficulty rapidly results in better learning and in better feelings about learning.

The extent of student discussion is a good indicator of the level of learning with this method. A good rule of thumb is that more discussion about mathematics means more learning. Thus, a good class can become quite noisy. If continuous dialogue is not present, then the following possibilities should be considered:

1. *Students in a group may become bored with each other.* Changing the membership of the groups with every chapter is a successful approach. Some students may not like it at first, especially if their first group experience is positive or they are sitting with friends and don't want the appearance of rejecting them. When they have experienced changing groups a few times, most students look forward to the new groups with anticipation. Consider changing the manner in which groups are formed, perhaps using a completely random selection. Some teachers use a deck of cards or numbered Ping-Pong balls from which each student draws to determine the groups. Or, you may count students at random (1, 2, 3, . . ., 9) four times for a class of 36, which is the quickest method of all. Or, in a class of 36 students, you might pick 9 students who have proven abilities and let the rest of the class form groups around them as they wish. Sometimes this method can backfire because of the suggestion of elitism. Or, students may not want to be in a group with a student you thought would be a good leader, which can be devastating to that student. Generally, it is preferable to let leadership evolve, rather than assigning it. It is imperative that each group have leadership and that group members change every three weeks or so.

2. *A group may have inadequate leadership.* One or more roles may be missing in a group. All the leaders may have formed a clique or joined the same group(s). Experience shows that it is

desirable to have students of like ability distributed throughout the room. In random grouping, groups with homogeneous abilities may be formed accidentally. This can be a special problem with students with low abilities because students can assess their abilities quite accurately, and these students already feel inadequate. Such a group will need extra attention from the teacher. On the other hand, if four strong students are in the same group, two or three of them may feel piqued because of fewer opportunities for leadership. There are times when a group of all strong students can be very stimulating for them, but only when they have a spirit of cooperation.

If there is a missing role in a group, the teacher may need to fill that role, especially the role of ego-builder. Many students lead a lonely life both at school and at home and don't actually know how to praise. Our society does not encourage compliments, but rather mimics the TV sarcasm and calculated insults. For optimum group learning, both teacher and students must be committed to caring more for each other.

3. *Students may feel abandoned by the teacher.* Because students may be accustomed to total teacher control, being told precisely what to do and when to do it, the teacher needs to move constantly among the groups to detect any common difficulty. Short lectures may be needed from time to time, or the teacher may wish to join a group as a fifth member for a few minutes. By staying close to the students as they work, the teacher will gain insights helpful in changing the course style.

4. *Students may feel defeated by a difficult exercise or bored with one that is too easy.* In this case, returning to a more traditional, teacher-directed approach for a time or encouraging a student to explain the problem to the entire class is a welcome change. A valuable attribute of small-group learning is the availability of immediate feedback. The alert, mobile teacher can avoid content and discipline problems by swiftly moving in to correct a difficulty. Whether the exercise is too easy or too difficult, change the pace immediately. Small-group learning allows the teacher to detect needs quickly. The teacher may simply ask a group or the entire class if they are having difficulty and receive an instant answer. Let students diagnose sometimes.

5. *Students may need a change of pace.* The teacher may need to allow a day or two for special projects or games. Encouraging students to bring in their own projects helps to relieve boredom and stimulates creativity. Or, if the material is simply too difficult, the teacher can return to a more directive style of teaching for a while by giving more hints. If the material is too easy, the teacher can increase the pace. Small groups provide an excellent way to detect the content value and pace of a course. If there is deadwood in the course, it will show. The teacher need not wait for the results of the next test to assess how the class is learning.

6. *Too much accuracy may be required at a given stage.* Students should be allowed to stumble and make mistakes, yet recover without stigma. This helps build self-esteem. Many of the difficult things we learn, such as walking, talking, and riding a bicycle, are achieved through stumbling and through trial and error. Yet in mathematics we often require too much accuracy too soon. Most mathematics we need in daily life involves estimation, and students need to discuss such examples. Teachers can't overemphasize the value of good estimation skills, which result from practice.

7. *Students may not be receiving adequate praise.* Many studies in the last generation demonstrate that self-image is the most important single factor in learning. We learn more and we learn more easily when we like ourselves. Perhaps the "ego-builder" is absent in a particular small group. Or, simply, students may be suffering from a society where it is acceptable to insult one another. Some students are so fearful of failure that they scarcely try at all. If the problem is not clearly defined in his or her own mind, the student may become passive (or belligerent) and avoid any attempt to solve the problem. The sensitive teacher will assist students who have low self-esteem in learning to appreciate themselves as well as mathematics by giving honest praise whenever possible.

8. *The teacher may feel uneasy because he or she is not the traditional central figure in the classroom.* This feeling will affect the students. Is the teacher lecturing to a class unnecessarily? To

find out, one only needs to ask the students—they will tell you! The role of the teacher constantly changes in small-group learning, just as the roles of the group members change. There are times when it is wise for the teacher to return to the role of the central figure in the classroom. However, when that occurs, the teacher should be efficient, remembering the goal of getting the small groups functioning again as quickly as possible. When the teacher realizes that the new teacher role is more challenging and the learning process more enjoyable—and that the old traditional role is actually embedded in the new role should the need arise—then that teacher will feel more comfortable using the small-group method.

9. *The teacher may be getting mixed feedback on how much students have learned.* A good method is to let the students first struggle with a new idea briefly in the groups, then lecture briefly, then let them discuss again in groups. That way immediate feedback tells one where the problems lie. The teacher might lecture again briefly if necessary; some classes require very little lecturing, others need more. I have had classes that go for as long as three days or more in new material without a lecture, whereas other classes have required as many as 20 mini-lectures in a single period. Students quickly learn to assess their individual and group needs and ask for assistance if the method of small-group teaching and learning has been clarified and is functioning.

10. *The teacher may not have explained the small-group method of learning and teaching thoroughly.* This difficulty is easily remedied. Reteach the basics of the method and test students' knowledge through oral questions as you would with any information you want them to use. *Caution:* You can't teach the process of learning. If you do teach it, it becomes rote. That process must be experienced.

11. *The style of testing may need to be changed.* Since the class routine is based on discussion of content, some test questions need to be essay type, asking students to explain concepts. Also, cumulative exams are desirable because they force the student to integrate the course into a comprehensive whole. The small

groups encourage the student to relate content in perspective, as opposed to repetitive rote learning, which evokes very little motivation for discussion. In order to encourage individual initiative, I still test students seated in rows. (On occasion, I have given a group exam for variety, but the character of that exam is more creative and challenging than one given to individuals. A group exam can be a disaster if the groups are not balanced in abilities.) I tend to give a test too late rather than too soon. Since all my exams are cumulative, this is consistent with the course style; the student has had sufficient time for questions before the exam is given.

Note: Working together in small groups, students can solve more problems than they can working individually. Although the quality of the solution may or may not be better than the independent work of the most talented group member, everyone benefits from discussions that lead to a solution. This is the power and essence of small-group learning. An unexpected bonus is that students comprehend more realistically the abilities of their classmates.

Contrary to what one might conclude from reviewing many secondary texts, mathematics can be learned without a heavy dose of technical jargon. The excessive use of symbols and jargon greatly confuses many students, because they must first master a vocabulary not unlike that of a foreign language before learning any mathematics. When symbols and technical words are kept to a minimum, students understand the mathematics better because the ideas are not hidden by esoteric language. By having students discuss mathematical ideas in everyday language before they learn too many technical names for those concepts, it is possible to avoid intimidating students who lack confidence in their mathematical abilities. Through student dialogue, misconceptions can be cleared up, new concepts tried, and confidence strengthened. There is plenty of time later for mastery of the essential vocabulary. Total precision too early in the course is usually futile and often reduces the students' enthusiasm for learning. Small-group learning is more successful because it is based on experiment and discovery; it is more exciting and motivating than a more axiomatic approach. Thus, to stimulate discussion, mathematical concepts need to be presented in a meaningful context and in everyday language whenever possible.

Sample Problems for Small Groups

A good problem for small-group learning possesses some attributes:

1. It is easy to state. That is, the problem is clearly defined, even though it may not be easy to solve.

2. It is easy to visualize physically. That is, it is not abstract, even though it may lead to an abstract generalization later.

3. It stimulates student questions that may be better than the original question. This is the most important attribute.

These attributes of a good problem are especially important when starting a new topic or starting new learning groups. A good problem ensures enthusiasm and dialogue.

The following are samples of good problems taken from texts designed for small-group learning (Chakerian, Crabill, and Stein, 1987; Stein and Crabill, 1986; Stein, Crabill, and Chakerian, 1986).

Problem. First, a problem from geometry.

A man has a campsite in a large flat clearing next to a straight river. He is at point A (600 ft from the river), and his tent is at point B (300 ft from the river). He sees a large spark leap from his campfire and set his tent aflame. The man has an empty bucket in his hand. *At what point P on the river should he fill his bucket in order to make the shortest possible path to put out the fire?*

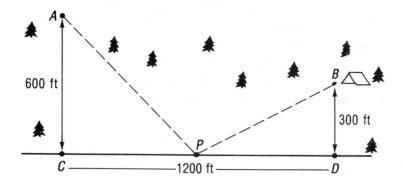

1. Using a protractor and a centimeter ruler, make a scale drawing of the situation in the problem (scale: 1 cm = 100 ft).

2. (a) Use your scale drawing in Step 1 and a centimeter ruler to estimate the total distance the man must go, AP + PB, when P is chosen to be exactly at C.

   (b) Record your estimate from part (a) in the table where CP = 0.

   (c) Do the same with point P chosen successively between C and D so that CP = 100 ft, 200 ft, . . . , 1200 ft.

   (d) In each case, also use your protractor to measure angle 1 (the angle at which he approaches the river) and angle 2 (the angle at which he leaves the river).

Copy and fill in the table showing the results of your measurements:

CP	Total Distance AP + PB	Angle of approach angle 1	Angle of leaving angle 2
0			
100			
200			
300			
400			
500			
600			
700			
800			
900			
1000			
1100			
1200			

3. (a) From your table in Step 2, guess how P should be chosen in order to make $AP + PB$ as small as possible.

(b) How do angle 1 and angle 2 compare when $AP + PB$ is as small as possible?

(c) Compare your conclusions in (a) and (b) with those of your classmates.

Comment. The preceding problem is known as Heron's problem and is rich in mathematical ideas. Heron's problem is easy to state and visualize; also, a great number of concepts are hidden in the problem, such as angle, distance, congruence, similarity, reflections, and the Pythagorean theorem.

Problem. The following is a sample of a classical problem for beginning algebra with geometric (and calculus) implications.

Suppose we have a square piece of paper 8 in. by 8 in. From the corners we first cut four small squares identical in size, then fold up the sides, and tape the corners. In this way we have made a tray (see diagram below).

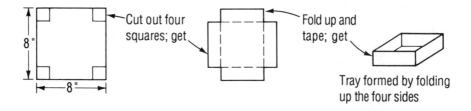

Tray formed by folding up the four sides

Many different trays can be made in this fashion, depending on the size we choose for the cutout squares. This raises our basic question: *What size squares should we cut out from the four corners of the paper to make the tray hold as much water as possible?* (Assume that the tray does not leak.)

The steps that follow will guide you while working on this problem.

1. With a ruler, make a paper square measuring 8 in. by 8 in.

(a) Draw lines to divide it into 64 squares, each 1 in. by 1 in.

(b) Cut out from each corner a 2-in. by 2-in. square.

(c) Fold up the four sides and tape them to make the tray.

(d) What is the length of a side (in inches) of the base (the bottom) of the tray?

(e) What is the area (in square inches) of the base of the tray? (*Hint:* Area equals length times width.)

(f) What is the height of the tray?

(g) What is the volume of the tray? That is, how many cubic inches of water could it hold? (*Hint:* Volume equals length times width times height.)

2. Fill in the table using a calculator and an 8-in. by 8-in. paper square. Use the same approach as in Step 1.

Length of side of cut out squares (in.)	Length of side of base (bottom) of tray (in.)	Area of base of tray (sq. in.)	Height of tray (in.)	Volume of tray (cu.in.)
0.0				
0.5				
1.0				
1.5				
2.0	4.0	16	2	32
2.5				
3.0				
3.5				
4.0				

There are many chances to make mistakes in Step 2. Check your answers with those of several classmates before you go on.

3. Fill in this smaller table, which selects the part of Step 2 that interests us most, namely, *how the volume changes as we change the size of the cutout squares.* (The piece of paper is an 8-in. by 8-in. square.)

Length of side of cut out squares (in.)	Volume of tray (cu.in.)
0.0	
0.5	
1.0	
1.5	
2.0	
2.5	
3.0	
3.5	
4.0	

4. On the basis of Step 3, what would you *guess* is the largest volume you can obtain?

5. (a) The table in Step 3 lists the results of nine experiments. Plot (graph) the nine points that record the information of this table.

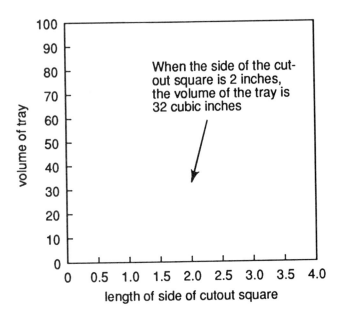

(b) Compare the points you have plotted with those of your classmates.

6. Compute the volume of the tray formed when the side of the cutout square is (a) 1.2 in., (b) 1.3 in., and (c) 1.4 in. Fill in this table:

Side of cutout square	Side of tray base	Area of base	Height of tray	Volume
1.2				
1.3				
1.4				

7. (a) Plot the three points on your graph that record the preceding data.

(b) Is there a tray of greater volume than that of your guess in Step 4?

You have now plotted 12 points on your graph. With more time and effort you could draw more and more points that show how the volume of the tray varies when you vary the sizes of the four cutout squares. If you were to do this, the points would begin to form a single curve, called the *graph of the volume of the tray depending on the size of cutout squares*.

8. Sketch the graph by joining the 12 points plotted in Steps 5 through 7.

Comment. The above problem is based on an experiment in beginning algebra. For good students, the problem may be extended as the course proceeds to an intuitive approach to the calculus.

Problem. The following is a problem from second-year algebra.

When a resilient tennis ball, golf ball, or super ball is dropped on a hard floor, it rebounds and continues to bounce many times. This exercise describes an experiment with such a ball.

Suppose a ball is dropped from 100 units (inches or centimeters) above a hard, level floor. Drop the ball several times. Observe the distance it rebounds on successive bounces.

1. Drop a ball with high rebound qualities from a point 100 units (inches or centimeters) above the floor. Watch the experiment carefully in order to answer the following questions.

    (a) On the first drop of the ball, how high does it rebound? (For precision, drop it several times from the same height. Average the heights of the rebounds.)

    (b) "Amount of rebound of the ball" is defined by the fraction

$$\frac{\text{height of rebound}}{\text{distance of fall}}$$

    On the basis of the results in (a), what is the amount of rebound of the ball in the experiment?

    (c) Use the results in (b) to *guess* the height of the second rebound if you were to let the ball bounce freely.

(d) Let the ball bounce twice, and measure the height of the second rebound:

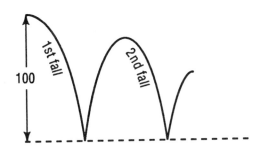

Was your guess in (c) close to the results you observed?

(e) What is the actual height of the second rebound?

(f) What do you *guess* the height of the third rebound will be? How does it compare with the experimental results?

(g) What is the total distance in a *downward* direction that the ball travels during the first fall? The first two falls? The first three falls? The first four falls?

2. (a) When the ball bounces freely, without being stopped, how many bounces can you count?

(b) How far would you guess the ball drops during the fifth fall? The ninth fall? The tenth fall?

(c) Compare your guesses in (b) with those of other students.

Imagine now a ball that rebounds exactly 90 units when it is dropped from a height of 100 units.

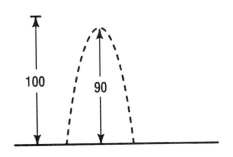

More generally, the ball always rebounds exactly 90 percent of the distance it falls.

(For the rest of the chapter, This ideal ball will be the model in exercises involving the bouncing ball.)

3. Assume an ideal ball is dropped originally from a height of 100 punits and that it will rebound 90 percent of the distance for each fall.

(a) Copy and fill in the following table.

Number of fall	1st	2nd	3rd	4th	5th	25th
Distance of fall	100	100(0.9)				

(b) Indicate the total downward distance the ball falls for each of the following. (Do not simplify the expressions; use exponential notation.)

First fall   =   100

First 2 falls   = $100 + 100(0.9)$

First 3 falls   = $100 + 100(0.9) + 100(0.9)^2$

First 4 falls   =   ___ + _____ + _____ + _____

First 5 falls   =   ___ + _____ + _____ + _____ + _____

First 25 falls =   ___ + _____ + _____ + _____ + _____

                   . . . + _____

(c) In your experiments in Step 2, about how many times did the real ball bounce before it stopped?

Comment. The preceding problem again involves an experiment, which can be done by a teacher demonstration or by each small group. The intuitive introduction to geometric progressions extends into many areas of mathematics.

Summary

Using materials that encourage discussion, a secondary teacher can experience many advantages when using small-group learning:

1. *Immediate feedback* is the result that teachers most commonly mention. The teacher can make an on-the-spot correction when a concept is not well understood.

2. *Discipline problems diminish* when the method is functioning, for students are less bored.

3. *Individual help is possible* without disrupting the rest of the class; even "counseling" a student who may be having difficulty is possible.

4. *Student digressions tend to minimize;* they are easily observed and can be corrected by the teacher, especially through selecting good problems.

5. *Students are not bored;* better students have roles to play, and less able students have help and leadership opportunities available.

6. *Student weaknesses are in the open;* the teacher must be sensitive and encourage peer tutoring where possible. Students are very adept in helping each other on remediation.

7. *A caring attitude soon develops* if the teacher is encouraging. Loneliness diminishes as students get to know more and more class members when membership of the groups changes.

8. *Everyone becomes more relaxed;* the comfortable environment of the classroom improves both teaching and learning.

9. *Deeper content* may be explored and understood because there is time for thought and discussion.

10. *Larger classes are easier to teach,* since everyone is involved in the teaching-learning process; the teacher has help in the classroom. Instantly every person, including the teacher, has as many helpers as there are people in the classroom.

11. *Ordinary language is encouraged;* hence, most students understand the concepts better and remember them longer.

12. *Neatness improves* because students are aware of peers' seeing their work. This is one of the more pleasant surprises!

13. *Students become active, rather than passive, learners* because they are completely involved in the teaching-learning process. There is a greater sense of identity and responsibility in a group of 4 than there is in a total class, a group of 36 students.

14. *Students enjoy mathematics more;* there is laughter and excitement about mathematics.

15. *Remediation can occur* naturally, in context, and immediately.

16. *Problem-solving skills improve* because students are more active in the learning process.

Finally, if students are excited about math, they are learning how to learn; they are experiencing the process of learning. They are learning much that we cannot measure. Since no two teachers are alike, they will use small groups in a slightly different manner, but the teacher's basic job is to make the small-group method work.

Most teachers will admit that teaching a subject is the best way to learn. If that is so, why not let the students in on the rewards? The amount of noise in the classroom may be irritating at first; however, if the students are talking about mathematics, what more can a teacher ask?

References

Chakerian, G.D., C.D. Crabill, and S.K. Stein. 1986. *Geometry: A guided inquiry.* Pleasantville, N.Y.: Sunburst Communications.

Davidson, N. 1985. Small-group learning and teaching in mathematics: A selective review of the research. In *Learning to cooperate; cooperating to learn,* edited by R.E. Slavin. New York: Plenum Press.

Davis, R.B. 1984. *Learning mathematics.* Norwood, N. J.: Ablex Publishing Corporation.

Gruber, H.E., and J.J. Voneche, ed. 1977. *The essential Piaget: An interpretive reference and guide.* New York: Basic Books, Inc.

Papert, S. 1980. *Mindstorms.* New York: Basic Books, Inc.

Stein, S.K., and C.D. Crabill. 1986. *Elementary algebra: A guided inquiry.* Pleasantville, N.Y.: Sunburst Communications.

Stein, S.K., C.D. Crabill, and G.D. Chakerian. 1986. *Algebra II/ Trigonometry: A guided inquiry.* Pleasantville, N.Y.: Sunburst Communications.

Calvin D. Crabill *is Lecturer-Supervisor in the Department of Education at the University of California, Davis. He has taught at the high school and junior/community college levels and, in recent years, has been involved in the retraining of teachers in the Northern California Mathematics Project and in the recruiting and training of beginning teachers. He is also coauthor of a secondary mathematics textbook series designed for small-group learning.*

8.

Real Maths in Cooperative Groups in Secondary Education

JAN TERWEL

First Encounters

My first encounter with cooperative learning in mathematics was in the early seventies, when I attended a conference in a small Dutch village. I was then a student and little realized how involved I was later to become in cooperative learning. The subject at the conference was "Innovation in Dutch secondary education." There were many German experts present, since they already had experience with a type of comprehensive education at the secondary school level (the *Gesamtschule*). At that time in the Netherlands, change was still only in the planning stage.

At this conference a central issue was "unity and diversity within the new comprehensive school." Our German colleagues suggested many possibilities for coping with individual differences among pupils. They spoke of streaming, setting, and intraclass differentiation. They also offered sophisticated models for flexible student grouping. This all seemed wonderful at first glance.

However, the German research data revealed a considerable problem. All models tended in the direction of maintaining inequality of opportunity among pupils. It did not bring an end to the internal selection process (that is, selection within schools) merely by postponing the between-school selection process. The only difference was that this now happened under one (school) roof. Thus the introduction of the new comprehensive school did not always have the desired aim of integrating children of different abilities and from differing backgrounds. Selection procedures within the German *Gesamtschule* still exist but are less noticeable than in the traditional elitist school system, with its separate schools for different "types" of pupils.

Some people were disappointed with the results of the German innovations. Among these was Prof. Hans Freudenthal, a well-known Dutch mathematician. In a lecture, he criticized the use of the traditional differentiation models. "Our German colleagues," he said, "differentiate the students before integrating them" (1973). This differentiation is merely a euphemism for separation. If this is to be the result of future innovations in the Netherlands, would it not be wiser to maintain the traditional school system here? There appears to be no difference between the old and the new systems.

Freudenthal, in his lecture, also suggested an alternative that could be used in the new comprehensive schools that were being established. He proposed having small, heterogeneous groups within the heterogeneous class. He further proposed guided discovery learning in mathematics and spoke about special opportunities within the subject area of mathematics. He referred to Van Hiele's theory about levels in the learning process. Students who work together may have different ways of solving a maths problem. If they discuss these differences with each other (reflection), they may make significant progress in learning mathematics.

Although when I first heard them I did not understand the meaning of such expressions as "levels in the learning process" or "reflection," I felt very interested and attracted. Freudenthal's ideas seemed to overcome many difficulties of other differentiation models.

Later on, I read other articles and books by Freudenthal. In these he is concerned with topics such as "mathematics for everybody" and "the relevance of mathematics." In Freudenthal's view, mathematics should be seen to have a closer connection with everyday reality and not be taught simply through abstractions. Freudenthal argues that mathematics is a human activity. What humans should learn is not a maths that is a closed system but one that is an activity, a process.

I am at present very involved with research into cooperative learning in mathematics. In our research project, "Mixed ability groups in mathematics for 12- to 16-year-olds," we evaluate a curriculum that is based on the ideas of Prof. Freudenthal, Van Hiele, and others; on cognition theories, both classical and recent, about teaching and learning; and on research findings that deal with problem-oriented learning in small groups in mathematics (Davidson, 1980, 1985).

Personal Viewpoint

My own view on education and my interest in cooperative learning arose from my experiences as a secondary school teacher. I have spent about nine years teaching in technical schools in the Netherlands. Most of my pupils were low achievers (although there were often bright children among them) for various reasons: They frequently had a very negative attitude toward school, and most of them came from low-income families. I find it a challenge to work on the development and improvement of programmes and practices in which students with different abilities work together.

I should like to explain how differences among students can lead to more than just difficulties for teachers in the classroom. Individual differences and common characteristics of students may also be seen as untapped potential. Cooperative learning is a way of exploiting this potential.

Personally I prefer an open, informal system of teaching, but I realize that it is unrealistic to suppose that all pupils will benefit from this. I therefore advocate a combination of open, informal elements together with more structured ways of teaching and learning. It seems wise to aim for a well-balanced curriculum that will provide all pupils with motivating experiences and with basic concepts and strategies.

After analyzing and comparing different approaches, I have developed my own viewpoint concerning maths in education. I have had discussions with such people as Freudenthal and Van Hiele, worked with educational specialists and teachers, and carried out my own research in different schools. And what I want to propagate is something called "real maths." What this means is that maths is not a separate distinct discipline but an activity that has a real-world context. It is often fruitful to carry out this activity in connection with others. I think that many pupils may come to understand what maths is about through concrete daily experiences. Maths needs to be integrated with other studies and other activities.

There are exciting teaching opportunities using maths and science in practical, technical situations (for example, designing, drawing, making, constructing, analyzing, or using technical objects, tools, buildings, or models).

I recently had this idea of mine confirmed when I visited the experimental schools in Redwood City, California, where Elizabeth Cohen's programme, Finding Out/Descubrimiento (FO/D), was being implemented. I was impressed by the results of this science and maths programme and the effects of special procedures to stimulate children with different backgrounds to work together (Cohen, 1986).

I shall now present a rationale for a maths programme that will realize some of the principles I have just mentioned.

Rationale for a Maths Curriculum

I should like to say two things before I describe the main features of this maths curriculum for 12- to 16-year-olds.

First, we did not develop this curriculum; we are the evaluators of this programme. Our research questions are (1) How does it work in classroom practice? (2) What are the learning results? and (3) What is the relation between processes in classrooms and learning results? The curriculum has been developed by the mathematics section of the National Curriculum Development Foundation (Dutch: SLO) in the Netherlands. The maths section of this foundation needed feedback based on theory and research. And so in 1981 we, a group at the state university of Utrecht, started a research project. It should be born in mind that the staff of the SLO are the ones who develop the curriculum; we, from the Department of Educational Research at the University of Utrecht, are the research workers. This is a typically Dutch division of labour, with related work carried out at different institutes. There are counterproductive aspects to this labour division, which we try to overcome by cooperation with the SLO and by adjusting our research to developmental activities (developmental research). But we still have our own tasks and our own responsibility: quality of research and theory building.

Second, I use the term *curriculum*, or *programme*, with a wide meaning. "Curriculum" refers to the whole arrangement of the teaching-learning process, not only on paper, but also in the classroom. In this sense, "curriculum" covers the goals, content, procedures, interactions, groupings, classroom management, organization, and more!

What Are the Main Characteristics?

This curriculum may be considered as an experiment, to teach mathematics to the majority, to reach a high level for all, and to present maths in real-life situations. Cooperative learning is an important aspect of this curriculum. The slogans are "Mathematics for All" (for everybody) and "Real Maths."

I shall now describe the eight characteristics of this "Maths for All" curriculum. This is a description of the rationale of the curriculum. This description contains the main features and theoretical standpoints of the curriculum on paper.

1. *Common goals.* All students are encouraged to reach as high a level as possible. Students who have difficulties with maths are given special attention. All students are required to attain a certain minimum level, but there are students who far exceed this.

2. *Teaching and learning in heterogeneous classes.* Maths for all means that in contrast to what is usually done in secondary schools, pupils are not permanently separated into classes or streams on the basis of achievement or ability in maths. There is no setting, streaming, or ability teaching. One teacher instructs students of different abilities (mixed-ability teaching) in one class. The teacher is an important figure. He or she gives systematic instruction to the class as a whole and leads class discussion and reflection.

3. *Cooperation in small groups.* Within the class, pupils work together in heterogeneous small groups of two to four. Freudenthal says: "I believe in the social learning process, and on the strength of this belief I advocate the heterogeneous learning group. My own ideas concerning the heterogeneous learning group, my appreciating it, and my arguments in favour of it, have arisen in observing mathematical learning processes and

thinking about my observations. The heterogeneous learning group comprises pupils of different levels collaborating on one task, each on his own level, a common task such as is often undertaken in society by heterogeneous working groups of people collaborating on different levels, each on his own" (Freudenthal, 1980, pp. 60–61). Freudenthal says that the structure of the mathematical learning process can be characterized by levels. From this fundamental idea of levels, he advocates learning in heterogeneous groups.

4. *Levels in the learning process: theory and examples.* But what are levels? Mathematics practiced on lower levels becomes mathematics observed on higher levels. Pupils apply ideas and rules until they become aware of them. If they reflect on their own problem-solving processes, they may reach higher levels of understanding. The results of this reflection may be the formulation of ideas, concepts, and rules in general terms. It is fruitful not only to reflect upon one's own learning processes but also on those of others.

5. *Maths in real-life situations.* This means that maths education is generated in everyday situations and deals with such topics as: sports, cycling, fishing, camping, traffic, TV, video, houses, weather forecasting—subjects that will be familiar to everyone. Figure 8-1 shows a task from a pupil's booklet that illustrates this.

6. *Maths: something people do.* In some concepts of mathematics, it is seen as an abstract logical system, as a fixed construction. The opposite view sees maths as an activity—something people do.

7. *Applicability.* Pupils need to realize that maths can be related to other aspects of the world, to other disciplines and techniques. Maths is not simply an end in itself.

8. *Registration of individual progress and additional help.* This last feature of the maths programme may be seen in close connection with the first characteristic (common goals). Common goals can only be attained if teachers recognize the dilemma of

Figure 8-1   Cycling

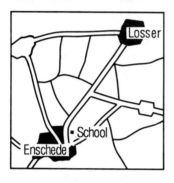

Many children from Losser go to school in Enschede. They usually go by bike.

Questions:
Below you can see four graphs and four stories. Which story goes with which graph?

Think about what Marijke might have said.

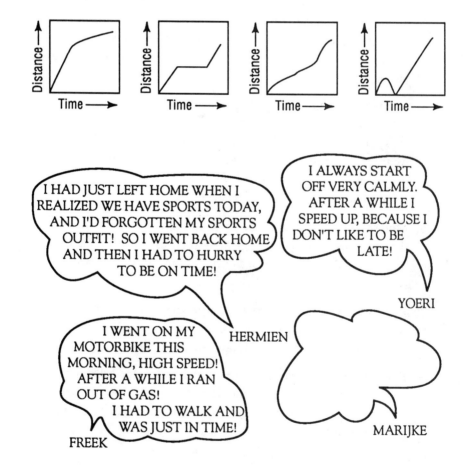

time and achievement. In order to achieve common goals, some pupils need more time and help. It is therefore necessary to register the progress of each student and to identify low achievers (by keeping records of progress and by giving feedback and additional help). If we accept that low-performing pupils constantly need more learning time, we are likely to approach "Maths for All."

We have now given a description of the main characteristics of the curriculum (a rationale). Such a description gives information about the ideas and intentions of the curriculum developers. But it is still a long way from transposing these ideas into curriculum materials or classroom practice.

In the following paragraphs we provide a more detailed description of some characteristics: levels in the learning process, classroom and group composition, the materials used, the teacher's role, and classroom practices. These are all clarified by concrete examples of maths problems and protocols of interaction processes in the classroom. This article ends with a summary of our research findings as well as some recommendations.

Levels in the Learning Process: Theory and Practice

Van Hiele, a Dutch maths teacher and educational researcher, has gained worldwide recognition with his level-theory. Van Hiele's work may be placed in the tradition of European cognition theory (Piaget, Selz, and Kohnstamm). There are also similarities between Van Hiele's work and Klausmeier's theory; however, Van Hiele has built his argument on his own experiences as a maths (geometry) teacher in secondary schools (Van Hiele, 1982). I shall try to explain his level-theory with examples taken from the SLO curriculum dealing with mathematical relations and functions. The maths problems in this curriculum have real-life settings. For example: Grandpop goes to the baker's in his car. They sell really good cookies at that baker's . . . . Students are given a map of the roads round the baker's (showing traffic lights and pedestrian crossings) and a graph in terms of speed and time representing Grandpop's drive. Then they are asked to fill in Grandpop's route on the map. (See Figure 8-2.)

Figure 8-2 Grandpop's Route

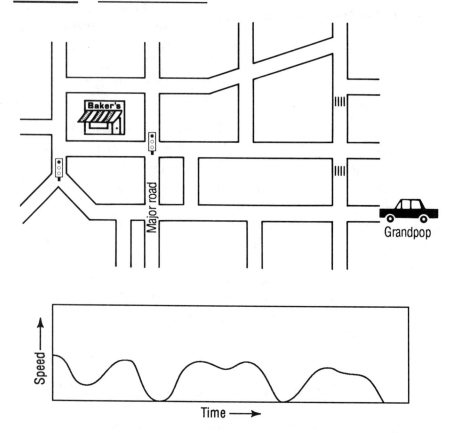

In other parts of the curriculum, students make graphs by themselves; graphs showing relations between (1) speed and time, (2) time and distance, and (3) speed and braking time (skid marks). In some of the small groups, we observed the phenomena of levels while pupils were doing this type of work. I shall give some illustrations of these taken from such examples as Grandpop going to the baker's—in particular, problems about speed and length of braking time.

0 Zero level or perceptive level. Students are on the zero level if they see or experience "going to the baker's" as a whole action ("gestalt"), without thinking or analyzing the elements that are involved. Sometimes pupils at this level may interpret a graph as a picture of their visual impressions, for example, as a road with curves, hills, and valleys.

1 First, or descriptive, level. A student is at the first level if he or she gives a description of the elements and their characteristics in the total situation: car, road, speed, and braking time. Intuitive notions may appear in this description about connections between those elements or characteristics. The pupils may express these intuitions via gestures, drawings, words, or numbers. But there is as yet no reflection upon the fundamental idea of functions as expressed in formulas.

2 Second, or theoretical, level. In the second level, these intuitive notions are more explicitly formulated, and they become objects of reflection in the following ways:

(a) In words: The greater the speed the longer the braking time, or the length of the braking distance is related to the quadration of the speed.

(b) In graphs:

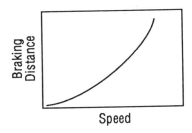

Speed

(c) In tables:

SPEED	BRAKING DISTANCE
10	1
30	9
50	25
70	49
90	81

(d) As a formula: $y = \frac{x^2}{100}$

When pupils reflect upon the connections between the different representations of functions in (a), (b), (c), and (d) and upon the mathematical concept of functions (for example, if they reflect upon different kinds of functions expressed in abstract formulas, such as $y = ax$, $y = ax^2$, $y = c/x$ and $y = ax + b$), we may say that the pupils are on the theoretical level.

In practice, there is not always a sharp distinction between the levels. Thinking about mathematical problems like this is a dynamic process. This process swings back and forth between naive, everyday experience with cars and traffic and more abstract representations. Misconceptions, such as seeing the graph as a sketch of a cyclist on a road with hills, may persist even after a pupil has already shown that he or she is able to analyze the whole gestalt, in terms of elements, characteristics, and their relations. A pupil may show a temporary "regression" to a lower level. This return to a lower level may have positive effects. For example, a pupil may recognize that the formula $y = \frac{x^2}{100}$ is too simple and crude because it doesn't take into account factors like driver's reaction time, type of car, brakes, roads, and weather conditions. All these are relevant factors affecting the slowing down of a car. When someone returns from using abstract formulas to the rich context of concrete experience, this may help to evaluate, improve, and refine the abstract formula. Thus, in fact, thinking cannot be adequately described in terms of distinct, static levels. In the thinking processes, levels may appear simultaneously, both in the problem-solving processes of groups of pupils and within the thought process of an individual. This is one reason why teaching and learning is so complex and exciting. This dynamic, simultaneous nature of thinking should be recognized and may be exploited in the teaching-learning process, especially when different levels are involved at the same time in small groups.

Van Hiele says that there are different languages on the various levels. This causes a serious problem in mathematics learning. There is a communication gap between pupils on different levels. They express themselves differently and the result may well be that they talk at cross-purposes.

But we need not be defeated by Towers of Babel. Van Hiele suggests a teaching-learning process in five stages: information, structured orientation, expliciting, free orientation, and interpretation. At the first stage (information), pupils receive materials, such as objects, figures, papers, drawings, photos, figures, and graphs, to use in exercises. In the second stage (structured orientation), pupils are given specific tasks. Each task aims to teach pupils one characteristic of the material they are using. At the third stage (expliciting), pupils express the characteristic in words. In the fourth stage (free orientation), pupils learn by general tasks to find their own way in the network of relations. In the fifth stage (integration), pupils reflect on the different solutions. They explore the relations between those solutions. They formulate the laws of the new, higher-level structure (Van Hiele, 1986, p. 54). Van Hiele points out that at this last stage in particular, confusion and cross-purpose talk may arise. In such cases, Van Hiele recommends that the teacher be patient: he or she should not force students to a higher level but wait a few weeks, take another topic, and try to return later (telescoped reteaching). See also Bruner's idea (1960) of the spiral curriculum and other ideas of a concentric curriculum design. The teacher is central in these processes, but cooperation between students may also be helpful.

Students of different levels, working together in small groups, may learn from each other even (especially) if confusion and/or crises (sociocognitive conflicts) arise. The teacher is a crucial figure in solving these conflicts: he or she may help pupils to verbalize their thoughts or express them in graphs or formulas. The teacher may foster the reflection process and so help pupils to attain greater insight into certain processes.

Composition of Classes and Groups

The schools that have adopted the "Maths for All" programme generally work with heterogeneous small groups within a heterogeneous class. "Heterogeneous" here means that pupils vary in ability and achievement. Pupils are not separated into different classes on the basis of ability. Instead of streaming or setting, there is mixed-ability teaching. But one of the schools in our research sample uses a type of streaming—overlapping ability classes like roof tiles! However, our maths programme is designed for mixed-ability teaching.

Within the class there are heterogeneous small groups of two to four (mostly four) pupils. How do they form these small groups? We saw this done in many different ways. (Dutch schools, and teachers, are relatively autonomous.) Sometimes pupils were free to choose their groups, and these groups remained the same throughout the year. This practice has the advantage of simplicity and stability. Pupils often want to work with their friends, which has some advantages, these being:

1. Less rivalry between pupils in the small groups

2. Easy communication and understanding

3. Teacher freed from making management decisions

But this free choice procedure also brings certain problems:

1. There are always people left out (so they don't have a free choice).

2. Cliques may develop, leading to rivalry and poor communication between the small groups.

3. Free choice may lead to homogenizing with the small groups, for example, all one sex; same background; same level, ability, or ethnic group.

4. Within stable small groups there are often static communication patterns and/or fixed hierarchies.

How the advantages and difficulties connected with free choice are evaluated depends on the goals and attitudes of a school and teacher. My own attitude is that the existing friendships between pupils should be used as much as possible, but that the composition of groups should not be a matter of free choice. Keep the groups well balanced, with regard to sex, ability, and background, in order to gain optimal profit from differences and avoid rigid interaction patterns.

In one of our research schools, groups were shuffled every six weeks. During the first period of the school year, there was free choice. Afterwards, teachers changed the groups, taking into consideration what the pupils would like but making the ultimate decision themselves. If this seems useful, teachers may create groups of pupils who need special attention from the teacher.

This practice avoids many difficulties. In those classes where the teacher did not intervene in the composition of the small groups, we observed definite Pygmalion effects between pupils. Pupils acquired fixed role patterns. As a result, some pupils were almost entirely ignored, even were they to produce good suggestions or solutions. This presents a serious problem; it also has a negative effect on such pupils' learning results. Cooperative learning in itself is no guarantee that such problems will not occur.

In the plan in Figure 8-3 we show the physical arrangement of a class. There are of course many other possibilities.

Figure 8-3 *Plan of Seating Arrangement*

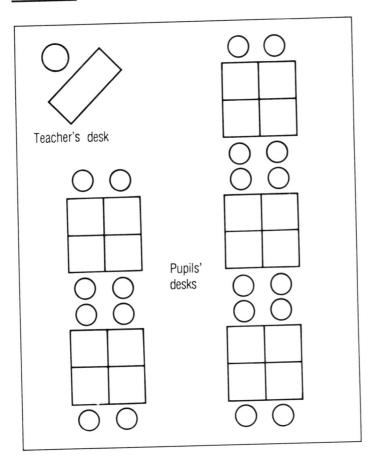

Teacher's desk

Pupils' desks

Materials for Pupils and Teachers

The written curriculum consists of different materials (see the Resources at the end of this chapter). There are teacher manuals with suggestions for classroom implementation of the "Maths for

All" programme. There are books/booklets for the pupils, dealing especially with relations and functions in maths. As I have said, all these materials have been developed by a team (mathematicians and instructional psychologists) from the Dutch Curriculum Development Foundation (SLO).

Although strictly speaking we as researchers at the University of Utrecht are not meant to develop materials, we did not limit our work to pure research. There are some spin-offs that are very interesting to teachers, curriculum developers, and policy makers. Based on our research reports we produced:

- Articles in journals for teachers, teacher education, and curriculum developers

- A videotape for teachers who want to work with the new programme and find out about recent research results

- A manual for teachers containing many practical tips and protocols of classroom situations and problem solving in small groups

There is more information about these materials at the end of this chapter. In the following paragraphs you will find problems from the pupils' books.

The Role of the Teacher

The teacher is an important figure. He or she organizes activities that involve the whole class, such as systematic instruction, Socratic discussions, and reflection. The teacher provides guidance for small groups.

In a task dealing with weather forecasting, the pupils try to find an answer to a question about data in a newspaper chart. The pupils are in the first class at secondary school, aged about 13 years.

Amsterdam	re	17	4
De Bilt	re	17	2
Athens	ob	32	0

The pupils have to answer the question: What does this all mean? There are no problems in interpreting "re" and "17." "R" and "e" are the two first letters of the Dutch word for rain—"regen," and "17 stands for 17 degrees Celcius. But what about the rest?

Teacher: What does 2 mean in this table?

Franny: Two millimetres of rain. (She blurts it out, as if frightened of herself.)

Karen: Never heard of it.

Trudy: It *is* possible, 2 millimetres of rain.

Karen: No, it's not.

Teacher: Possible or not?

Karen: Not.

Trudy: Yes.

Teacher: Why not, Karen?

Karen: It's just not.

Teacher: Franny, can you explain it to Karen?

Franny: It means 2 millimetres of rain has fallen.

Karen: Two millimetres is hardly anything—that's not a shower of rain.

Franny: That's what it means.

Karen: If it pours with rain you have much more than 2 millimetres.

Mary: The area where the rain falls is actually much bigger.

Teacher: How deep is 2 millimetres? Is it deep?

Karen: No, of course not, you can't have 2 millimetres of rain.

There is a lot of confusion in the class. Some of the pupils look for other meanings of 2.

Sandra: In the night the temperature drops 2 degrees.

Karen: Two! That means 2 degrees below zero.

Teacher: Look at the table again, and compare data in the first and third columns.

Light begins to dawn. For Athens, there are no clouds and no rain. But Karen does not understand. The teacher describes how the amount of rain is measured.

Karen: It doesn't pour with rain all over the place. A downpour is much deeper, even more than 1 centimetre.

The teacher and Mary try to explain it to Karen. But it is not clear whether she understands it yet.

In this example we see that it was important that the teacher was there to lead the discussion. The teacher detected a misunderstanding and tried to sort it out, using the other pupils to help. At first this did not work. Some pupils became confused, but a hint from the teacher helped to sort things out for them. But Karen cannot manage to look at things in a new way. She is on what Van Hiele calls the "zero level." For her, rain is only visualized in one way, as a heavy downpour. What she cannot manage (yet) is to think of rain in terms of something that can be measured in a container.

Generally speaking, the teacher is an important figure. He or she helps to solve differences in representations and language between pupils. And the teacher has many other functions as instructor, manager, and evaluator. We found strong correlations between the time-on-task in learning in small groups and the extent to which teachers give systematic instruction and organize discussion and reflection in the class as a whole. What we found was that in classes where the teacher gives little instruction to the class as a whole (in which small groups work for long periods on their own), there is more noise, off-task behaviour, and quarreling in the small groups than in classes where the teacher spends more time on instruction and reflection with the whole class. We discovered great differences between classes in the time spent on group work: variations between 23 percent and 96 percent of lesson time. The largest proportion of group work was found in classes having many low-performance pupils and inexperienced teachers. In such classes there was a tendency for teachers to avoid teaching the whole class because of management problems and negative reactions of the pupils and also because there were frequent requests for help from individual pupils and small groups. We wonder if there is an ideal balance between group work and whole-class instruction. We cannot answer this question by generalization. It depends on varying factors, such as the pupils (start competencies, experience in group work), the teachers (experiences, resources), and the mathematical content. There is no unicausal relation in this respect. Quality of instruction in whole class and quality of interaction in small groups are more important than quantity of time spent on different activities. In many cases it may be wise to work toward a golden mean, say about 50 to 70 percent of the time available, to be spent in group work.

We also found strong, significant correlations between time engaged in learning (task-orientation) and learning results. The conclusion is clear. Cooperative learning needs to be very well organized by the teacher. Without coordination, systematic instruction, and management from the teacher, cooperative learning may turn out to be neither cooperative nor learning.

Lesson Outline and Examples

In this section I give a brief outline for lessons and four example lessons that illustrate each aspect of the model. The examples are fragments from lessons we observed during some of our investigations. The observations were made at secondary (comprehensive) schools. The pupils were aged 12 to 14 years. The problems (or tasks) given to the pupils are in a textbook (Dutch: *Regelrecht* means "all straight"). In this section the pupils are introduced to linear functions. The lesson (or series of lessons) generally consists of the following three successive parts:

1. *Introduction*. The teacher introduces the problem to the whole class. He or she may motivate the pupils by placing the problem in their world. The teacher gives the general outline of the problem, explores the various aspects of it, and may give hints about the solution.

2. *Group work*. The pupils are instructed to work in groups. The teacher observes and supervises their cooperation and tries to solve problems that originate in differences of pace or level between pupils. When required, he or she deals with individual problems.

3. *Reflection and evaluation*. Following the group work, the results and the actual process of the group work are discussed in the class. This discussion contains the following elements:

   ▪ An inventory is made of the different ways of solving the problem and of various solutions.

- The different ways of solving the problem and the solutions are considered.

- Using questions, the teacher tries to investigate other ways of handling the problem.

- The solutions are reformulated and summarized.

- If necessary (and possible), generalizations are found.

These three aspects make up the lesson outline. Each part deserves great attention. As well as these things, the teacher should evaluate the progress of individual pupils and when necessary take some didactic measures (do some teaching). We now have an outline of the characteristic moments in the lessons. Now let us look at the practical situation.

Introduction: Lesson Example

The following example is a fragment from the beginning of a lesson. The pupils are sitting in a circle. They are not (yet) looking at their books. The teacher asks questions about the following problem:

Once upon a time there was a young man called Jim, with a keen nose for business. He saw that badges were all the rage—pinned on jackets, shirts, and so on—so he thought he'd start up a business making and selling badges. He could make the designs himself or find them in old newspapers and magazines. Anyway, he was good at drawing and could design them himself. If you know the right address, you can order badge-making kits and get the parts you need. Jim finds the right address.

In the illustration you can see the graph in Jim's papers.

Figure 8-4   Graph in Jim's Papers

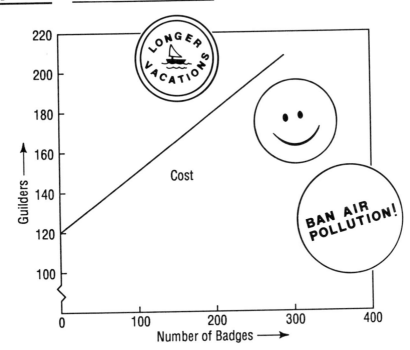

Questions:

1. How much will it cost Jim, according to his own calculations, to make 250 badges?

2. What does the gadget cost that you press badges shut with? And what does an empty badge cost?

3. Jim tells his friend Chris, "You can work out my costs by looking at this graph. I'm going to sell the badges for a guilder a piece. They ought to sell well, because that's cheaper than the usual price. I'll make a mint, man!"

   Chris isn't so sure. He says, "If I look at your graph, it costs 150 guilders to make 100 badges. If you sell them at a guilder each, how are you going to make any profit?"

   "Man, you don't get it!" says Jim. "Look . . . ." (What will Jim say to explain?)

The teacher starts the lesson:

Teacher:	Let's think about what you need to make badges. Who can tell me something? What would you need?

Several pupils respond to this question. Some say "a pin."

Teacher:	Yes, a pin. What else?

There are various answers: iron, a picture, plastic.

Teacher:	OK, one at a time. What else would you need?
Nadja:	The thing you put the picture in.
Teacher:	Yes, if you want to make a luxury badge, that's right; what else?

Other answers: paper, a photo.

Nadja:	That's not what I mean.
Teacher:	Not what you mean?
Nadja:	The picture that's in the badge.
Teacher:	Oh, you mean a message in the badge, like "Ban Air Pollution" or "Longer Vacations."

(Loud cheers at this point from the class)

Teacher:	Well, we've got several things now. If you have all these, can you make a badge, just like that?
Several pupils:	Yes.
Teacher:	Well, I suppose you could do it all by hand. But imagine you want to set up a small business. Would you make all the badges by hand?
Pupils:	No.
Eddy:	You can get those little gadgets, you push on it and then, snap.
Teacher:	That's right. There's a special gadget on the market to make badges with. So if you want to

start up a badge-making business, what would a gadget like that cost?

There are some guesses.

Teacher: Sam, have a guess.

Sam: Five thousand.

Teacher: That's probably a bit high, but it doesn't matter.

This conversation goes on for a while. The teacher also asks for estimates of the cost of materials needed and the cost of producing 1 or 2 or 0 badges. The pupils estimate the cost of one badge at 0.50 guilders. The teacher introduces the subject before the pupils have seen the story of Jim and his badges in their booklets (Figure 8-4 and questions). With the first questions of the teacher, the pupils are placed in the role of Jim: They want to make badges. The subject becomes alive for them, as can be seen from their spontaneous reactions.

The teacher asks the question about making the badge (with your own hands) and this prompts the reply about the gadget. One boy, Eddy, has seen a gadget like this and knows how it works. The questions about the cost of such a gadget, about the materials needed, about the production of, for example, 1 or 2 or 0 badges, try to elicit mathematical ideas from the pupils. Their answers show that they understand the principle of fixed and variable prices.

Teacher: How much does it cost to make 1 badge?

Patty: 5000.50 guilders.

Now all the important elements have been discussed.

Group Work: Lesson Example

Two pupils, Lucy and Meg, work together on this problem:

> There are two shops in our district where you can rent video tapes: Video-All-Inn and La Bonne Video. In one of the two, you have to buy a membership card first. The other shop does not have these cards; you simply pay per tape. Both have a daily charge (rate per day). The graph showing the costs is given in Figure 8-5.

Figure 8-5   *Video Shops*

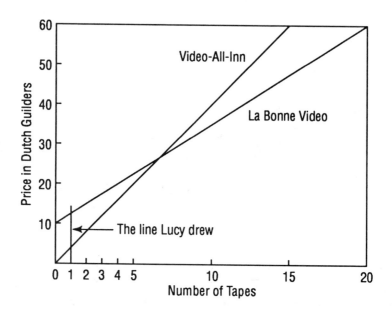

Questions:

1. In which of the two shops do you have to buy a membership card?

2. How can you see that on the graph?

3. What does the membership card cost?

4. What is the charge per day per videotape in Video-All-Inn?

5. What is this charge in La Bonne Video (once you have a membership card)?

6. The lines in the graph cross at a certain point. What does this mean for people who often rent videotapes?

7. Video-All-Inn has a special offer this month: rent 3 tapes, pay for 2. What do you have to pay if you rent 15 tapes this month?

8. If you rent 40 tapes from La Bonne Video, how much do you have to pay?

Questions 1–4 do not present any problem and are quickly answered. At question 5 something happens, which later proves to be very significant. Lucy draws a thin vertical line from the x-axis (from point 1 tape) parallel to the y-axis. This line crosses the graph of La Bonne Video. From this crossing point she makes a move horizontal to the y-axis and calculates 3 guilders per tape. Lucy and Meg both write for question 5 the answer 3 (the correct answer is $2\frac{1}{2}$). Questions 6 and 7 get a correct answer. At Question 8 it becomes interesting. Meg follows a global strategy—she takes big steps along the axes. Lucy uses a precise strategy and works from the basis of the price per tape.

Meg: (moves with her finger upward from 20 tapes on the x-axis) Twenty tapes cost 60 guilders; 40 tapes cost 120 guilders.

Lucy: You'd better go like this: you have to pay 4 guilders per tape. $40 \times 4 = 160$. Plus a card costs 10 guilders. So you have to pay 170 guilders. Oh no, it's 3 per tape. (She points to the graph of La Bonne Video.) That means you have to pay $3 \times 40 + 10 = 130$ guilders.

Meg: That doesn't make sense to me. And that's not the same result as I had. (She points to the right of the graph.) If you start here you get 50. So without taking this into account (she indicates the 10 guilders for the card) you would have $50 \times 2 = 100$. (She is pointing to the left where the line of La Bonne Video starts on the y-axis.) It doesn't make sense!

Lucy: Yes, it's dotty! Don't ask me!

Meg: We start here (points to right side of graph). That's 100.

Lucy: Plus 10.

Meg: Yes, that makes 110. But we've just said it was 130 or 160 . . . funny, funny, funny.

Lucy: I think the small dots on the x-axis (1, 2, 3, 4, 5) aren't right. You have to look at the price of one tape without the card. For example, 3 guilders per tape . . . if you want 40 tapes . . . $40 \times 3 + 10 = 130$.

Meg: Well, maybe the card is already paid.

Then they look at the whole process; they recapitulate. Lucy does not like Meg's approach.

Lucy: Probably this is what is making the difference. (She points to the line she drew earlier.) It is not 3 guilders per tape but 2 guilders! If the graphs were drawn on graph paper, you could see it precisely. You have 110. I have 130. A difference of 20! Look (points to her vertical line at point 1 tape), if you go upward from this point—I think that's 3 guilders per tape.

Both girls maintain their own solutions and verbalize them very accurately. They listen to each other very carefully.

Meg: (repeating) 2 × 20 tapes = 40 tapes. That makes 100 guilders (2 × 50) plus card is 110 guilders.

Lucy: (Her face lights up . . . silence.) What's 100 divided by 40? Is that $2\frac{1}{2}$?

Meg: Yes.

Lucy: Then that's the answer. Now it works. This part of the line is $2\frac{1}{2}$. (She points again to the line she drew and moves her finger horizontally from the meeting point of her line and the line of La Bonne Video to the y-axis.) Look! Look! If this part is $2\frac{1}{2}$, then it's OK. See—one tape costs $2\frac{1}{2}$ guilders, 40 tapes cost 100 guilders, plus 10 for the card is 110 guilders.

Meg: Yes, the problem was you couldn't see whether this part of the line was 2, 3, or $2\frac{1}{2}$. But now we've solved it. The answer is 110 guilders. We did it different ways. But your first answer would have been right, if you take into account that the graph wasn't very clear.

This account demonstrates clearly the benefits of cooperation. Lucy and Meg are friends. They motivate each other and give each other direct feedback. Although strictly speaking, Meg was the first one to have the right answer, at the end she sums up the value of Lucy's solution. Both are satisfied. In their problem-solving process they initially made a lot of mistakes, but they both were able to reflect not only on their own method of solution but also on the other's. Finally, in the confrontation of the different answers, Lucy had a moment of "Eureka!" She suddenly realized what was causing the difference between the two answers. The strategies of both girls proved to be adequate. Lucy and Meg even criticized the task—the graph wasn't clear enough.

Group Work: Lesson Example

The group being observed in this case had been working for some time on the same type of problems. In the following example, the most difficult part deals with the question about delivery charges.

Yesterday I saw an ad in the paper from a large do-it-yourself firm, PRISKA. They had a special offer for garden (patio) tiles.

PRISKA DO-IT-YOURSELF

Patio Tiles at Bargain Prices!

- 50 for 135 Guilders
- 100 for 255 Guilders

Quantities over 500 even better bargains!

PRICE INCLUDES DELIVERY

Questions:

1. Does PRISKA charge delivery costs? If so, how much?

2. What is the price of one tile?

One of the pupils is puzzled about the first question. Why is the answer 15 guilders? Here is a fragment from the discussion. Monique, Vanessa, and Colin are pupils.

Monique: I don't understand the 15 guilders.

Teacher: Think about it. The set of 100 tiles costs 255 guilders and 50 tiles cost 135 guilders, but that's not half the price for 100 tiles, is it?

Colin: There's a difference of 15 guilders.

Monique: Ooh, I see.

Colin: So in fact the delivery costs are included in the price.

The next problem is to find out the price of one tile. Monique thinks she knows the answer and wants the teacher to confirm this.

Monique: Please, is the price of one tile 85 cents?

Teacher: How did you figure that out?

Monique: 135 minus 50.

Teacher: Minus 50? 135, what's that?

Vanessa: Money.

Teacher: And what is 50?

Colin: Tiles.

Teacher: You're subtracting tiles from money?

Monique: Oh, stupid!

Teacher: So that won't work, will it? Now, you know exactly how much 50 tiles cost, excluding delivery cost.

Monique: 120.

Teacher: So how do you work out the cost of one tile?

Monique doesn't yet know the answer.

Teacher: How much do 50 tiles cost?

Colin: 120.

Teacher: Yes, that's what you pay for 50. So you can work out what you have to pay for one tile, can't you?

Monique: 120 divided by 50.

Teacher: What's that?

Colin: 2 point 4 (reads this from a calculator).

Teacher: What does that mean?

Colin: Two guilders and four cents.

Here it becomes clear that both Colin and Monique think that 2.4 means 2.04 guilders. The teacher asks them to write down 2 guilders and 40 cents. When they do this, they see their mistake. The teacher repeats the question.

Monique: Two forty—it's 2.40 guilders for one tile.

Teacher: Are you sure?

This group can only solve the problem when guided by the closed questions of the teacher. Cooperation among the three group members is not very good. Sometimes they start off well, but they soon stop cooperating and work individually.

In this fragment we see how the teacher assists the group with very directed questions. He understands the problems these pupils have in cooperating but also wants them to achieve a minimum level in their maths and not fall behind because they work too slowly. So he gives them a lot of help.

Reflection and Evaluation: Lesson Example

The pupils had worked on a certain problem during the preceding lesson. Now the teacher is trying to find out the solution to the problem and how the answers are reached.

Figure 8-6   *Twenty-two Guilders*

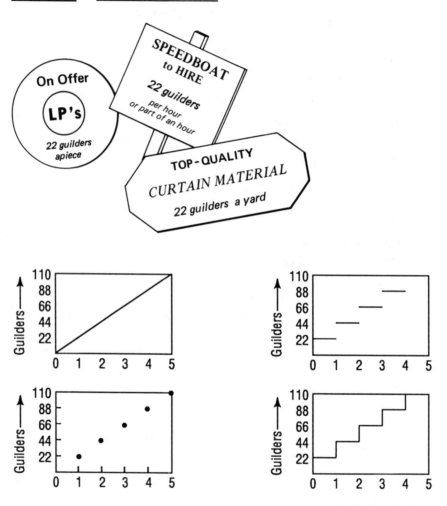

Question: Which graph fits best with which sign, and why?

Teacher: Now let's take a look at the graphs and the notices. LP's (long-playing records) cost 22 guilders; you can rent a speedboat for 22 guilders an hour; you can buy top-quality curtain material for 22 guilders a yard. Now we can take these graphs . . . Alice, where are your LP's?

Alice: In the third graph.

Teacher: Alice puts them in the third graph—are there any other suggestions?

Tom: I've got them in the first.

Teacher: (reacting to various pupils) You've got them in the first, you've got them in the second, and you've got them in the fourth . . . right. Alice, why do you think it's the third?

Alice: Because you can only buy 1, 2, or 3 LP's, not $1\frac{1}{2}$.

Teacher: How do you see that in the graph?

Alice: There are no dots at $2\frac{1}{2}$ LP's, are there? I mean, you can't buy half a record.

Several pupils agree with this. The teacher makes a joke about a broken record.

Teacher: If I look for $2\frac{1}{2}$ LP's in the first graph, it would be 55 guilders, wouldn't it? But we know that's nonsense. How about if I look in graph 4 for $2\frac{1}{2}$ LP's? According to the diagram it would be 66 guilders, right? And what about here? (Points to the third graph.)

Various different answers are heard.

Teacher: What do you think, Alice?

Alice: 55.

Teacher: How do you read a graph? I start off at $2\frac{1}{2}$ LP's and move up. . . look left, and I can see the amount. How far do I have to move up before I can see what it costs to buy $2\frac{1}{2}$ LP's? I can't, can I? The graph only shows whole numbers—is that clear to everyone?

Step by step the pupils are confronted with the different aspects of the problem. The teacher does this through questioning. She wants the pupils to tell her ways of solving the problem. In the last part of this extract she explains how to read a graph. She wants to be sure that all the pupils understand why graph 3 is the right answer in this case. We may suspect from Alice's answer that she did not really understand her own solution. She knew that you cannot buy half a record but was not really clear how a graph translates information.

Experiences, Problems, and Recommendations: A Summary

Since 1981 we have made many observations in secondary schools that are implementing the new maths programme. We have looked at the learning results of this new system, using pre- and post-tests. We have collected data from five secondary schools. With the help of these observations and test results, I have made the following summary of the positive experiences as well as the problems we have to deal with, together with proposals for improvement.

By and large, our experiences and research findings are positive. Cooperative learning is like a rich gold mine. Learning in cooperative groups is really a way of exploiting an untapped potential. We observed excellent discussions between pupils in small groups. The quality of interaction was in many cases remarkably high. Differences between pupils proved to be a positive factor instead of a hindrance in the teaching/learning process. Pupils offered and received explanations from each other. These explanations were often very useful in providing insight and in reaching a higher level of understanding. Most of the teachers we saw were very stimulating in motivating and guiding the class in small groups. Our test results show significant progress from pre- to post-tests. But there were some problems, too.

1. In some classes there were problems of organization management and discipline. Changes from group work to whole-class activities were particularly difficult. Where the class is difficult, teachers seem to avoid changes by cutting down on whole-class activities and letting the pupils work for long periods in small groups. But in the long run this strategy seems to produce more problems.

2. We sometimes observed what can be called "escapism." Pupils in small groups were often very happy doing almost anything but maths—just laughing and talking. They were often bored and did not know how to use their time. This could be seen most often in classes where there were low start competencies in maths.

3. Some pupils hardly took part in the group work. There are several possible causes for this. They then become low-status members of the small group.

4. There were great differences in how teachers implemented the maths programme. These differences applied mainly to the amount of time spent on group work, as opposed to time spent on whole-class activities. There were also differences in the proportion of time spent in learning. In classes where teachers organize relatively few whole-class activities (such as systematic instruction, evaluation, and reflection), the proportion of time spent in learning in the small groups is lower than in classes where there is more teacher-directed instruction to the whole class. Thus the quality and effectiveness of pupils' work in small groups depends on the extent to which the teacher supports cooperative work in small groups by giving instruction to the whole class (in, for example, introductions, concept clarification, evaluation, rules for cooperation, and reflection).

   Our research clearly shows that the proportion of time engaged in learning (time-on-task and task orientation) is positively related to learning results. I therefore suggest an optimal balance between open, informal self-discovery activities in small groups and teacher-structured activities, such as systematic instruction and registration of individual progress. The first will not flourish without backing from the second. The teacher-structured activities may be directed in the class as a whole, but in heterogeneous classes one can also form subgroups with special needs—for example, a group of low achievers who gain instruction in basic concepts of strategies while the rest of the class works in small groups on their own (Slavin, Madden, and Leavey, 1984).

5. Sociocognitive conflicts may foster and intensify the learning process. But sometimes the crises can become too intense. Pupils misunderstand each other, and irritation and frustration may result.

6. Real-life situations cause interference. Pupils do not always see what the core of a question is. They become so involved in the examples given (deep-sea diving, cross-country racing, and

so on) that the mathematical content of the exercise tends to be obscured.

7. In general, the learning results taken from the pre- and post-test scores showed a firm gain. But the differences were striking in pre- and post-test outcomes between classes, individual pupils, and schools. Although in general the pupils make significant progress, the curriculum does not yet achieve the aim of mathematics for all: Not all pupils reached an acceptable minimum level. We found high correlations between pre- and post-test scores (0.70–0.88). This means that (roughly speaking) the differences between pupils are still there, even after they have taken part in this new maths programme.

8. There was not always systematic registration of an individual pupil's progress. This could be seen in the case of lack of help offered to exceptionally gifted pupils or pupils who in some way had special learning needs. The teachers underestimate the dilemma of time and achievement. The curriculum developers did not provide teachers with diagnostic instruments or remedial procedures.

9. In education there are no easy victories, and cooperative learning cannot be seen as the latest cure-all. But it does offer exciting perspectives, especially in maths education. We should not be pessimistic about this new maths curriculum. Most of the pupils who use it make significant progress and attain the set goals. This kind of maths is what they enjoy, and they also enjoy cooperation in small groups. Teachers are also enthusiastic about this new programme. It does mark a real innovation in maths teaching in the Netherlands. It is worth remarking that among those pupils who failed to attain a minimum level using the new programme were children with very low start competencies (who lacked the requisite preknowledge in terms of concepts and skills) and/or unfavourable learning conditions. With the best will in the world, a new teaching programme cannot counter years of failure. If we really want to make maths for everyone, these children need to be given extra time and help. And perhaps

content changes are required. This maths programme has a paper-and-pencil character, with strong emphasis on verbalization and reflection. I believe in these strongly, myself, as ways of gaining insight, but we should not ignore the fact that some people have difficulties either with paper and pencil or with verbalization and reflection.

I should like to suggest building more practical or technical aspects into the programme. There should be more emphasis on learning through doing: manipulating, constructing, drawing, and making. Many children cannot sit still for very long, cannot listen to the teacher for very long, and get restless and bored. Bring objects into the classroom that they can do things with, such as (bits of) bikes and boats. Use things like wood, iron, and water. These things are alive and real and stimulate pupils because of their reality.

Resources

Teacher Manuals

SLO* : *Situatie beschrijvingen in wiskunde teksten* (Real-life situations in mathematics)

SLO: *...het werken in kleine heterogene groepen* (Learning in heterogeneous small groups)

SLO: *...een introductie op functies via verbanden* (An introduction to functions through connections)

Posthuma de Boer, M. *Werken met heterogene groepen* (Working with heterogeneous groups)
Guidelines for teachers
Utrecht, University of Utrecht, 1986

---

* The SLO is the National Curriculum Development Foundation in the Netherlands. The SLO curriculum developers involved are: Wim Kerkhofs, Hans Krabbendam, Jos ter Pelle, Jan Speelpenning, and Piet Verstappen.

Student Materials

These are all SLO productions and take the form of small textbooks.

Grafiekentaal

Grafieken en verbanden

Regelrecht A en B

Vlak voorbij

Uitstippelen

Videotapes

Mathematics for all

Lessons on video (University of Utrecht)

Project Information

The research project "Mixed ability teaching in mathematics 12–16" (ID 12–16) is sponsored by the Dutch National Foundation for Education Research (SVO) in The Hague. It is a project run by the University of Utrecht in the Netherlands. The members of the research team are: Rijkje Dekker, Paul Herfs, Dirk van der Ploeg, and Jan Terwel. University students also take part in research into specific topics, as well as the project team (ID 12–16). The protocol extracts in this chapter are taken from observations of Minke Postuma de Boer, Johan Gademan, Wytse de Jong, and Jan Terwel.

Author's mailing address:
  Dr. Jan Terwel (project leader, Research Project ID 12–16)
  University of Utrecht
  Department of Educational Research (VOU)
  Heidelberglaan 2
  3584 CS Utrecht
  The Netherlands

References

Bruner, Jerome. 1960. *The process of education*. New York: Vintage Books.

Cohen, E.G. 1986. Treating status problems in the cooperative classroom. Paper presented at the American Educational Research Association Annual Meeting, San Francisco, Calif.

Davidson, N. 1985. Small-group learning and teaching in mathematics: A selective review of the research. In *Learning to cooperate, cooperating to learn*, edited by R.E. Slavin, et al., 211–30. New York: Plenum.

————. 1980. Small-group learning in mathematics: An introduction for non-mathematicians. In *Cooperation in education*, edited by S. Sharan et al., 136–46. Provo, Ut.: Brigham University Press.

Freudenthal, H. 1973. De niveaus in het leerproces en de heterogene leergroep, met het oog op de middenschool. In *Gesamtschule conferentie 1973*. Purmerend: Amsterdam. APS Muusses.

————. 1980 *Weeding and sowing*. Dordrecht/Boston: Reidel.

Hiele, P.M. van. 1982. Fasen en stadia in de ontwikkeling van het denken, zoals die door Piaget worden geconstrueerd, vergeleken met de denkniveaus geintroduceerd door Van Hiele. *Pedagogisch Tijdschrift Forum voor Opvoedkunde* 7 (5): 207–18.

————. 1986. *Structure and insight: A theory of mathematics education*. Orlando, Fla.: Academic Press.

Simon, H.A. 1983. Otto Selz and information processing psychology. In *Otto Selz. His contribution to psychology*, edited by N.H. Frijda and A.D. de Groot. Den Haag: Mouton.

Slavin, R.E., N.A. Madden, and M. Leavey. 1984. Effects of team assisted individualization on the mathematics achievement of academically handicapped and nonhandicapped students. *Journal of Educational Psychology* 76 (5): 813–19.

Treffers, A. and F. Goffree. 1985. Rational analysis of realistic mathematics education. In *Proceedings of the Ninth International Conference for the Psychology of Mathematics Education* (vol II), edited by L. Streefland, 97–121. Utrecht, Noordwijkerhout, July 22–July 29.

References (Project)

Mixed-ability teaching in mathematics (Dutch: Interne Differentiatie 12–16)

Dekker, R. 1985. Maths for all? Just have a look. In *Proceedings of the Ninth International Conference for the Psychology of Mathematics Education* (vol. I), edited by L. Streefland. Utrecht, Noordwijkerhout, July 22–July 29.

Dekker, R., P. Herfs, and J. Terwel. 1986. Niveaus in het leerproces als differentiatieprincipe bij het werken in heterogene groepen bij wiskunde (Levels in the learning process as differentiation principle in small-group learning in mathematics.) *Onderwijs Research Dagen* (ORD) Utrecht (mei).

Dekker, R., P. Herfs, J. Terwel, and D. van der Ploeg. 1985. *Interne differentiatie in heterogene brugklassen* 's Gravenhage, SVO-selecta reeks.

Terwel, J. 1986. Mathematics for all: Between dream and reality. Presented at the Annual Meeting of the AERA, San Francisco.

———. 1984. *Onderwijs Maken. Naar ander onderwijs voor 12–16 jarigen.* (Educational development for secondary schools). Harlingen, Flevodruk. Foundation for Educational Research/University of Utrecht (diss. with an English summary).

Jan Terwel *is Assistant Professor in the Department of Education and Educational Research (VOU) at the University of Utrecht. He is an experienced classroom teacher and is currently a member of a research team investigating the impact of changes in curriculum and classroom practices in the Netherlands.*

9.

Integrating Computers as Tools in Mathematics Curricula (Grades 9–13): Portraits of Group Interactions

CHARLENE SHEETS AND M. KATHLEEN HEID

Computers can be used in a wide variety of ways in the mathematics classroom. Although computers are most frequently used for tutorials and for computational drill, mathematics curricula can be designed to take full advantage of computers as tools for mathematical explorations and as adjuncts to problem solving. With computer access to graphs, spreadsheets, and symbol manipulations, extended investigations of mathematical ideas can become an integral part of mathematics curricula. In such curricula, opportunities for collaborative work can arise naturally with increased opportunity for open discussions and shared decision making.

This chapter discusses in depth the group work that emerged during the implementation of two such mathematics curricula[*] —one at the beginning algebra level and a second at the introductory calculus level. In each discussion, the authors trace the growth of student collaborative work throughout the course. Special attention is paid to the nature of the lab environment, the tasks that seemed to foster group work, and the emergence of a variety of new teacher and student roles.

[*] The Algebra with Computers curriculum project, directed by Dr. James T. Fey of the University of Maryland, Department of Mathematics, was funded by a grant from the National Science Foundation under NSF award number DPE 84-70173. The computer-based applied calculus course was supported by the joint National Science Foundation/National Institute of Education Program on Mathematics Education Using Information Technology under NSF award number FED 80-24425 (DISE). Any opinions, findings, conclusions, or recommendations expressed herein are those of the authors and do not necessarily reflect the views of the National Science Foundation or the National Institute of Education.

The chapter begins with a discussion of group interactions in the first-year field test of an experimental algebra curriculum (Algebra with Computers) and follows up with a recounting of the group work that occurred in a computer-based applied calculus curriculum.

Group Work in Algebra with Computers

Traditional treatments of secondary school algebra focus almost exclusively on the development and routinization of symbolic procedures for the solution of linear and quadratic equations. The 1985-86 version of the Algebra with Computers (AWC) curriculum provided high school students opportunities to use computer simulations, graphics, and simple spreadsheets to explore mathematical ideas and solve real-world problems. The algebraic activities provided in this computer-driven curriculum focused heavily on the development of the concept of mathematical function and explored ways in which functions arise naturally in a variety of real-world settings.

Four algebra 1 classes implemented the first-year field-test version of the AWC curriculum. Most class sessions were conducted in a standard high school classroom with the occasional use of a microcomputer and a large-screen monitor. Each class of about 30 students also had on-demand access to an adjacent lab with 15 microcomputer stations.

One striking feature of both the classroom and computer lab settings was the frequent discussion of mathematical ideas. The tightly woven fabric of the computer-driven investigations and the very real necessity to share computer facilities fostered collaborative work.

Natural Opportunities for Collaborative Work

Computer Simulation of a High School Talent Show

The very first computer lab activity in the Algebra with Computers curriculum presented students with a mathematical model of a fairly complex problem-solving and decision-making task—the planning of a high school talent show. Students were given repeated lab opportunities to explore the cause-and-effect relations built into a computer simulation of this fund-raising event and to generate questions of interest about those relations. Based upon data collected from several trial simulations, students were encouraged to discover an optimal combination of quantitative decisions for the talent show planning. This lab activity was set up by the following tasks:

The following situation is very much like the problems that face a new business. We will ask you to make a first attempt to answer the questions that are given. Using the computer, we will show and let you work with a mathematical model of the situation. We hope that the following chain of events will give you a first look at the uses of algebra and computers in complex problem-solving and decision-making tasks.

Task 1.
Think about the things that might happen before and at a talent show at school. List several decisions that must be made and several jobs that must be done for things to go well at the show and to make a profit.

DECISIONS	JOBS

Task 2.
Each decision that must be made in planning the talent show will have consequences. The situation involves *variables*. You can choose the price for tickets. But if you charge too much, attendance will be low. If you charge too little, you will have very little income. Price and attendance are variable factors.

Look back at your list of decisions and jobs in the first task. Identify any numerical variables that you've listed and name them below in two columns. In column 1 list those variables that *you* can decide on. In column 2 list those that are affected by your decisions. Then draw arrows between variables that influence each other.

COLUMN 1 (VALUES YOU SET)	COLUMN 2 (VALUES THAT FOLLOW)
1. ticket price	1. ticket sales
2. _____	2. _____
3. _____	3. _____
4. _____	4. _____
5. _____	5. _____

Task 3.

Go to the computer lab and call up the program named "Talent Show." This computer program is a simulation of the decision process that you began earlier. The variables and relations built into that model might be different from what you would have chosen. But they should seem reasonable.

Run the simulation several times to become familiar with the choices it offers. Then run a series of tests to study the *cause-and-effect* relations that you suspect must be built into the program. Look for the "best" choice of value for each variable.

When completing the first Talent Show lab assignment, students were directed by their classroom teachers to share a computer with one or two others. To help them keep track of "what affects what, and how," the students were given copies of the following table to record their trials.

RECORD OF COMPUTER-SIMULATION TRIALS

Decisions

Hire a D.J.	_____	Sodas ordered	_____
Ticket price	$_____	Soda price	$_____
Number of ads	_____	Candy ordered	_____
Number of posters	_____	Candy price	$_____

Results

Attendance _____

Tickets	$_____	Print tickets	$_____
Sodas	$_____	Print programs	$_____
Candy	$_____	Posters	$_____
Total	$_____	Newspaper ads	$_____
		Chaperones	$_____
		Soda	$_____
		Candy	$_____
		D.J.	$_____
		Total	$_____

Profit = revenue − costs = _____

Did these trials give any unexpected results? If so, note them briefly.

How can you explain these results?

Without guidelines for working within the computer lab pairs or triples, these high school students began assuming specific lab responsibilities within their lab groups. For a period of time, one student would be mostly responsible for typing in data, while the other helped to provide a "watchful eye" or running commentary on the computer screen displays. Following an initial "play period" where students familiarized themselves with the software options, students focused upon clarification of the task and interpretation of computer screen displays.

Although some students were primarily concerned with ways to keep track of their results, others puzzled over the meaning of basic economic terms like *revenue* and *profit*. A few students questioned the occasional appearance of negative values for profit.

Although students appeared to be working together on the simulation, in fact they were for the most part engaged in completing individual lab reports with little attention paid to producing a group report. Throughout this early stage of students' computer lab experiences, the teachers functioned most frequently as technical assistants, responding to students' questions about hardware and software options, and as task masters—clarifying the nature of the assigned tasks and monitoring students' progress.

While the preceding vignette describes students' first experience with the Talent Show simulation, it characterizes first encounters with each new computer tool introduced in this computer-intensive algebra program.

As the curriculum progressed, a variety of computer lab work styles became apparent. Some lab partners would reach consensus before entering data, whereas in other pairs one partner would be more or less responsible for initially entering the data. For these pairs the other partner often served as critic of the computer output. Discussions about the consequences of the initial inputs were not uncommon for these students. Within computer pairs, role definition appeared to be a function of students' stylistic differences, the mathematical talents of the students, and the nature of the task as well.

Throughout their second opportunity to test hypotheses about the nature of the relations built into the Talent Show simulation, most students explored avenues for improving the profits they'd earned on earlier trials, as indicated in the following lab task sheet.

FOLLOW-UP TALENT SHOW ACTIVITY:
LOOKING BACK

After having worked with the simulation, you should have some ideas about how it works. Which decisions (inputs) influence which results (outputs)?

Give your summary of your best hunches below.

1. Should a D.J. be hired? What effect does that seem to have?

2. What ticket price seems best? What does the ticket price seem to affect?

3. What numbers of newspaper ads and posters seem best? What do those decisions seem to affect?

4. What candy and soda prices seem best? What order for each seems best?

5. What variables seem to affect the revenue from tickets, soda, and candy?

6. What factors seem overlooked by the computer model of the talent show planning task?

Students completing the Looking Back activity deliberated over their choice of input values instead of hurriedly working through the simulation as they had done in the first lab. More than three quarters of the students stopped to discuss why they had chosen particular input values. The rationales for their decisions ranged from insights gained from studying data collected during their first lab experience to personal intuitions about the context itself.

For instance, about one half of the students never experimented with the effects of raising ticket prices above $5. There was some rather heated debate among a few pairs of students about the likelihood of any student paying more than $5 per ticket. Occurring less frequently were discussions about systematic approaches to test the effects of their inputs on total profit earned. One pair announced at the end of the lab that by selling no concessions, having no advertisements, hiring a D.J., and raising ticket prices, they could make profits exceeding those earned by all the other students.

As the students became more comfortable with the nature of the computer assignment, the hardware/software options, and collaborative work, they seemed more able to shift their attention toward mathematical ideas.

Somewhat later in the curriculum, students were introduced to a piece of software called *Gravity of the Planets*. This program functioned in a spreadsheet-like fashion providing output values for given input values. The students were asked to discover the function rules for computer-generated input-output pairs. Sample student input and computer output are as follows:

	EARTH WEIGHT	URANUS WEIGHT	
	25	22.75	
Student	55	50.05001	Computer
input	125	113.75	output
	500	455	

Students were required to make reasonable estimates of the earth weights for a variety of objects ranging from bowling balls to automobiles. Although the focus of the lab was intended to be guided discovery of the relation between earth weights and weights on other heavenly bodies, the initial estimation task consumed most students' attention. Considerable discussion took place between computer lab partners about how to produce reasonable estimates of the weights of cars and of the total weight of the class.

Two students, Pat and Chris, were busily estimating the earth weights of each item on their task sheet. Chris would ask Pat to provide the estimates and then Chris would type them in. Chris never challenged Pat's estimates until they reached the last item on their list—the total weight of their class. Pat reasoned aloud that since there were so many students in the class, the average weight per student would have to be great. Pat suggested that they take 150 as the average weight per student and multiply that amount by the number of students in the class. Chris staunchly maintained that there was no way that this could possibly be right and refused to enter any new data. Chris argued that no single student in the class could possibly weigh 150 pounds. And although Pat may not have fully appreciated Chris' insight, Pat willingly abandoned her line of reasoning and followed Chris' lead.

New Student and Teacher Roles

Peer Tutoring and the Formation of Computer Lab Teams

Computer lab work modes were not entirely restricted to collaborative efforts demonstrated within computer pairs and triples. One striking phenomenon, observed in several of the first labs dealing with computer-generated graphs, involved the *pooling of resources* between computer pairs to form lab teams. Occasionally it appeared that the formation of computer lab teams (two pairs or one pair and a triple) revolved primarily around purely social considerations, but more frequently students appeared to provide one another the specific mathematical or technical capabilities needed to carry out a task at hand. It was not uncommon to find stronger students repeatedly offering to help less-able students.

Particularly challenging lab activities appeared to foster repeated opportunities for peer tutoring. One area of difficulty, surfacing early in the computer labs that focused on displaying data, was the choice of scales for coordinate graphs. Students quickly gained an appreciation of the dramatic effect of scaling on the apparent shape and slope of function graphs.

Varying the scale units from the standard choice of $x = 1$ and $y = 1$ proved to be troublesome for many students when the input-output data were of different orders of magnitude (for example, providing plots of ticket price versus ticket revenue for the high school talent show). See Figure 9-1.

Figure 9-1

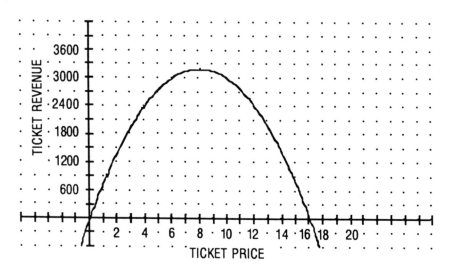

$$R(x) = -50x^2 + 800x$$

In each class at least one student voluntarily offered to help students (other than lab partners) choose and interpret decimal scales. Sometimes the "student specialist" overheard other students having trouble with a graphing assignment. Other times the troubled students themselves sought the aid of their fellow classmates.

The Johnny Appleseed Phenomenon

As the students progressed through the curriculum, they talked more about the nature of the task at hand: outlining their plans of attack, sharing their findings as they carried out their plans, and discussing their conclusions. The computer lab configurations began to serve as forums for students to present, critique, and refine one another's mathematical understandings. Within the context of this algebra curriculum, computer labs provided a learning environment where *engaging in pair and small-group decision making* and *utilizing fellow students as legitimate resources for learning* increasingly became the order of the day.

The teacher's role began to take on a more collaborative dimension—one we refer to as the Johnny Appleseed phenomenon. The teachers found that one fruitful vehicle for refocusing many students' problem-solving efforts was to move from computer pair to computer pair, planting the seeds of problem-solving insights or approaches gleaned from the work of two or more students in the lab.

The following vignette suggests ways in which the Johnny Appleseed phenomenon was played out very early in the first field test of the Algebra with Computers curriculum. Insights into students' problem-solving processes are also provided.

One lab activity entitled "Finding Rules Relating Variables" required that students write function rules for given input-output tables. This lab activity preceded any formal study of linear, quadratic, or higher-order polynomials. Most of the tables of $(x, f(x))$ pairs were generated by linear rules.

INPUT	OUTPUT	CHECK
2	7	
3	11	Yes
4	15	Yes
5	19	No
10	23	
20	q	

Want more clues to rule (y or n)? y
  How many clues? 2
  Start clues at input = 6

6	23	
7	27	

Now you give inputs and outputs

8	31	Yes
10	39	Yes

Rule: _____

Two students, Jeff and Phil, adopted the following working arrangement for suggesting and testing function rules. They consistently began each function search by multiplying the first input value by some positive integer. Jeff usually suggested the value of this constant. Then they added a positive integer to the resulting product in hope of obtaining the corresponding output value given in the table of values. The boys took turns carrying out the computations. Sometimes Phil performed the necessary computations mentally or with paper and pencil, talking aloud as he worked. Jeff usually double-checked Phil's work by also performing mental or "by-hand" arithmetic. When Jeff and Phil were unable to come to agreement on their calculations, they would ask another student to double-check their work.

When the classroom teacher overheard this pair discussing their efforts, she began circulating around the room sharing this strategy with students who were having little success at identifying linear function rules. One pair of students, Adam and Brian, were quick to adopt the new strategy. They were also the first students to point out that the method didn't seem to work for all the tables of input-output values. Another pair of students, Jon and Marc, also adopted the new problem-solving strategy. They successfully identified the patterns developed in the input-output tables but had difficulty writing the function rules. Jon and Marc didn't hesitate to ask other students for help with this part of the assignment. There was a lot of sharing in the computer lab that day. Each computer pair in the room remained on task until the end of the class period.

The preceding computer lab cameos illustrate a variety of ways in which the AWC curriculum fostered cooperative pair and group work. The quality of students' collaborative efforts reflected in these scenarios is not an upper bound for the degree to which high school students will actively seek and value one another as resources for learning. Rather, in our opinion, each of the AWC lab vignettes is a modest but promising move toward a classroom environment fostering greater student initiative, responsibility, and commitment to task accomplishment.

Group Work in Computer-Based Applied Calculus

The evolution of group work, the unfolding of individual work styles, and the dramatic shift in teacher and student roles as seen in the Algebra with Computers project echoed trends observed in a seemingly quite different setting. The setting was a conceptually oriented, computer-based calculus course taught to business and architecture majors at a large university. The course was designed to acquaint nonmathematics majors, through the use of computer tools, with the importance of calculus concepts in their chosen fields. As in the algebra course, it centered on applications and concepts rather than on a singular development of procedural skills. Unlike the algebra course, however, the calculus course did not have in-class computer time during which to complete assignments. Instead, students were able to avail themselves of a large number of out-of-class computer lab hours. Whereas the algebra students almost always had to share a computer station with at least one other student, students in the calculus course were free to choose whether or not to work alone.

For students in both courses there was a gradual evolution of group working styles and a new variety of teacher and student roles, but these phenomena, as played out in the two courses, differed in important ways. As the semester progressed, for instance, not only did a large number of students in the calculus class engage in group work, but they seemed actively to seek opportunities to work in groups. With the lack of an imposed group structure, students in the calculus course were also freer to develop their own varieties of group work. The following pages describe insights into group work as it unfolded in a computer-based college mathematics course.

The computer-based introductory calculus course was developed on this premise: If the computer were used as the primary tool for the execution of routine procedures, concentrated attention could be given to developing a broad-based understanding of calculus concepts. During class, as well as on most assignments, students used computer tools to generate a variety of representations for each calculus concept. Derivatives, for example, were viewed through their symbolic representation (using a computer symbol manipulation program, *muMath*), through their graphical representation (using a computer function grapher), through their numerical representation (using a table-of-values generator), and through applied settings (using a curve fitter to provide the link between real data and the functions that describe them). Since it was not until the last three weeks of class that students were introduced to by-hand techniques for executing calculus procedures, the computer was a necessary tool for active class participation.

Beginnings of Collaborative Computer Lab Work

The computer room (a small office, large enough for four Apple II Plus computer stations) was open at least 34 hours a week, spread throughout weekdays, evenings, and weekends, and was staffed either by an instructor or by a student aide. In a rather unexpected way, the computer room, its physical setup, the scheduled hours, and the nature of the computer assignments interacted to produce a unique working situation for the students involved. From the start, limited facilities led naturally to group work. As a student aide wrote after her first few hours in the computer room: "Two people were here at 9:00, but we had only one *muMath* disc. Solved this by having the two work together." During the first few weeks, whenever the instructor observed a student waiting for an empty machine, she encouraged him or her to join a working group, while encouraging the group to open up for the newcomer.

A first example of natural group work arose from an assignment (due at the end of the third week of class) that did not actually require work with the computer. A summarized version of part of the assignment follows.

For the following computer output, answer each of the following questions:

1. Translate the computer output into algebraic representations.

2. Use the computer output (and other y-values you may compute) to identify: x-intercepts, y-intercepts, maximum points, minimum points, inflection points, asymptotes, intervals of upward concavity, and intervals of downward concavity.

3. Sketch a graph of the given function, making sure your graph reflects the characteristics identified in Step 2.

4. Relate a real-life situation that might be described by part of your graph.

Computer (*muMath*) output* for the function $f(x) = x^4 - 4x^3$:

(Algebraic translations shown in this column are given for the convenience of the reader. They were not provided for the students.)

? ⟦FX:X ∧4 –4*X ∧3$⟧

The name FX (a mnemonic for $f(x)$) is assigned to the function rule

$$x^4 - 4x^3$$

? ⟦FDX: DIF(FX,X);⟧

The derivative of $f(x)$ with respect to x is computed to be

$$4x^3 - 12x^2$$

@: 4*X ∧3 – 12*X ∧2;

The name FDX (a mnemonic for $f'(x)$) is assigned to the first derivative function rule.

? ⟦SDX: DIF(FDX,X);⟧

The derivative of $f'(x)$ with respect to x is computed to be

$$12x^2 - 24x$$

@: 12*X ∧2 – 24*X

The name SDX (a mnemonic for $f''(x)$ is assigned to the second derivative function rule.

? ⟦EVSUB(FX,X,0);⟧
@: 0

The value of $f(0)$ is 0.

? ⟦SOLVE(FX == 0,X);⟧
@: {X == 0,
    X == 4}

If $f(x) = 0$, then $x = 0$ or $x = 4$.

? ⟦SOLVE(FDX == 0,X);⟧
@: {X == 0,
    X == 3}

If $f'(x) = 0$, then $x = 0$ or $x = 3$.

---

* In actuality, the user must type in the commands enclosed by boxes. The unboxed symbols in the left-hand column represent computer responses to the user commands.

? SOLVE (SDX == 0,X); @: {X == 0, X == 2}	If $f''(x) = 0$, then $x = 0$ or $x = 2$.
? EVSUB(SDX,X,0); @: 0	The value of $f''(0)$ is 0.
? EVSUB(SDX,X,3); @: 36	The value of $f''(3)$ is 36.

Unlike calculus assignments in typical courses, this one focused clearly on translation and interpretation instead of on computation. Students needed to translate computer language into algebraic notation, to interpret the algebraic information graphically, and to concoct a real-life situation representable by part of their graph. Sample answers to parts of the assignment appear here and in Figures 9-2 to 9-4.

x-intercepts: Since $x = 0$ or $x = 4$ when $f(x) = 0$, then the x-intercepts are 0 and 4.

y-intercepts: Since $f(0) = 0$, then the y-intercept is 0.

Maximum points, minimum points, inflection points, and intervals of upward and downward concavity:

> The x-values of interest are 0, 2, and 3, since the derivative functions take on values of 0 there. Candidates for maximum and minimum points are 0 and 3, since $f'(0) = 0$ and $f'(3) = 0$. Since $f''(3) > 0$, the curve is concave up at $x = 3$. So $(3, f(3))$ is a minimum point. $f(3) = 3^4 - 4(3)^3 = -27$, so $(3, -27)$ is a minimum point. Since $f''(0) = 0$, we cannot determine whether $(0, 0)$ is an extreme point by examining concavity at that point. Instead, we can examine the values of the second derivative at nearby points. Using the computer's formula for $f''(x)$, we can compute $f''(-1) = 36$ and $f''(1) = -12$. The graph of $f(x)$ is concave up below 0, concave down between 0 and 2, and concave up for x greater than 2.

The graphs in Figures 9-2 to 9-4 show $f(x)$, $f'(x)$, and $f''(x)$ on equally scaled coordinate systems.

Figure 9-2

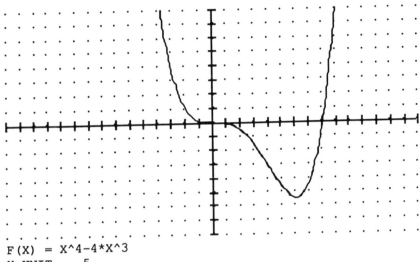

```
F(X)  =  X^4-4*X^3
X-UNIT  =  .5
F(X)-UNIT  =  5
```

Figure 9-3

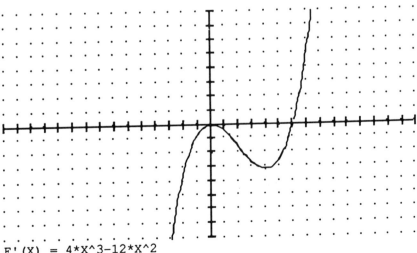

```
F'(X)  =  4*X^3-12*X^2
X-UNIT  =  .5
F'(X)-UNIT  =  5
```

Figure 9-4

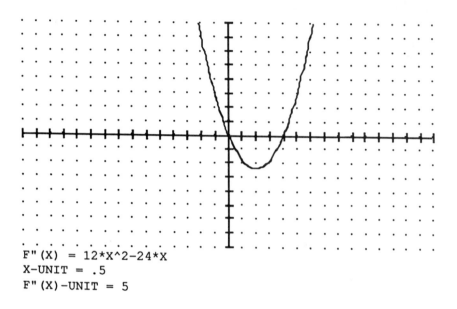

```
F"(X) = 12*X^2-24*X
X-UNIT = .5
F"(X)-UNIT = 5
```

It was student work on this early assignment that first brought the potential of group learning to the instructor's attention. Four students had come to the computer room two nights before the assignment was due. Two of the four immediately started working together, and (although the assignment did not require a computer-generated graph) the instructor suggested that they graph the function. With the instructor's attention on another student, these two graphed the function $f(x)$ just discussed. They soon drew the third student into their discussion, and when the instructor's attention refocused on their work, the three students were looking at a single screen with two superimposed graphs. They quickly pointed out to the instructor that the derivative function did not reflect the slope of the original function (zeros of the derivative did not match critical points of the function). Locating and correcting an error in typing, the three spent the rest of the evening graphing the other four functions on the assignment. Throughout the evening, their discussions were lively, punctuated with disagreements about procedures and exclamations of surprise. At times, they adjusted and readjusted scales, challenging each other to read values of critical points more accurately. At one point in the evening, they called the instructor's attention to three differently scaled versions of the same function (constructed on three adjacent computers). (See Figures 9-5 to 9-7.)

Figure 9-5

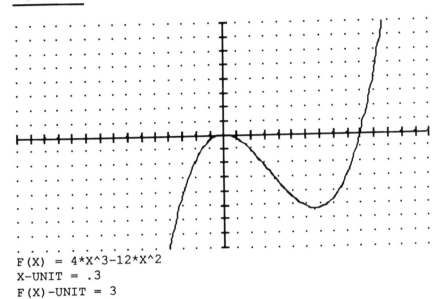

```
F(X) = 4*X^3-12*X^2
X-UNIT = .3
F(X)-UNIT = 3
```

Figure 9-6

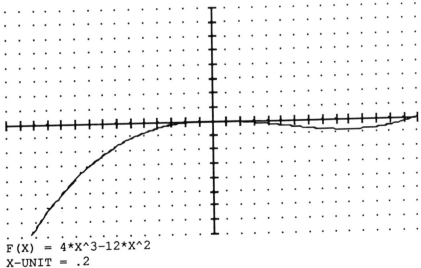

```
F(X) = 4*X^3-12*X^2
X-UNIT = .2
F(X)-UNIT = 20
```

Figure 9-7

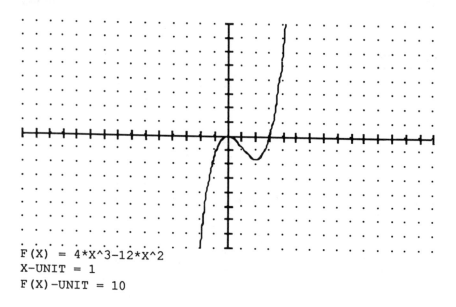

```
F(X) = 4*X^3-12*X^2
X-UNIT = 1
F(X)-UNIT = 10
```

One of the students expressed astonishment at how different a function could look, depending on its scale. Essential to the group work that evolved that evening was the nature of the assignment as well as the flexibility of the computer tool. The assignment required interpreting symbolic, graphical, and numerical information. The function grapher was a convenient vehicle for answering the questions posed in the assignment, provided an excellent impetus for the generation of questions, and enticed the group who worked that evening into a variety of related explorations.

In equally important ways, other computer-based assignments promoted discussion and exploration. Students were given assignments for which they did not have procedural recipes. As the semester progressed, they worked in groups with greater frequency and with seemingly greater efficiency.

Emerging Work Styles

After the first two weeks, a description of a typical session in the computer room would show three or four machines in use, with one, two, or three students working at each machine. Throughout the three to four days before the due date on an assignment, however, each machine seemed to have been in use every available hour. During those peak times, it was not uncommon, particularly during evening or Saturday hours, for 8 to 12 students to arrive early at the computer room and to continue work until the very end of the scheduled hours.

A number of predominant work styles emerged through the semester. Students who worked together in groups seemed to develop methods based on a shared responsibility. As one student aide described a work session: "It is like a 'let's find it out together' atmosphere." At times the motivation for a particular style of group interaction seemed to be efficiency, with each student taking responsibility for a separate division of the work (typing, proofreading, analysis of graphs, initial direction, and critical analysis of decisions made). More often, however, each student seemed to take responsibility for criticizing, analyzing, and understanding group efforts. Even those who did not appear to be taking an active part in the initiation of the problem solving would often stop the action of the group for an explanation or a criticism of the chosen line of action. One assignment that resulted in a considerable amount of group work required the analysis of a mathematical model of a business situation. The assignment began with a display of data:

A new professional baseball team is in the process of determining the optimal price for a special ticket package for their first season. A survey of potential fans reveals how much people are willing to pay for a special 20-game ticket package. The data from the survey are displayed in the following chart:

20-GAME TICKET PRICE	NUMBER OF TICKET PACKAGES THAT COULD BE SOLD AT THAT PRICE
$96.25	5,000
90.00	10,000
81.25	15,000
56.25	25,000
50.00	27,000
40.00	30,000
21.25	35,000

The problem continues with a series of queries about the situation:

1. Find a quadratic relationship that describes the price p as a function of the number of tickets sold (let x = the number of thousands of packages that could be sold at price p). (Students used a curve-fitting program to produce $p(x) = -0.05x^2 - 0.5x + 100$.)

2. Determine the number of ticket packages that must be sold in order to maximize revenue. What package price will maximize revenue? (Students used *muMath* or the table generator and calculators. The revenue function was $R(x) = -50x^3 - 500x^2 + 100,000x$.)

3. Assume the total cost function is described by

$$C_1(x) = 200,000 + 23,000x$$

(where $C_1(x)$ is the cost (in dollars) when x thousand packages are sold). How many packages must be sold to maximize profit? What package price will maximize profit? (Students used *muMath* and calculators. The profit function was $P(x) = -50x^3 - 500x^2 + 77,000x - 200,000$.)

4. If fixed costs are lowered to $150,000, determine the effect on the maximum profit. (Students examined superimposed graphs of the revenue function: $(R(x) = -50x^3 - 500x^2 + 100,000x)$, the old cost function $(C_1(x) = 200,000 + 23,000x)$ and the new cost function $(C_2(x) = 150,000 + 23,000x)$. See Figure 9-8.

Figure 9-8

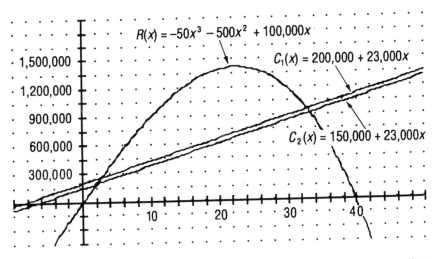

5. What will be the effect of an increase in variable cost to \$30 per package on the maximum profit? On the optimal price? ($R(x) = -50x^3 - 500x^2 + 100,000x$, $C_1(x) = 200,000 + 23,000x$, and $C_3(x) = 200,000 + 30,000x$.) See Figure 9-9.

Figure 9-9

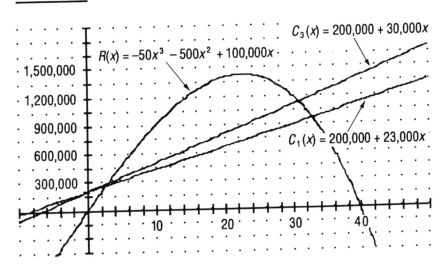

This assignment required student work with each of the computer tools encountered (a function grapher, a curve fitter, a table generator, *muMath*, and a calculator). Students needed to identify and use appropriate computer tools and to interpret their output in an applied setting. Although the concepts of cost, profit, and revenue functions had been introduced to students in class, the bulk of the work was in planning and executing appropriate strategies. The assignment fostered group sessions with each of three or four members of the group taking an active role in the decision making and interpretation. A student aide described what she perceived to be a typical group work session for the assignment:

> On the far left corner of the room three people are working on Graph Functions. (Graph Functions was a function plotter. The user would input a function rule and scales for each of the variables, and the computer would output a function graph.) They appear to interact on an equal level, one person will make a suggestion and they will all discuss it and then act on what they discussed. The two males next to them were doing about the same thing. When answers were wrong, they would discuss them and how to correct them.

As much as computer room facilities and hours encouraged group work, there was apparently still enough flexibility to accommodate a variety of other working styles. Some students seemed to prefer working alone at times, often waiting for a machine to empty in order to begin their work. One student invariably sat back and watched for the first half hour in the computer room and then completed his or her own work in about a third of the time the task would have normally required. Another student sometimes floated back and forth between groups, giving corrective input at times. Other students seemed to move freely in and out of groups in a single session. Whatever their working styles, students seemed at times to be inexorably absorbed in their computer activities. A student aide described this concentration:

> None of the students seem aware that I'm taking notes on them. They give me no attention—that is, they don't look at me. They are completely absorbed in their work. I don't think their eyes ever stray from the screen or from their writing pads.

Evolving Teacher and Student Roles

As groups worked they frequently consulted the instructor for corroboration of their process, for interpretation of alien output, or for guidance on problem solution. Although the instructor seemed to be their first resort for checking answers or errors, by the middle of the semester students seemed equally comfortable in enlisting the help of other students when they confronted difficulties. That some students would use the available assistance as a substitute for working the problems out on their own was, perhaps, inevitably true. The feeling that they needed to do the problems individually in order to understand the material seemed to have prevented this tactic from becoming a predominant recourse. One student commented on a group having gotten together to plan the division of work on a particular assignment: "There were eight of us, each agreeing to do two of the ten problems. But when we got back together, six of the eight had worked out every one of the problems! And of those six, four of us did very well on the exam!"

Although working groups seemed always to welcome new members, certain students were consistently hesitant to join in group work during the first few weeks. One student explained that if he understood the material well, he preferred to work alone. He explained that he avoided working with someone else for fear of losing time in having to defend his methods. By the end of the first month, this student—along with all but a few others—engaged in group work at the computer. As the semester evolved, it became more and more evident that limitations on facilities were not the sole motivation for students continuing to work in groups at the computer. The limited number of computers and the set schedule of computer hours served instead as a convenient initial reason for group work. One student described the development of his working relationship with another student:

The computer brought us together because we were forced to share one. There weren't enough. And then we realized that if I thought and he typed or if he thought and I typed, that we could move faster. So rather than him working on it and me watching and waiting and then me working on it, we would just work together.

He said that working together on the computer led later to working together on problems that did not require the computer. He summarized as follows:

> *The computer started the working relationship. It's a way to get to know someone—a way of getting annoyed at someone also! The computer is sort of a . . . focus—it gets people working together—that's true for other people I've seen.*

Even those students who did not seem to develop close working relationships with other particular individuals claimed that they purposefully came to the computer room when they knew lots of people would be there. One such student claimed that working with certain other individuals helped her develop a better overall understanding of particular assignments. She said she especially benefited from working with individuals whose mathematical strengths complemented her own and with individuals whose pace of work matched hers. She described a particularly enlightening session with another student: "It was beneficial to me because we took the time to discuss and compare problems (instead of just following an algorithm)." Other indications that students valued finding appropriate workmates came from student comments and from the structure of their work groups. Students commented on the strengths of individuals with whom they worked, citing ability to translate *muMath* commands, typing ability, algebraic facility, and ability to analyze problem situations. Students entering an active computer room seemed most often to choose to work with groups with whom they had previously worked successfully. During the last month of the experimental portion of the class, it was not uncommon for students to choose to work with a group rather than to use one of the unoccupied machines, even when the unoccupied machine was set up and ready for use. During the last days of computer use, a sense of efficiency and community pervaded the room. The following field notes reflect this characterization:

> *Although nine students are in the computer room, only two machines are in use. One of the students points out that the groups have split by class, and there is some good-natured joking about which group will "wreck the curve." The noise at times gets so loud that one group*

tells the other to quiet down. There are no spectators tonight. Each student seems to have an active role.

As the semester progressed, then, it was clear that both the instructor and students took on new roles. The instructor was no longer the only source of authority. Students actively sought opportunities to consult with other students about course assignments. They recognized and used the strengths of their classmates through the informal group structure that arose during the semester.

The Computer Room Atmosphere

To define the computer room as a place where students came to execute the computer portions of their assignments would be an understatement of no mean variety. As one watched an older student station himself near groups of students where explanations were being given (after he had missed the first two weeks of class), one might have described the computer room as a place for catching up. As one observed that another student seemed content to sit in a corner of the room, working out the answer to old class handouts with no apparent intent to use a computer, one might have described the computer room as somewhat of a tutoring room. As one noticed two students discussing problems in chairs they have pulled together on the noncomputer side of the room or noted that as the computer room gets crowded students move into the hallway to discuss problems, one might have described the computer room as a group study room. Perhaps a better description than any of those yet proposed lies in one student's summary description of what he termed "the computer room atmosphere":

> *The computer room atmosphere—where you or some math student is available—or just being able to work with other students—means a lot more ideas get thrown around, and you're exposed to a lot more ideas.... It's a community. You get this group of people working on a common problem. And you have to share often because there aren't enough computers, which means it's not just the computers that get shared. It often creates discussions over the keyboard. You can get a good working relationship and a sense of shared responsibility.*

Conclusions

Both the algebra and the calculus computer lab environments appeared to foster natural opportunities for the development of collaborative work in small groups. The Algebra with Computers lab setting provided numerous openings for students to engage in small-group decision making. The computer-based calculus assignments encouraged open discussion about concepts and their applications by directing students to compare results obtained through different computer tools. Although in both courses there remained a few students who preferred working through assignments on their own, most students appeared to have discovered "workable" lab configurations at some time during the course. With the computer serving as a tool for the computer-based activities, students were afforded repeated opportunities in both courses to test their conjectures actively and to hypothesize about results obtained. With the increased support provided by students working with students to accomplish single goals, students appeared to invest unusual efforts in carrying out computer-lab assignments. As students became more comfortable with collaborative computer lab work, they appeared increasingly to take advantage of opportunities for discussion of such key components as multiple representations, selection of appropriate mathematical procedures to solve problems, and interpretation of problem results.

One cannot, of course, assess the real effect of a curriculum by focusing on a single facet of its implementation. The two computer-based curricula discussed in this chapter were characterized by philosophies that promoted work in small groups. The nature of the software, the type of problems assigned for work at the computer, and the in-class development of concepts prior to computer lab work all contributed to an environment in which small-group work thrived. The curricula described here nourished collaborative work in unpredicted and intriguing ways.

Resources

Readers interested in obtaining copies of the computer symbol manipulation program *muMath* are encouraged to contact:

Soft Warehouse
3615 Harding Avenue, Suite 505
Honolulu, Hawaii 96816

Another excellent source of computer software for the classroom, distributing both *Green Globs* and the *Geometric Supposer*, is:

Sunburst Communications, Inc.
39 Washington Avenue
Pleasantville, NY 10570

References

Fey, J.T., ed. 1984. *Computing and mathematics: The impact on secondary school currricula*. Reston, Va.: National Council of Teachers of Mathematics.

Heid, M.K. 1985. An exploratory study to examine the effects of resequencing skills and concepts in an applied calculus curriculum through the use of the microcomputer. (Ph.D. diss., University of Maryland, 1984). *Dissertations Abstracts International* 46, 1548A.

Sheets, C., Fey, J., and M. Matras. 1985. Teaching in a hi-tech mathematics curriculum—New substance and new style required. Paper presented at the Columbus Regional Meeting of the NCTM, December.

Charlene Sheets is Assistant Instructor of Mathematics at the University of Maryland, College Park. She has been a research assistant on the NSF-funded projects Algebra with Computers and Computer-Intensive Algebra at the University of Maryland. She has also worked in curriculum development and evaluation of secondary school mathematics programs. She is currently pursuing her doctorate in Mathematics Education at the University of Maryland.

M. Kathleen Heid is Assistant Professor of Mathematics Education in the Division of Curriculum and Instruction at the Pennsylvania State University, University Park. She has served as director of evaluation for the NSF-funded Algebra with Computers project and as project director for the NSF-funded Computer-Intensive Algebra project at the Pennsylvania State University. Her research has included several studies on the use of computer tools (including symbolic-manipulation programs) in the reformulation of introductory calculus and beginning algebra.

10.

Cooperative Learning Using a Small-Group Laboratory Approach

JULIAN WEISSGLASS

Introduction

Why are some children enthusiastic about mathematics and others not? Why are some students "good at math" and others almost nonfunctional? In order to understand why a small-group laboratory approach can enhance mathematics learning, we need to consider these questions. We could assume that some people have the potential for learning mathematics and some do not (and "where were you when the brains were passed out?"). This is often the assumption, articulated or not, that underlies many approaches to math instruction. It has had unfortunate consequences.

To be frank, we have been doing a disastrous job in mathematics education. For example, the Second Mathematics Assessment of the National Assessment of Educational Progress (1981) reports that "For the 9-year-olds mathematics was the best-liked of five academic subjects . . . and the least-liked subject of the 17-year-olds." My observation is that many, if not most, students come to perceive math as a system of techniques that someone else has invented, which they need to memorize in order to get the right answers on a series of problems that are not particularly interesting to them so they can graduate and stop studying mathematics.

It is time to change how we teach mathematics. These changes will require conscious decisions on our part. Because our assumptions about learning affect the decisions we make and because people often mean different things when they talk about learning, it is worthwhile to consider definitions and assumptions at the beginning.

Learning is the process of taking in new information from the environment, comparing and contrasting it to past experience and previously understood information, evaluating, organizing, and storing it so that the acquired information is available for use in new situations. (Weissglass and Weissglass, 1987).

This distinguishes learning from rote memorization of facts and from conditioned behavior. Learning is a complex, high-level activity of the human brain.

I believe that every child whose brain has not been damaged has a natural enthusiasm and a great potential for learning and has the desire to learn with others. The evidence for this comes mainly from looking at young children who have had good nutrition and a caring environment. Think about how much such children learn in the first three or four years of life. They learn to recognize people and objects, to communicate their needs, and to understand language and then to use it (no small feat when you consider that people talk to them using different accents and syntax). They learn the physical coordination necessary for reaching, crawling, walking, and climbing. They learn social skills. They develop an understanding of number, topological and geometric concepts, quantity, and the rudiments of cause and effect. Anyone continuing to learn at the same rate as a three-year-old would become a genius by current standards.

Children's enthusiasm and natural curiosity are also obvious. They seem to have a biological drive to understand their environment. From the first days of life, babies are exploring their surroundings, stretching their muscles, sticking their fingers in places, and grasping. Older children want to know everything. They explore with an intensity that make adults uneasy or impatient or both. They ask questions incessantly.

Children like to communicate what they have learned. In the beginning, of course, this is nonverbal. They will show their excitement over a new discovery through sounds or a look. As they get older, if you are attentive, they will tell you about the things that they have done and learned.

Some adults have preserved their enthusiasm and curiosity for learning. You probably know adults who learn for the fun of it. I know people who love mathematical puzzles or games and are always eager for more information. They love listening to my discoveries and communicating their own to me. But not everyone has kept their full enthusiasm for learning. As a result, educational institutions have used external pressure instead of relying on our inherent interest in learning.

Because learning is affected by personal feelings, the external situation, and the past experience of the learner, most people do not realize their full capabilities as learners. The school experiences of most children damage their inherent curiosity about mathematics and their ability to learn it. In order to achieve quality mathematics learning, it is necessary to set up learning situations that take account of both the inherent eagerness to learn and the damage that students have suffered.

I advocate having students explore and discuss mathematics in small groups, whenever possible using appropriate concrete mathematical models. These are physical objects that provide a concrete model for investigating abstract mathematical concepts. For example, colored rods, squares, and cubes can be used to model arithmetic, geometric concepts, and even algebra; base ten blocks model place value; geoboards model plane geometry and the arithmetic of irrational numbers; attribute blocks model set theory; and pattern blocks model fractions and can be used to explore sequences and functions. It is particularly important that prospective elementary and secondary teachers have experiences with concrete models so that they can provide these experiences to their students. At advanced mathematical levels there are fewer concrete models available, and students will need to rely on diagrams or computer models, but even at the advanced level it is worthwhile to make the effort to start with a concrete model. For example, colored rods model the Peano postulates for the natural numbers as well as various topics in combinatorics (such as Pascal's triangle) and number theory; pattern blocks can be used to investigate symmetry groups; and tiles or cubes can be used to study sequences.

Free exploration and guided discovery using a variety of concrete models should accompany the learning of any mathematical concept at all age levels. (See examples of lessons at the end of the chapter.) The relationships between the concrete models and the mathematical concepts should be explored and students encouraged to rely on the concrete models whenever they are unsure of themselves or feeling confused. Connections must be explored and explained among concrete models and representational forms, such as pictures or diagrams and abstract notation. In this way, students will see the real nature of mathematics—that it develops from the concrete and moves to the abstract and that it is a playful subject.

This chapter describes how children's natural potential for learning is interfered with, the distorted view of mathematics that is provided most students, and how cooperative learning in a laboratory setting helps alleviate these obstacles to learning.

Interference with Learning

Students' difficulties with and bad feelings toward mathematics are a result of the way they have been mistreated as learners and the incorrect view they have been given about mathematics. I want to be clear at the outset that I do not blame anyone for this mistreatment. No one intentionally wants to interfere with another's learning. Adults interfere with children's learning because their own learning was interfered with and they have not had a good learning method modeled for them.[*]

The following are some ways that adults and schools interfere with children's learning.

1. *Children are made to be passive in many learning situations.* They receive much instruction and information instead of exploring, experimenting, and figuring things out for themselves. They watch television for long hours. In school, students get used to being told answers, shown how to do problems, or entertained by others. As a result, it becomes difficult for them to do mathematics actively.

2. *Children are not respected as learners.* Adults often find a child's investigation inconvenient or disturbing and stop it. For example, children's exploration of a mud puddle may be

[*] This is further explored in *Learning, Feelings, and Educational Change*, Part 1 by Julian Weissglass and Theresa Liebscher Weissglass.

interrupted because they might get their shoes wet. Children want to spend a long period of time lining up blocks or sorting buttons, but parents get bored. Instead of allowing children to make mistakes and encouraging them to "mess around" with materials or concepts, impatient adults often just do the job. In school, teachers under pressure to increase test scores and "cover material" do not pay attention to the needs of their students. Students are pressured to learn at a pace set by adults. They are not allowed to take the time necessary to develop their own understanding of the world. This results in lack of self-confidence and lowered self-esteem.

3. *Children are often confused by the world around them. They are not given opportunities to express their feelings about this confusion.* The confusion might be about family matters (for example, parents fighting), worldly matters (for example, war or poverty), or attitudes (for example, parents being prejudiced) or might be a result of their level of cognitive development (for example, not being able to understand adult vocabulary). Whatever the cause, the feelings resulting from the experience, whether grief, fear, or anger, are often repressed by ridicule from adults ("don't be a sissy"), threats ("go to your room until you can act like an adult"), or criticism ("don't talk to your elders that way"). Repressing these feelings produces emotional and physical tensions that hinder learning. In addition, when a confusing experience is encountered later in life, it may trigger the feelings from previous incidents. Because learning mathematics is bound at times to be confusing, it is likely that a variety of feelings will be stimulated.

4. *Children are frequently criticized.* As a result of this criticism, they often feel bad about themselves and their abilities. They may feel that adults don't regard them as intelligent. Furthermore, as a result of frequent testing and outside evaluation, children come to mistrust their abilities to evaluate their own learning. Many children end up pretending that they understand things when they don't in order to avoid criticism (or worse). When students don't understand mathematics, an inevitable part of learning it, they need to feel free to admit it, to express their feelings, to ask questions, and to

take their time to explore. However, they will not do so if they feel that this will open them to more criticism.

5. *Learning is often presented as memorizing, copying, and filing instead of as an active, complex process of integration, construction, and reevaluation.* Children are often coerced into memorizing facts or seemingly arbitrary procedures without understanding. New information is presented abstractly instead of in relationship to concrete understanding. Students come to believe that their job is to memorize what is in the textbook and reproduce what the teacher does. Although it can be efficient to memorize some things, it should only be done after understanding and with the learner making the decision to memorize because he or she sees the effectiveness of doing so. Students must have the opportunity and the time to construct their understanding of abstract relationships from concrete experiences. When they memorize without understanding, their self-confidence and intellectual integrity are undermined. A striking example of this is reported by S.H. Erlwanger (1975):

> A student (I.Q. 123) had been working through an individualized mathematics program. He was judged by his teacher to be above average in math. When he was asked to compute
>
> $$\frac{3}{4} + \frac{1}{4}$$
>
> the student had two answers:
>
> (1) $\frac{3}{4} + \frac{1}{4} = \frac{4}{8} = \frac{1}{2}$
>
> (2) "If I divide a circle into 4 parts . . .

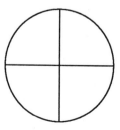

and then add $\frac{1}{4}$ and $\frac{3}{4}$ [student shades respective regions]

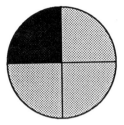

. . . it's a whole."

He then wrote

$$\frac{3}{4} + \frac{1}{4} = 1$$

When asked about the differing answers, the student responded: "I don't know! That's the way it is. . . . You get a different answer every method you use." When asked, "How do you know which answer is right?" the student responded: "It depends on which method you are told to use. . . . And you use that method and you come out with the answer. And that's what answer is in the key. . . ."

When asked to choose between the two answers, he chooses "the one where you add the denominators and numerators, because that's what method they've taught me to do it, in my booklet, and they didn't teach me to do it with diagrams."

The tragedy here is not that the student cannot add fractions. He will be able to learn that when he needs to. The tragedy is that his intellectual integrity has been compromised.

6. *The relationship between disciplines is not adequately explored.* In school, there is often a strict schedule. At 9 a.m. everyone studies math, at 10 a.m. everyone is reading, and so on. Children need to explore the relationship of mathematics to art, social studies, science, and language, not just study it as an academic subject that has no vitality or relevance to their own lives.

7. *Success in school or ability to perform is often a condition for receiving love, affection, or recognition.* Children are set up to compete with classmates and friends. In competition, when one person wins, others lose. This creates considerable stress, which interferes with learning. Furthermore, because mathematics is a prerequisite for so many other respected disciplines, it often becomes the focus of intense pressure by parents. An upper-grade or college teacher, in particular, needs to be aware that students' previous competitive experiences affect their willingness to work cooperatively exploring mathematical concepts in small groups.

Although the practices just described affect all areas of learning, the nature of mathematics can intensify the harmful effects for mathematical learning.

The Nature of Mathematics

Mathematics is a powerful and useful tool for understanding the world. It is a beautiful and creative endeavor that has fascinated people for the past three thousand years.

The creativity of mathematics consists in the possibility of using mathematics to invent structures to invent and explore or to solve problems. In some ways mathematics is closer to art than it is to science. However, most school children rarely get to be creative with mathematics. If schools taught art the way they usually teach mathematics, students would spend their time memorizing the wavelengths of the colors and what happens when you mix different wavelengths. Perhaps they would do a little mixing of paint. But they would rarely pick up a brush, a crayon, or a stick of charcoal. If schools taught writing the way they teach mathematics, students would spend most of their time studying grammar and analyzing sentences and very little time writing creatively.

Mathematics is powerful because it is a language that permits one to concisely capture the essence of complex phenomena. The conciseness and therefore the power of mathematics springs from its abstraction, which is also the source of much of the difficulty for learning and teaching it. The abstraction of mathematics consists in its being separate from any particular phenomenon or application. If a mathematical theory or technique is developed abstractly, then it can be applied to a variety of situations. For example, the techniques for solving equations can be applied to equations about astronomy, economics, or biology. The concepts of statistics are used by political pollsters, quality-control engineers, and social scientists.

However, in presenting the abstract concepts of mathematics to school children, the meaning and the creativity are often lost. People usually develop meaning by relating new concepts to their own experience. But most children's (or even adults') experiences are not abstract—they deal with concrete objects, examples, or situations. In an effort to provide access to the powerful techniques of mathematics, schools have presented abstract concepts to students too soon and too fast. We have developed courses that require students to memorize how to compute and manipulate mathematical symbols without truly understanding what they are doing or having confidence in their thinking.

Adults do mathematics either because it helps them solve real problems, because of its inherent beauty, or because they enjoy the challenge of problem solving. Students see too little of these facets in the classroom. In order to preserve students' natural interest in mathematics as they progress through school, we need to (1) increase the breadth of mathematical content and (2) alter the methods of instruction. I have found that using a small-group laboratory approach enables me to do so in a way that both the students *and I* can handle the changes.

Mathematical Content

What we teach is as important as how we teach it. Certainly, a cooperative learning approach can be used to improve computational skills. If this, however, is its main focus, we are not presenting an accurate view of mathematics. Students at all grades levels and from all socioeconomic backgrounds deserve to have a wide range of mathematical experiences, to be prepared to apply mathematics to a variety of situations and come to see that arithmetic is only part of mathematics. If we teach only arithmetic, we are not providing students with the experiences and knowledge necessary to succeed in many careers. In addition, they will miss seeing some of the most fascinating parts of mathematics—areas in which some of them might have considerable talent that is going unrecognized. I presented an extremely challenging geometric puzzle to a fourth grade class of "slow learners." One boy solved it in ten minutes, although I have never seen an adult capable of doing it that fast. Another time I was introducing tangrams (a geometric manipulative) to a seventh and eighth grade remedial class. One girl showed particular talent and stayed during lunch to continue her explorations. I asked her if she liked mathematics. She replied, "I am not good in it." I said, "It seems as if you are good in geometry." She replied, "We don't do geometry in here."

Topics such as patterns, functions, measurement, geometry and topology, statistics and probability, logic, and algebra can all be explored using concrete objects in small groups at all levels of mathematical development. Using a small-group approach will allow the teacher time to observe students' reactions and thought processes in these areas. (Because many of these subjects are unfamiliar to elementary teachers, the small-group approach allows innovation to begin at the elementary level without providing years of in-service education. A teacher does not have to know everything about the subject in order to have students working together in small groups. The teacher only needs to have some background knowledge and be willing to approach learning cooperatively with his or her students.)

Developing an understanding of abstract mathematics is a major goal of mathematics instruction. But if children are to learn abstract mathematics, they should do so because they want to—because they see it as something interesting and relevant to their lives and as something that they can understand. Because new understanding must be related to what is already understood, we need to lay a good foundation for abstract understanding. This requires that we address the method of instruction.

Method of Instruction

The method of instruction has a significant effect on the learning of children. When I go into a classroom to teach mathematics, I am often told something like, "Ignore Maria and Raul. They can't learn mathematics." Usually these warnings are about females or members of minority groups. And almost without fail, one or more of these students will respond in ways that startle the teacher and myself and show that the student has great potential for mathematical learning. I do not attribute this to my skill as a teacher but rather to my setting up learning situations that tend to contradict experiences that have interfered with learning. If we refer back to the section "Interference with Learning," we can describe the advantages of the small-group laboratory approach.

1. The small-group laboratory approach provides the opportunity for students to talk about mathematics instead of being passive listeners. Having concrete objects available for use also contradicts passivity.

2. Students are more likely to ask questions of peers than they are of teachers, and through questions and their contribution to the group discussion, they can be more in charge of their own learning time. The approach encourages students to construct their own understanding through dialogue instead of accepting the explanation of an authority. Children are respected as learners. Their opinions are taken seriously.

3. In a traditional classroom structure, students have little opportunity to talk about their feelings. They rarely get to express their excitement *or* frustration. They often feel alienated or isolated. Students working in small groups will develop friendships, discuss mathematics, and talk about their feelings. Interaction about mathematics in the classroom encourages students to talk about mathematics outside of the classroom as well. They teach each other, which, as most teachers know, enhances understanding. In this way they have the opportunity to clear up their areas of confusion.

4. The combination of laboratory equipment and a cooperative approach can make the mathematics classroom a more relaxed place, where learning can occur amidst play and free exploration. As friendships develop among the members of a group, the sense of safety increases, and the students are free to ask questions and admit they don't understand. They are less afraid of criticism. The approach can also help students

develop confidence in their ability to evaluate their own learning and to learn self-discipline. One way to assist students in this area is to have members talk to their groups about the group process, how they work in the groups, how they can be more helpful to the groups, how the groups have been helpful to them, and what they still need help in understanding.

5. The experience with manipulating concrete models is relevant to students (everyone enjoys playing with interesting physical objects) and helps lay the foundation for more abstract learning in the future. Taking the time to develop a solid foundation will enable students to *understand* mathematical concepts and processes instead of just be able to reproduce facts or algorithms from memory. The discussion of mathematical ideas, the arguments of students with different points of view, and the richness of the concrete models all communicate to students the complexity of the learning process. Students come to see themselves as problem solvers, capable of using a variety of mathematical tools (concrete objects, pictures, diagrams, simplifying examples, or equations) to solve problems. They no longer spend their time just memorizing, copying, and computing. They see that mathematics is a powerful and useful tool for their lives and a beautiful and interesting subject.

6. Once cooperative groups are established in mathematics, it is possible to extend them to other subject areas and to integrate areas. Groups can participate in projects that integrate mathematics with art (for example, the graphic work of M. C. Escher), social studies (for example, the statistics of opinion surveys), language (for example, writing about their discoveries), or science.

7. By working in small groups, the students develop friendships with their classmates that extend outside the classroom. Their needs for affection, belonging, and recognition are no longer dependent on superior academic performance. The group develops a spirit of camaraderie. They learn how to help each other learn. Teachers know the good feeling that comes from helping someone learn. Students can experience that, too.

The Role of the Teacher

The essence of the small-group laboratory approach is students working together in groups of four or five, using concrete objects whenever possible to explore mathematical concepts, discuss mathematical ideas and processes, and solve routine and nonroutine problems. For most teachers, the decision to use this approach is a significant change. We teachers have typically been taught by the lecture method and most of our colleagues teach that way. It is always challenging to change. Furthermore, the small-group approach usually involves more than a change in teaching techniques. My own experience has been one of gradually changing my attitude about my responsibilities as a teacher. Instead of viewing my primary role as one of imparting information, I now see it as one of setting up situations that facilitate learning. I have come to believe that the experiences my students have in class and the attitudes they develop about mathematics will be as important to them as any information that I present.

The small-group approach changes the teacher's focus from being answer-oriented to being process-oriented. The teacher no longer collects worksheets to assess students' progress; instead, the teacher becomes an observer and facilitator of small-group interaction, paying attention to the ongoing learning process. This is often rewarding and sometimes frustrating. I have found that when I lecture, it is easy to isolate myself from reality and ignore the fact that many students do not understand what I am talking about. When I observe them in small groups, I get to see what they don't understand and to participate in their struggles and their triumphs.

Interacting with small groups is different from interacting with a whole class. The students for the most part will be helping each other learn. The teacher's task is to (1) provoke discussion of mathematics without telling everything to the group, (2) notice when learning is not taking place and intervene, and (3) observe difficulties in the group's interaction and find creative ways of resolving them. One way of encouraging group discussion and assisting learning is to help students "discover" the answer by asking a series of appropriate, well-paced questions. Although it is difficult to resist the temptation to tell students the answers, it turns out that questions are often more fruitful than answers. This questioning technique can be used by the students also, and your using it will be a good model for them. To be sure, it doesn't always work, but it is often more effective than explaining the situation and then discovering that you have overwhelmed the learners with too much new information. Be aware, however, that each learning situation is unique. Sometimes it *is* appropriate to explain. For example, it makes sense to explain what a certain notation means, how a term is defined, or how a diagram or concrete object might be used to model a situation.

Another method to improve group interaction and effectiveness is for the instructor to stop the mathematical activities periodically and ask each member of the group to address the following questions, while everyone else listens: (1) *How are you contributing to the successful operation of this group?* (2) *What can you do to make it function even better?* These questions give students the opportunity to analyze their own behavior. They will often take the opportunity to state exactly what they need to do to improve the situation and then do it.

The change of function from delivering information to setting up learning situations does not mean that we abandon the students to "do their own thing." It means thinking to the best of our ability about what will help each group and each individual learn. The teacher has a crucial role to play both in establishing a favorable environment for learning and for setting up situations that challenge the intelligence of the learner.

I have personally found it helpful, on the first day of class, to let the students get to know me by telling them about myself and my ideas about mathematics. Also, I've found it beneficial to get to know the students by visiting each group on the first day and discussing nonmathematical subjects. One way of doing this is mentioned in the following section on class organization and operation.

The small-group approach will provide you with the opportunity to encourage your students individually. It is helpful to approve of and appreciate their efforts whenever you have the opportunity. Remember that many students lack confidence in themselves and may have experienced failure and criticism in previous mathematical learning situations. By appreciating their efforts and accomplishments, you will help them overcome any negative feelings that they may have.

The attitude you show about mathematics and learning is extremely important. If you are enthusiastic, it will be contagious. If you believe students can learn, they will develop self-confidence. If you show that you like mathematics, they will come to like it.

You will have the opportunity, if you use the small-group approach, to observe the thinking process of students—how they learn, where they get stuck, and how they misinterpret definitions and explanations. This can be frustrating, but it can also be informative. We can learn a lot by observing how people learn.

I have found it helpful to be quite direct when interacting with students. Students having difficulty often become passive. This is almost always a result of their having been criticized in previous learning situations. More criticism is not the answer, but neither is neglect. Be thoughtful in approaching students who have problems, but *do* approach them. For example, students who are not participating in a group can be asked why they aren't participating, what their feelings are about the group or working in groups, and what their previous educational experiences have been like. If you really listen, the students may talk through the problems. At least you will be establishing relationships from which you can make suggestions for improvement.

Class Organization and Operation

I have used the small-group laboratory approach at the college level, both with mathematics majors and with pre-service elementary teachers. I have also used it at in-service workshops for teachers and to a lesser extent with elementary students. I use it when I am well prepared and have written material to guide students carefully through the development of a concept, the discovery of a theorem, or the learning of an algorithm. I also use it when I am less prepared, by verbally posing a question or a textbook problem for students to discuss in groups. Some of my classes are predominantly small-group discussion with about 10 to 15 percent of the time devoted to my providing perspective, background, and explanations. In other classes the ratio is almost reversed, and the small-group activities take up 15 to 20 percent of the time. I find that I use the lecture method more when I am less comfortable with the course content.

I have found that having four or five students in a group works well. The best way I've found to organize the groups is to divide the class size by four to obtain the number of groups and then have the students number off by counting up to $\frac{n}{4}$, where n is the number of students in the class. For example, if there are 26 students in the class, there will be six groups. The students number off 1, 2, 3, 4, 5, 6, 1, 2, 3, . . . , by each student saying a number in turn. Then the 1's form a group, the 2's form another group, and so on. You will end with six groups (two of them will have five people and four of them will have four people). If there is a small group of students with a native language different from English, I have them form a group before numbering off. This makes it possible for them to use their native language in discussing difficult concepts.

I usually have groups work together for at least five weeks, sometimes for as many as ten weeks. However, if there are serious problems between group members, I will reorganize the groups. A note of caution: It is not a good idea to reorganize groups late in the term.

It is important that the groups get to know each other before they start learning together. On the first day, have them introduce themselves and say something about themselves. In fact, it is a good idea to start *each* class with a nonmathematical activity that will get the students talking to each other. I start each class by having each student talk to his or her group about a topic. Sometimes these topics are general:

- Something enjoyable you did or that happened recently

- Something you are interested in

- A memory of reading a good book

- Something you like about yourself

Sometimes they are related to the mathematics we are studying:

- A memory of learning something about counting

- A memory of playing with mazes or trying to find your way through a fun house

- A memory of measuring something

- A memory of seeing or touching a pleasing pattern

- A memory of seeing something symmetrical, or of looking in or playing with a mirror

Using these class-starters, or other ones you invent, may feel awkward at first. My experience has been, however, that if you persist, both you and your students will come to recognize the value of these activities. You and your students might feel that the time spent on class-starters is not "on task"—and therefore wasted. My observations are different. I find that taking the time to do this helps students feel good and improves their attention for learning. A research study (Weissglass, 1977) I conducted with pre-service elementary teachers showed that gains in basic concepts were roughly equal for students using a lecture approach and students using a small-group laboratory approach, and the attrition rate was less for the small-group approach.

Class-starters should be positive. It is a good idea for the instructor to participate in these exercises. This is particularly important on the first day. When you go to each group, you can have them repeat the introductory exercise with you. On subsequent days you can attend the groups alternately during the class-starter. Your participation in these activities will help establish good relationships between you and your students.

I have found that I can handle a maximum of 32 college students (8 groups of 4 students) in a class. However, it goes better if the class has only 28 students, and 24 is ideal. During the class, I circulate from group to group observing how each group is functioning. Then I ask whether the students have any questions. If they do, I either try to get them to discover the solution or give them some information. If they do not have any questions, I will often ask them to explain certain concepts or exercises. I try to make sure that everyone in the group understands the main concept. If someone does not understand, I encourage him or her to ask more questions in the group.

The main difficulty in using a small-group laboratory approach is that students must take responsibility, often to a greater extent than ever before, for their own learning. Older students who have grown up accustomed to the traditional method of listening passively to lectures often take a while to adjust to a small-group approach. It is helpful to hand out and discuss the following remarks.

Remarks on Learning Mathematics in Small Groups

Successful evaluation of new information requires that it be presented in a way that its relationship to information already assimilated is understood. A useful tool to ensure that new information is presented to you in context and at the appropriate rate is "asking questions."

In addition, asking questions is a basic tool of mathematical research. Simple questions about a situation can lead to interesting results. "A good question is worth a thousand answers."

I urge you to take the responsibility for asking questions about situations you don't understand or about those you would like to learn more about. I offer some suggestions for encouraging question-asking in your group.

1. Do not evaluate or criticize a question. Respond to it cheerfully.

2. Verbally appreciate the person who asks the question.

3. Validate each other's intelligence and ability to ask questions.

4. If you see someone is lost, urge him or her to ask a question. Or ask a simple question of that person to bring him or her back to the group.

5. Ask questions yourself. Be a model for the entire group.

6. Try explaining something by asking a series of simple questions. (This is often more effective than just telling someone the answer.)

7. Remember that the facts are not as important as the process of investigation and communication taking place.

8. Smile and be cheerful. It will make it easier for someone to ask you a question.

9. Arrive on time.

10. Come prepared. This doesn't mean knowing all the answers. It means knowing what questions you have.

11. Approach the group each day thinking that you are going to be responsible for (a) helping everyone else to learn, (b) asking interesting questions, and (c) making the experience an enjoyable one.

Learning is enjoyable. Remember what it was like when you were three years old? If you don't, observe a young child exploring his or her environment. Learning can be just as enjoyable for you.

I find it useful to remind the class of at least one or two of these guidelines each week. Sometimes students' reluctance to ask questions or actively participate in the group persists. When this happens, I have them pair up and each relate their childhood memories of asking questions, what it was like for them, and why and when they stopped. This is followed by class discussion of what they remember. This process often releases some tension and enables students to work better in the groups.

Lesson development can be complex or simple depending on your resources and desires. Under ideal circumstances you would think about the mathematical experiences you want the students to have and the concepts or processes that you want them to understand. You would determine all the prerequisite activities and the concrete objects that are necessary for understanding. Then you would devise activities appropriate to the age and developmental level of the students that would provide these prerequisite experiences. You would write out instructions to a small group that would enable it to work through the activities and learn the concepts. In your instructions you would promote small-group interaction as much as possible. You might even write activities that require small-group cooperation. Project EQUALS (Lawrence Hall of Science, SPACES, 1982), for example, has developed logic activities in which each group member has a part of a logical problem. My book *Exploring Elementary Mathematics: A Small-Group Approach for Teaching* was written specifically for small-group interaction. (Three extracts from this book are found at the end of the chapter.)

Writing your own activities is the ideal situation. At the other end of the spectrum, you can tell your class to "form groups and discuss exercises 23–26 on page 68 of the textbook." I do this as well. I believe it is better than their doing the exercises individually or seeing me present the solution. Usually, my lesson development is somewhere in between these two extremes. I might start by introducing a problem—for example, "How many different Cuisenaire® rod trains can you find equal in length to the purple rod? Get together in groups and discuss it." Often I take an activity with manipulatives from the many excellent books available and use it as is or modify it to make it suitable for small-group activity. I observe the progress of the lesson, make adjustments as necessary with the class, and make notes as to how to change it next time. Adequate preparation time is always a problem, but if you wait until there is enough time or until there is a textbook using a small-group approach for your particular course, change will be very slow indeed.

Sample Lessons

The following excerpts are beginnings of three lessons from my book *Exploring Elementary Mathematics: A Small-Group Approach for Teaching*. The first lesson is an introduction to probability. The small-group approach is effective in exploring random phenomena because lots of data can be generated fairly quickly while students discuss what they are doing and observe the outcomes. The instructor can summarize the data from the various groups on the chalkboard. After the introduction contained here, the lesson goes on to explore probability in various ways. The second lesson involves area on the geoboard. The third excerpt is the beginning of a lesson on numbers. You can observe from these lessons that the curriculum can be quite standard. The main difference is that students are working together in a group and are encouraged from time to time, either in the textual material or by the instructor, to be talking to each other about what they are learning.

PROBABILITY

"The True Logic of This World Is in the Calculus of Probabilities."—James C. Maxwell

Lab Exercises: Set 1

Equipment: One die and two coins for each person.

We start with a discussion of the different uses of the word "probability," and then proceed to explore the mathematical concept of probability using dice and coin flipping.

1. (a) Each person think of a sentence that uses the word "probable," "probably," or "probability." Explain your use of the word.

   (b) Below are three statements. Discuss in your group the use of the word "probability" in each sentence.

      (i) The *probability* of rolling two 6's with a pair of dice is 1/36.

      (ii) The *probability* that a child born in the United States will be a boy is slightly better than half.

      (iii) The *probability* is high that the president will be reelected.

   ▪ The use of the word "probability" differs in each of the above statements. In (i) we are concerned with calculating the ratio of certain outcomes to the total possible outcomes. The statement (ii) is based on statistical information about previous births. The statement (iii) is a statement of belief or judgment.

   (c) Make up another sentence that illustrates each of the above uses of the word "probability."

   ▪ Although each of these statements uses the word "probability," the mathematical theory of probability is concerned primarily with statements similar to (i). Therefore, in this chapter we will concern ourselves with analyzing certain processes with a view to predicting the likelihood of a certain event.

2. Suppose you were to roll a die 30 times. What would you guess as to the number of times a 3 would appear? _____ A 6? _____ An even number? _____ Answer the same questions for 60 rolls, for 120 rolls, and for 480 rolls.

3. What *percentage* of the rolls would be a 3? _____

4. (a) Each person perform 30 rolls of a die. Record the frequency of occurrence of each number in the following table and the approximate percentage of the total number of rolls.

30 Rolls of a die

Outcome	1	2	3	4	5	6
Frequency						
Percentage						

(b) Which number occurred most often? _____

(c) Would you expect this number to appear most often if you repeated the experiment? _____ Compare the table with the predictions you made in Exercise 2. Are there differences? _____ Why might these be?

_____

5. (a) Obtain the data from the other people in your group and record the information below.

30 Rolls of a die

Outcome	1	2	3	4	5	6
Frequency						
Percentage						

30 Rolls of a die

Outcome	1	2	3	4	5	6
Frequency						
Percentage						

30 Rolls of a die

Outcome	1	2	3	4	5	6
Frequency						
Percentage						

30 Rolls of a die

Outcome	1	2	3	4	5	6
Frequency						
Percentage						

(b) What do you notice about these data? _____

_____

(c) Do any of the experiments agree with your predic-
     tion? _____ Summarize the results for all rolls in the
     table below, entering the number of rolls in the space
     provided. Compute the percentage that each number
     appears.

_____ Rolls of a die

Outcome	1	2	3	4	5	6
Frequency						
Percentage						

(d) Compare the observed percentages with the predicted
     percentages. What do you observe?

6. (a) Obtain the data from the other groups in your class
        and summarize the results in the table below,
        entering the total number of rolls in the space pro-
        vided.

_____ Rolls of a die

Outcome	1	2	3	4	5	6
Frequency						
Percentage						

(b) Compare these percentages with your predictions. What happens as the number of rolls increases?

7. Suppose you are going to roll a *pair* of dice. How many ways are there for the dice to come up? _____ (*Hint:* Suppose one die is red and the other is white. How many ways are there for the red die to come up? _____ The white die? _____) A complete analysis of this experiment will be carried out in the following exercise.

8. Since the possibilities for the red and white die are {1, 2, 3, 4, 5, 6}, we can fill out the following table by entering the sum in the appropriate square. We will then have displayed all the possible ways the dice can turn up, and the resulting sum.

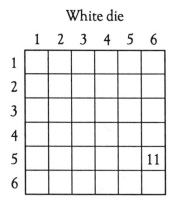

White die

	1	2	3	4	5	6
1						
2						
3						
4						
5						11
6						

▪ Exercises 9–15 involve tossing two dice.

9. Use the chart to determine the number of ways there are of rolling a 7. _____ An 11. _____ The probability of rolling a 7 is equal to

$$\frac{\text{Number of ways of rolling a 7}}{\text{Total number of ways the dice can occur}}$$

10. What is the probability of rolling a 7? _____ An 11? _____

11. Express each of the above probabilities as a percent. _____ ____

12. If you rolled the dice 100 times, about how many times would a 7 occur? _____ An 11? _____

13. Fill in the following table, using the information in Exercise 8.

Sum of two dice	2	3	4	5	6	7	8	9	10	11	12
Number of occurrences											
Probability											
Probability expressed as a percent											

14. If you and a friend were to each roll a pair of dice simultaneously, would you be willing to bet that you would roll a 5 before your friend would roll a 4? _____

15. What is the probability of rolling a 7 or an 11?

- In the experiment of rolling two dice, it was easy to determine the number of outcomes of each event and the total number of outcomes. Other situations may be less routine. For example, consider the problem of determining the probability of being dealt a straight flush in a poker game. It would take a long time to list all the possible 5-card hands for a deck of 52 cards. In fact, there are 2,598,960 possible 5-card hands and of these 40 are straight flushes. So the probability of being dealt a straight flush is

$$\frac{40}{2,598,960} = \frac{1}{64,974}$$

Fortunately, we can determine this without listing all the possibilities. It is not very difficult to develop the mathematics to do this, but we will limit ourselves to simpler problems.

In the following exercises we will develop the tools to answer questions of the following type.

(1) If a coin is tossed 10 times, what is the probability that it will come up heads every time?

(2) In a family with 3 children, what is the probability that at least one is a boy?

16. Let us begin by tossing two coins. Guess the probability of getting two heads. _____ Based on your guess, what percentage of a large number of tosses of two coins would be two heads? _____ Each person perform the experiment 10 times and record the data below by entering H or T in the appropriate space.

For example, if two heads were flipped on the first toss, you would write H/H next to (a). If a head and a tail were flipped, you would write H/T or T/H. If two tails were flipped, you would write T/T.

(a) _____   _____

(b) _____   _____

(c) _____   _____

(d) _____   _____

(e) _____   _____

(f) _____   _____

(g) _____   _____

(h) _____   _____

(i) _____   _____

(j) _____   _____

Record the information below, together with the totals from your group and lab.

	YOUR TOSSES	TOTAL OF GROUP	TOTAL FOR LAB
Total outcomes with both coins heads			
Total outcomes with both coins tails			
Total outcomes with both coins one head and tail			

In what percentage of the outcomes for the entire lab do two heads appear? _____ Two tails? _____ One head and one tail? _____ How does this compare with your guess? _____

AREA AND THE GEOBOARD

"If you don't read poetry, how . . . can you solve equations?"
—Harvey Jackins

Lab Exercises: Set 1

Equipment: One geoboard for each pair of students.

In these exercises we will explore the concept of area. We will determine formulas for the area of familiar geometric figures and develop a method for finding the areas of regions on the geoboard.

Definition: *The area of a plane region is a number that measures the size of the region.*

Let us investigate the concept of area on the geoboard by assigning an area of 1 to the square region indicated in Figure 1.

Figure 1

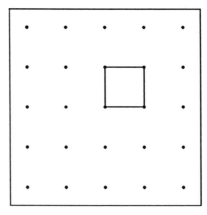

1. Determine the area of each of the following regions.

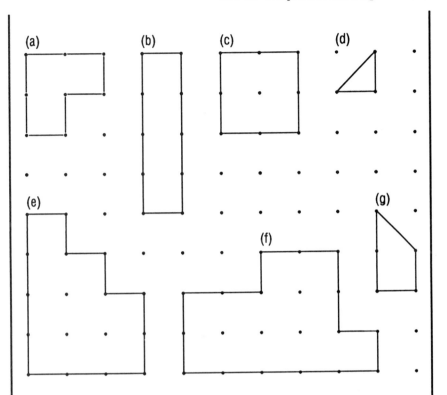

2. (a) Construct rectangles of areas 2, 3, 6, 8, and 12 on your geoboard.

   (b) Verify that the area of each rectangle is the product of the *base* and the *height*.

▪ We use A to denote the area of a region and write

$$A \text{ (rectangle)} = \text{base} \times \text{height}$$

$$A = b \times h$$

3. On your geoboard construct the parallelogram shown by the solid line in the following figure. Discuss in your group how you would explain to a young person that the area of the parallelogram is the same as the area of the rectangle (dotted line). What is the area of this parallelogram? Construct a parallelogram of area 6 and verify its area by indicating a rectangle of equal area. (Be sure you construct the figures on the geoboard.)

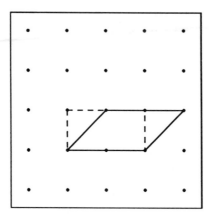

Are you convinced that the area of any parallelogram is the product of its base and height? If not, do some more examples. Be sure to note that the height of a parallelogram is the distance between the two sides (Figure 2).

Figure 2

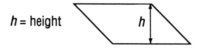

4. (a) Discuss in your group how to find the area of a triangle on the geoboard. For example, how would you determine the area of triangles (i), (ii), and (iii) below?

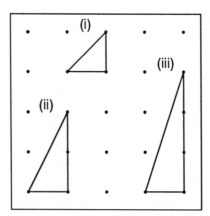

(b) How would you find the area of triangles (iv) and (v) below?

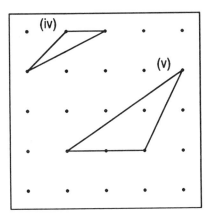

▪ A simple method for finding the area of the above triangles is to notice that for each there is a parallelogram that has an area twice the area of the triangle. If you did not discover this method, do Exercise 4 again.

5. Construct another triangle on the geoboard, and have a partner determine the area using this method. Then reverse roles and repeat.

▪ Since the area of a triangle is always $\frac{1}{2}$ the area of its associated parallelogram, we know that the area of a triangle is $\frac{1}{2}(b \times h)$, where b is the length of the base and h is the height of the triangle.

6. Construct triangles on the geoboard having areas 3, $4\frac{1}{2}$, 6, and 8.

7. Areas of more complicated regions can be calculated by partitioning the region into triangular and rectangular regions of known area and adding. Discuss this method in your group and use it to find the area of each of the following regions.

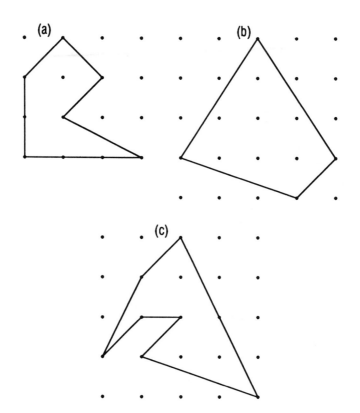

• In (c) above, finding a workable partition is challenging. It is usually easier to enclose such a figure in a rectangle and subtract the appropriate numbers from the area of the rectangle. For example, to find the area of the region in Figure 3, enclose it in a rectangle (dotted line) and calculate $6 - 2\frac{1}{2} - 1 - 1 = 1\frac{1}{2}$, which is the area.

Figure 3

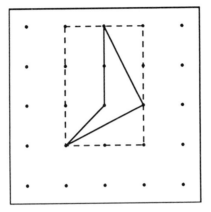

8. Find the area of the figures in Exercise 7 using this method.

9. Find the area of each of the following figures using this method. In (c) you will have to apply the method a second time in order to find the area of one of the figures you want to subtract.

(a)

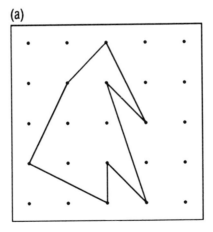

(b)

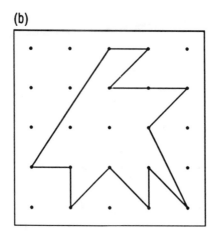

(c)

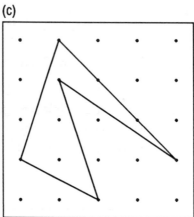

10. Will the method in Exercise 8 work for finding the area of any figure on the geoboard? _____ If it does, you can conclude that any figure on the geoboard made with one rubber band that does not cross itself has area equal to an integer or an integer plus $\frac{1}{2}$. Why is this statement true?

_____

_____

COUNTING AND NUMERALS

"The number 2 is the first step in the boundless frontiers of counting."—Student modification of a quote from Karl Menninger

Lab Exercises: Set 1

Equipment: For each group, one set of multibase arithmetic blocks (MBA-blocks) (Base 2, 3, 4, or 5) and a die.

In this set of exercises we will discuss and explore the origin and meaning of words for numbers. We will use the multibase arithmetic blocks to investigate the underlying patterns of numeral systems.

1. Everyone in the group take a turn relating a memory having to do with counting or learning about numbers.

2. Each group should have one box of Base 2, 3, 4, or 5 (rectangular) MBA-blocks. Examine the blocks. Discuss the following questions in your group.

   (a) What do you think they might be good for?

   (b) What would a child do with these blocks?

   (c) Make a list of some of the things a teacher or child might do with these blocks.

3. (a) Set aside a handful of the smallest blocks and count them.

   (b) How would you explain what you did to an intelligent being from another planet who did not know any mathematics?

   (c) What would a Spanish-speaking or French-speaking person say in part (a) above? (If anyone knows another language, ask that person to count in that language.)

   (d) In what way is what they would do different from what you did?

(e) How is it similar?

(f) Discuss what human civilization would be like without words for numbers.

4. In Figure 1 are the number words an Australian tribe uses for the indicated sets. What do you think are the number words for the sets in (e) and (f)?

Figure 1

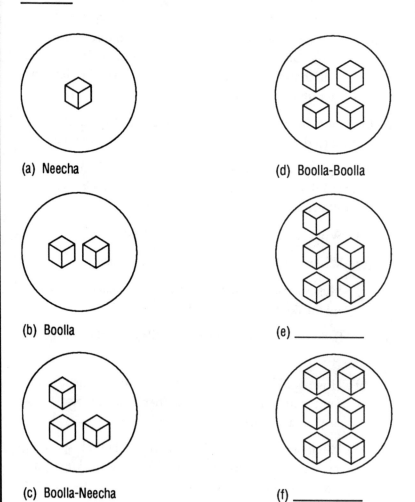

(a) Neecha

(b) Boolla

(c) Boolla-Neecha

(d) Boolla-Boolla

(e) _____

(f) _____

5. Each of the MBA-blocks has a certain volume.

   (a) Select one block of each volume and arrange them in order of increasing volume.

   (b) How would you describe the pattern of the arrangement to a blind person? That is, what is the rule for going from one block to the next block?

   (c) Draw a picture of a set of Base 7 blocks.

6. Obtain a set of blocks of a different base and do Exercise 5.

■ The diagrams in Figure 2 illustrate Base 2 and Base 3 blocks. The names are suggested by the designer of the MBA-blocks. How would you extend this naming system to the next two blocks in the sequence? What do you think they would look like? Since it is impossible to use another dimension, we extend the pattern as exhibited in Figure 3 for Base 2.

Figure 2

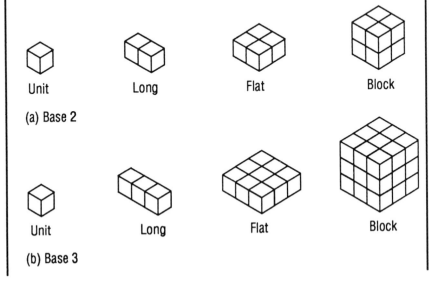

Unit   Long   Flat   Block

(a) Base 2

Unit   Long   Flat   Block

(b) Base 3

Figure 3

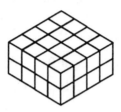
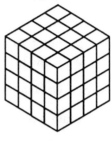

Long-block   Flat-block   Block-block

7. *Game: Win the Block.* For this game use a set of MBA-blocks of Base 3, 4, or 5, and a conventional die. Players alternate rolling the die and taking as many units as indicated by the number on the top face of the die. They then may exchange units for longs, longs for flats, flats for blocks, always maintaining equal volume. The first player to obtain a block in this process wins the game.

It is *not* necessary to play this game in order to answer the following questions.

   (a)   What is the fewest number of rolls necessary to win a block? _____

   (b)   What is the greatest number of rolls necessary to win a block? _____

   (c)   Is it possible to get a long on the first roll? _____ A flat? _____

   (d)   Is it possible to get two longs on the first roll? _____

   (e)   Answer the same questions for the other bases.

8. *Game.* This is a game for two people. Use the unit MBA-blocks as counters. (Coins, buttons, or matchsticks would work as well.) Decide who is to go first. Form two groups of counters. In this game, a move consists of taking any number of counters from either one of the groups. At any

time you can remove counters from only one group, but at each turn you may choose either group. The person who takes the last counter wins the game.

Play the game a few times, alternating the person who makes the first move. See if you can find a winning strategy. If you were going to move first and could arrange the piles any way you wanted, what would you do? It is likely that a young person could master the winning strategy before learning how to count. How would such a person describe the winning strategy? Try to describe it without using the word "number" or "equal."

References

Corbitt, M.K., ed. National Council of Teachers of Mathematics. 1981. *Second mathematics assessment of educational progress.*

Erlwanger, S.H. 1975. Case studies of children's conceptions of mathematics, Part I. *The Journal of Children's Mathematical Behavior* 1: 199–277.

Lawrence Hall of Science. 1982. SPACES. Berkeley, Calif.

Weissglass, J. 1985. *Exploring elementary mathematics: A small-group approach for teaching.* For information about this book, contact the author at Tri-County Math Project, Department of Mathematics, UC Santa Barbara, Calif. 93105.

———. 1977. Mathematics for elementary teaching: A small-group laboratory approach. *American Mathematical Monthly* 86: 377–82.

———. and T.L. Weissglass. 1987. *Learning, feelings, and educational change, Part I.* Santa Barbara, Calif.: Kimberly Press.

Julian Weissglass *is Associate Professor of Mathematics at the University of California, Santa Barbara. He is the Principal Investigator for the Tri-County Mathematics Project and Project T.I.M.E. (Teachers Improving Mathematics Education) staff development programs in mathematics education. He is the author of* Exploring Elementary Mathematics: A Small-Group Approach to Teaching *and coauthor of* Hands on Statistics: Explorations with a Microcomputer. *Dr. Weissglass is on the Committee on the Mathematical Education of Teachers of the Mathematical Association of America.*

11.

The Small-Group Discovery Method in Secondary- and College-Level Mathematics

NEIL DAVIDSON

Introduction

Let me begin with a personal story with three strands, which, when woven together, led me to develop the small-group discovery method. In 1966, I thought that I needed a course in experimental psychology but was denied admission because of lack of prerequisites. On my way out of the psychology building, I noticed something that riveted my attention: a class with small groups of students sitting and talking with each other. After watching in amazement for a few moments, I approached the professor, explained my status as a doctoral student, and asked permission to join the class, whatever it was. The teacher, David Bradford, generously agreed, and I enrolled as a student in theories of social and organizational change and later in his course in group dynamics. Thus began my exposure to group processes in learning.

During this same period of time, I was tantalized by Dewey's (1916, 1938) philosophy of education, which emphasized learning through active personal experience; learning by doing nonroutine, thought-provoking activities; learning as a social process; and much more. This philosophy actually provided the impetus for much of the work in classroom group dynamics. The philosophy seemed highly appealing and yet not quite practical in mathematics, or so I thought at the time.

For several years prior, I had taken a series of graduate courses in point set topology, taught by the Moore method (Moise, 1965). This is a highly competitive, individualistic method in which students independently develop conjectures, prove theorems, and construct counterexamples to propositions in topology. The students work alone outside of class, without recourse to books or to other people, and then are called upon to present to the entire class the problems that they claim to have solved. This method has produced some spectular successes, including a number of world-renowned topologists (Moise, 1965). It also produced among many of my classmates a sense of isolation and discouragement, even though they did well in other branches of mathematics. I wondered whether there might be a way to retain the challenging problems and intellectual excitement of the Moore method but to change the social patterns to foster more human contact and greater success for the majority of students.

One day, in a moment of insight, I saw an answer: Using Dewey's philosophy as the theoretical foundation, I would try to combine the intellectual challenge of the Moore method with the social support inherent in the group dynamics approaches. That insight, which was perfectly obvious after the fact, was the beginning of the small-group discovery method. Little did I know that others, whose work is represented in this volume, were beginning to develop different forms of small-group teaching in mathematics at about the same time. In retrospect, it seems this was an idea whose time had come, perhaps a seed in the collective consciousness of humanity.

After a semester of informal experimenting with teaching calculus by small-group problem solving, I was ready for my first systematic attempt at small-group teaching. This was a year-long course in calculus of one variable, taught by the small-group discovery method. That first trial took place under favorable conditions: a small class with better-than-average students. After the first anxious month, I could see that the method really was working and had some promise. Since that time, other instructors and I have used the method in a number of secondary- and college-level courses, including precalculus, calculus, math for elementary teachers, linear algebra, abstract algebra, number theory, foundations of geometry, advanced calculus, topology, and complex variables.

The remainder of this chapter is organized as follows: a description of principles from Dewey's philosophy, an overview of classroom practices, an elaboration based on practices in group dynamics, a description of the interaction between the students and the mathematics content in calculus, and an evaluation of the strengths and limitations of the method.

Practices Derived from Educational Philosophy

Let us turn our attention to the philosophical basis of the small-group discovery method. Polya (1965) placed emphasis upon student thinking, active learning, discovery learning, and interest in mathematics. These factors are particular aspects of a general philosophy of education and of life, whose foremost advocate in education was John Dewey (1916, 1938). While a description of Dewey's philosophy is beyond the scope of this paper, there follows a summary of classroom practices derived from Dewey's philosophy and applied in the design of the small-group discovery method.

In this method, students learn through personal experience; they learn mathematics by doing mathematics. The students, with limited subtle guidance from the teacher, formulate some definitions, make conjectures, state theorems, prove theorems, construct examples and counterexamples, solve specific problems, and develop techniques for solving various classes of problems. (For any given class, these challenges are realistically adjusted to fit the background and capabilities of the students.)

The approach to the subject matter is one of guided discovery in which thought-provoking topics are introduced as questions for investigation by the students. Some questions in calculus are: *How can we find the tangent line to a curve? How can we find the area under a curve? How can we find the volume of the surface obtained by revolving a curve around an axis?* Questions such as these can be raised in brief discussions with the entire class to set the stage for group explorations and activities.

The classroom activities take place in small groups of students. Within each group there is to be a cooperative atmosphere in which students can freely discuss mathematical ideas and work together to solve the problems at hand. The work is done "... as a social enterprise in which all individuals have an opportunity to contribute and to which all feel a responsibility" (Dewey, 1938, p. 56).

The teacher adopts a democratic leadership style by facilitating the activities of the students in a manner that is not highly directive. The teacher spends most of the class period with the small work groups, providing guidance and support in a variety of ways to be described later.

Motivation

Interest in mathematical topics and activities is intended to provide the major source of motivation. Problems are often given that arise in real life or in concrete physical situations, such as projectile motion, velocity and acceleration, distance required to stop a car, spring displacement, radioactive decay, and profit or loss functions. An occasional paradox is introduced, such as the arrow that never seems to hit the target because it always travels half of the remaining distance. Whenever possible, visual images are linked with and used to enliven symbolic expressions. Many situations involve a search for hidden patterns and relationships in data.

The teacher attempts to determine which topics are of intrinsic value, which appear to be useful (instrumental), and which have little interest or value from the student viewpoint. The ideal goal is to provide a learning environment in which all topics are perceived as interesting, valuable, or useful to the students. (This is not easy to achieve in practice, as is described later.)

Approaching the Mathematics

The sequencing of subject matter proceeds from the more concrete to the more abstract, as seen from the viewpoint of the learner. Abstract, theoretical considerations are postponed, pending the occurrence of a good deal of concrete experience. For example, students gain facility in finding limits of many functions and combinations thereof before encountering the definition of the limit and theorems about limits.

Emphasis is placed upon the discovery of new ideas, more than upon the expression of the ideas in the most impeccable form. Professional standards of rigor are not imposed upon the beginner, and the initial development is informal in character. The need for increased precision and theoretical security becomes apparent to the students with the handling of increasingly difficult and abstract problems over the course of time. For example, the need for proofs or counterexamples becomes clear when there is genuine doubt about the truth of a conjecture. This is one of the greatest departures from more formal traditional teaching.

Skills are formed under conditions where thought is necessary. Whenever possible, the students themselves develop the techniques for solving each class of problems. The remaining practice occurs with problems that differ from one another and that require some judgment for the solutions. The skills are attained, whenever possible, by solving problems of intrinsic value for the students.

The teacher proposes problems and questions in order to guarantee that all major and essential topics are covered during the course. Within this basic framework provided by the teacher, many questions occur to the students. The investigation of student-generated questions is a frequent activity of the class members.

Emphasis is placed on learning rather than upon evaluation. The teacher can often rely on students' internal sources of motivation—such as curiosity, interest in the mathematical topics or activities, and desire to develop a sense of competence or mastery. Some teachers may choose to reduce concern about external motivators such as grades by giving the students some voice in determining grading policies—for example, the frequency, timing, and type of exams or projects.

Classroom Procedures

In this method the class is divided into small groups, usually with four members each. Each group has its own working space, preferably including a section of the chalkboard. Each group discusses mathematical ideas and solves problems cooperatively during class. In some courses, group members also prove theorems, make conjectures, and construct examples and counterexamples. The teacher moves from group to group, checking the students' work and providing assistance as needed.

To facilitate cooperative group problem solving, the teacher states a set of guidelines, such as the following:

1. Work together in groups of four.

2. *Cooperate* with other group members.

3. Achieve a group solution for each problem.

4. Make sure that everyone understands the solution before the group goes on.

5. Listen carefully to others and try, whenever possible, to build upon their ideas.

6. Share the leadership of the group.

7. Make sure that everyone participates and no one dominates.

8. Take turns writing problem solutions on the board.

9. Proceed at a pace that is comfortable for your own group.

A teacher with small groups introduces new material and poses problems and questions for discussion or investigation. This can be done orally with a class discussion at the beginning of a period or with individual groups at appropriate moments. New material can also be introduced in written form via teacher-made worksheets or special texts designed for small-group learning. There are texts in elementary algebra (Stein and Crabill, 1986), plane geometry (Chakerian, Crabill, and Stein, 1986), algebra II/trigonometry (Stein, Crabill, Chakerian, 1986), abstract algebra (Davidson and Gulick, 1976), and mathematics for elementary-education or liberal-arts majors (University of Maryland Mathematics Project, 1978; Weissglass, 1979).

In discussions with the whole class, the teacher may need to answer certain questions, serve as discussion moderator, and clarify and summarize what the students have found. An overall synthesis by the teacher is needed from time to time, since students in the groups sometimes "see the trees but lose sight of the forest."

The teacher provides guidance and support during small-group activities. The teacher observes the group interaction and solutions on the board and, in visits to particular groups, checks their solutions, gives hints, clarifies notations, makes corrections, answers some questions, provides encouragement, and helps the groups function more smoothly. It is to be hoped that the teacher behaves in a friendly and constructive manner and strikes a balance between giving too much and too little assistance.

Forming Small Groups

There are several options for forming small groups.

1. The teacher can form groups that are as heterogeneous as possible in terms of mathematical achievement, sex, and race (Slavin, 1980).

2. The teacher can form homogeneous groups based on some criteria such as mathematical achievement or aptitude. This tends to be disastrous for the very slow learners.

3. The teacher can use random assignment or some arbitrary numerical scheme to form the groups.

4. Groups can be formed on the basis of natural seating patterns in the class.

5. The teacher can administer a psychological test and use the results to form groups. For example Schutz's (1966) FIRO–B instrument can be used to form groups of persons with mutually compatible needs for inclusion, control, and affection.

6. Students can participate in choosing their own group members. If students do not know each other at first, the group membership can be switched daily for several class periods. In one variation of this procedure, students are helped to get acquainted by talking together in pairs for a few minutes each day. After this initial period, students then choose groups in one of two ways. In one procedure, the students stand up and form themselves into groups during class. In a second procedure, the sociometric choice method, the students write confidentially on paper the names of those people with whom they prefer to work and perhaps those they would rather avoid. The teacher then forms groups that respect these written preferences and avoidances.

Space does not permit a detailed discussion of the pros and cons of the various group-formation procedures. Generally, if greater care and attention are given to group formation, there will be better group functioning and less need to switch groups later on. There is some experimental evidence showing positive effects of mixed-ability heterogeneous grouping (Slavin, 1980; Webb, 1985), sociometric choice procedures (Stam, 1973; Grant, 1975), and random assignment (Cohen, 1986). My personal preference is the use of sociometric choice after several days of group switching and interaction exercises.

In college-level courses that meet only once or twice per week, it may be best to choose groups that remain together for the whole semester. However, in courses such as calculus, which meet every day, the groups may rotate members every few weeks.

An experienced teacher can usually work comfortably with as many as six or seven groups. In very large classes, the teacher may need an aide for help in group supervision; a more advanced student can often be an effective aide.

Pacing and Evaluation

Some groups move more quickly than others. If all groups begin each new topic on the same day, the teacher should have some challenging extra problems ready for groups that finish early.

The small-group method can be used as a total instructional system or in combination with other methods. Groups can be used all the time, on specific days of the week, during portions of any class period, or for specific topics. I personally prefer to use small groups for most of the class time, except in a few multisection departmentalized courses taught on a rigid time schedule at breakneck pace with uniform hour exams.

A variety of grading schemes are compatible with small-group instruction. These include in-class tests and quizzes, take-home tests, group tests, group projects, homework, classwork (attendance, participation, cooperation), self-evaluation, and peer evaluation. If a teacher gives tests on a specific date, that date should realistically allow all groups to finish the material beforehand without rushing. If a teacher gives grades for classwork (attendance, participation, cooperation), he or she should *not* grade individual mathematical performance during class—doing so will foster competition and destroy group cooperation.

Classroom Practices Derived from Social Psychology

Supporting evidence and further elaboration for the previously described practices are provided by empirical studies in social psychology and group dynamics. This chapter includes a few major findings from these studies and inferences drawn from them in the design of the small-group discovery method.

White and Lippitt (1960) and Anderson (1963) found that the use of a democratic (learner-centered) style of leadership, in contrast to an autocratic or laissez-faire style, produces higher morale and satisfaction in groups. Accordingly, I recommend the use of a democratic leadership style by the teacher with the small-group discovery method. This is done as follows. The teacher provides a perspective on each day's mathematical activities in a brief discussion with the entire class. He or she spends most of the period working with the small groups, as described earlier. The teacher refrains from giving orders or disrupting commands. There is only a minimal amount of objective, constructive praise and criticism, usually directed to the work group as a whole rather than to particular individuals. The teacher offers guiding suggestions at times when they are needed and might be appreciated; these include mathematical hints and suggestions about work organization and group functioning. The teacher sometimes provides technical information upon request and stimulates self-direction by encouraging group members to think through and elaborate upon their ideas and to detect group errors. The teacher develops a friendly relationship with the students and behaves in an egalitarian manner, which might, for some teachers, include being on a reciprocal first-name basis. Finally, certain policies in the class, such as the timing of exams and the frequency of switching groups, can be arrived at through group discussion and decision making by a majority vote.

Decisions about cooperation or competition within the work groups are made on the basis of a classic study conducted by Deutsch (1960) at MIT. He found that in a cooperative situation, as compared with a competitive situation, the group members were more friendly, listened more attentively, better understood the ideas of others, and had fewer conflicts. Moreover, the productivity of the cooperative group discussion was higher in terms of the quantity and quality of ideas agreed upon for solving the problem. In accordance with these results, the mathematics teacher can promote cooperation within each work group by stating guidelines for cooperative group behavior, as given earlier. When interacting with a group, the teacher can check the group solution without asking who was responsible for it. He or she emphasizes the need for joint efforts to solve difficult problems, the importance of listening carefully and building upon the ideas of others, the fact that one person's good idea helps the entire group, and the goal of solving the problem in such a way that all members understand the group solution.

Studies have shown that conformity pressure to go along with a group can lead to the modification or distortion of individual judgment or perception (Asch, 1960). Fortunately, it is possible to reduce conformity in problem solving by developing group standards that encourage members to respect their own judgment. The teacher in a mathematics class develops such standards by emphasizing the importance of independent judgment, the legitimacy of disagreement, and the obligation of group members to give reasons to support their statements. The teacher intervenes as a mediator when students look puzzled or confused or when several group members put undue pressure on a dissenting member. The teacher emphasizes the distinction between thoughtless conformity and a change of opinion based upon a thoroughly understood argument. Moreover, he or she discourages conformity without promoting the other extreme of stubborn refusal to listen to the views of others.

A commonly held misconception is that every group must have a leader (Cartwright and Zander, 1960). In a discovery-oriented mathematics class, there is no clear case for establishing the need for a leader in each group. Therefore, the work groups operate without designated leaders. Although it is not possible to create a completely egalitarian work group in which all members have exactly the same influence, it is possible to place some limitations upon the discrepancy in power between the most active and the least active group members. No person is allowed to dominate the discussion in a manner that excludes or severely limits contributions from others.

Whenever necessary, the teacher influences the dynamics of particular groups by drawing certain members into the discussion, by suggesting that different people assume primary responsibility for writing the solutions to different problems on the chalkboard, and by using other techniques to promote cooperation.

It is necessary to keep work groups small, since the opportunity for active participation decreases as the group size increases. There is some empirical evidence available concerning the effects of group size upon group interaction in nonmathematics discussions. In two-person groups there is no one to resolve differences, and either member can bring the group to a halt by disagreement or withdrawal (Bales and Borgatta, 1961). Three-person groups tend to break up into a pair and an isolated member. Four-person groups can split into two subgroups of equal size and thereby produce a protracted argument or deadlock (Bales and Borgatta, 1961; Mills, 1960). Groups with five, six, or seven members entail the possible dangers of competition, exclusion of members from the discussion, and the need for a definite leader (Slater, 1958).

The experimental evidence, combined with my classroom experience, points to the following tentative generalization: Groups of four are large enough to generate ideas for discussion and solution of challenging problems, and large enough not to be bothered by the absence of one member. Groups of four are small enough to permit active participation, to allow clustering around a chalkboard panel, and not to require a leader or elaborate organizational structure. Groups of four can also split into pairs for occasional computational practice or simple application problems.

Examples of the Leadership Style of the Teacher

In giving a perspective on each day's mathematical activities, the teacher might raise questions for investigation such as these: *What happens at a high or low point on a curve? What can you say about a function that vanishes at the endpoints of its interval of definition? Let's see if we can find a formula for the derivative of a product.* These questions set the stage for the main activity of student problem solving in groups. Just enough input is provided in class discussions so that the groups can function productively for the rest of the class period.

This discussion period may be reduced if special texts or developmental worksheets are employed.

The teacher finds it easy to keep track of group progress if students write their problem solutions on the chalkboard. With experience, the teacher learns when to wait for a request for assistance and when to jump in and offer a suggestion. Often, a visit with a particular group takes a minute or less—for example, if it is necessary only to point out an arithmetic mistake, ask the reason for a step, or check a simple solution. However, on difficult proofs the groups need considerable assistance, and visits last longer. If the teacher stays too long with any one group, members of the other groups may begin calling for help.

The teacher checks the group solutions of all the *difficult* problems or theorems. In other problems, checking preferences vary. Some members always want their group's solution checked; other group members are quite confident and erase their solutions without teacher checking. When enough board space is available, some groups leave one solution up for checking while working on another problem.

Guiding suggestions of a mathematical nature are given in the form of hints, sometimes using the heuristic techniques of Polya (1965). Here are a number of examples in calculus:

1. The teacher frequently asks the students to concentrate on the given data, the desired result, and relationships between the two. This helps, for example, in the proof that differentiability implies continuity and in many proofs that involve the definition of the limit.

2. The teacher sometimes suggests use of an analogy with previous results. For example, if students have trouble deciding whether a function such as

$$f(x) = \begin{cases} 2 \text{ if } x \geq 0 \\ -2 \text{ if } x < 0 \end{cases}$$

has no limit or two limits at $x = 0$, the teacher might suggest a comparison with certain sequences such as 2, –2, 2, –2, . . . , where a similar issue has previously been settled.

3. General results are sometimes formulated by considering special cases. The students can correctly conjecture the fundamental theorem of calculus after computing:

$$\int_a^b x^k \, dx, \quad k = 1, 2, 3$$

This is described in more detail later in the chapter.

4. It is sometimes useful to suggest that the students discover or confirm results by drawing pictures. This is suggested, for example, in stating the mean value theorem or when students cannot remember if $\frac{d}{dx}(\sin x)$ is $\cos x$ or $-\cos x$.

5. A slight shift in notation occasionally makes a big difference in problem solving. In their first encounter with implicit differentiation, students may have great difficulty in finding $\frac{dy}{dx}$ for $x^2 + y^2 = 1$. The hint to replace y by $f(x)$ readily enables students to find $f'(x)$ if they are more used to functional notation.

6. The suggestion to guess the answer to a problem sometimes leads to some surprises. Students are usually convinced that the derivative of a product should turn out to be the product of the derivatives.

7. Sometimes, there are occasions when a hint is given only once and it does not need to be repeated for the remainder of the year. In the proof of the formula for the derivative of a product, the hint can be given to add and subtract the same term. For the rest of the year the students tend to use this technique correctly as needed.

8. It is sometimes helpful to suggest that students consider a simple instance of a general problem. This is done with $n = 2$ and $n = 3$ in guessing the formula for the derivative of a product of n functions.

The teacher sometimes offers guiding suggestions with respect to the work organization and functioning of a particular group. Students often write four or five attempted solutions all over the board, and no one can tell where one idea ends and the next begins. Many students omit key symbols—for example, writing sin x = cos x instead of the equation

$$\frac{d}{dx} \sin x = \cos x \quad \text{or} \quad \int \cos x \, dx = \sin x + c$$

This causes great confusion on complicated problems. Hence, suggestions about chalkboard technique and recording on paper are definitely needed.

The teacher provides technical information on request if the development or recall of that information is not a key part of the problem at hand. For example, a request for an approximation of the number e to five decimal places might be honored. A request to provide the formula for $\frac{d}{dx} f(x)^n$ is not honored. Other items of information, for example, an identity for cos 2θ, are provided for some problems but not others, depending on the context.

The teacher attempts to stimulate self-direction by encouraging students to look for errors in their group's solutions. Many errors are caught by the students themselves; others are detected by the teacher. There are computational errors, incorrect applications of basic formulas such as ($\frac{d}{dx} \sin 3x = \cos 3x$), errors in basic algebraic facts, logical errors of many types (circular reasoning, proving a conclusion without using the hypothesis, and so on), errors of overgeneralization ($\frac{d}{dx} e^x = xe^{x-1}$), and errors of notation (if $f(x) = x^3$, then $f'(x^3) = 3x^2$). The teacher might be surprised by the students' frequent shifts from erroneous to insightful thinking and back again.

The Interaction Between the Students and the Mathematics

This section includes a number of additional examples of student responses to the mathematics content. For simplicity, this discussion is limited to the subject matter of calculus; numerous examples could also be given from abstract algebra, foundations of geometry, topology, and the like. I have selected examples from the first-year course in calculus, which I have taught for a number of years using the small-group discovery method. On the whole, the students were successful with limited guidance in making conjectures, proving the main theorems of calculus, developing techniques for solving various classes of problems, and in coming up with problem solutions and proofs not previously known to the teacher. The students sometimes alternated between moments of brilliance and moments of ineptitude. This section begins with a number of success stories and concludes with accounts of difficulties and surprising responses to the subject matter of calculus.

Situation 1

Rolle's theorem was introduced as an open-ended problem for exploration by the students. The problem was stated as follows: "Let f be a function defined on $[a, b]$ such that $f(a) = f(b) = 0$. Assume that f is differentiable on the open interval (a, b) and continuous at the endpoints. What conclusions can you draw about f?" The groups then generated a collection of conjectures involving the existence of a positive maximum or a negative minimum under certain conditions—numbers of zeros of the functions, existence of inflection points, and so on. They also correctly stated Rolle's theorem: There is a point c in (a, b) such that $f'(c) = 0$. However, they were disappointed to find this result labeled as a theorem. "You mean the least interesting theorem is the one with the name?"

Situation 2

The mean value theorem was introduced with the following question. "Let f be defined on (a, b) satisfying the hypotheses of Rolle's theorem, but remove the restriction that $f(a) = f(b) = 0$. What conclusions can you draw about f?" When the students had difficulty formulating a conclusion, the hint was given to draw a picture and to state the conclusion of Rolle's theorem in geometrical language. After stating that the tangent line at some point was parallel to the x-axis (in Rolle's theorem), a student in each group made the appropriate analogy and stated that the tangent line at some point was parallel to the chord line joining the endpoints of the curve.

After the groups expressed their conclusions as mathematical statements involving a derivative, the hint was given to begin the proof by constructing a new function that satisfied the conditions of

Rolle's theorem. Within a few minutes, someone in each group set $h(x) = f(x) - g(x)$, where $y = g(x)$ was the equation of the line joining the endpoints $(a, f(a))$ and $(b, f(b))$. Until this time, matters had progressed roughly in accordance with the expectations of the teacher. However, each group then made the following argument: By construction, $h(a) = h(b) = 0$. By Rolle's theorem, there is a point c in (a, b) such that $h'(c) = 0$. Then $f'(c) = g'(c)$, and $g'(c)$ is just the slope of the chord line, namely, $[f(b) - f(a)] / (b - a)$.

Much to my surprise, the groups had completed the proof without any of the usual complications involving the equation of the line $y = g(x)$. Their proofs were more clear and comprehensible than the one found in many calculus books.

Situation 3

Exploration: Let f be a continous positive function on $[a, b]$. How can you find the area under the curve (that is, the area between the graph of f and the x-axis from a to b)?

Students came up with a variety of approaches for finding the area. In one group, three members wanted to compute the area under a curve by making approximations with the areas of rectangles. The fourth member insisted that it was better to use little squares (as in the double integral). The argument went on rather intensely for a few minutes. I then intervened and attempted to lower the tension level by pointing out that both sides were right but in different ways. The majority was right, as shown by several previous problems, in claiming that it was computationally easier to use rectangles than to use little squares. The fourth member was right in claiming that the use of little squares theoretically gave the same answer as the use of rectangles. This illustrated that there may be more than one right way to solve a problem.

In other groups, there were heated arguments about the merits of approximating the area by rectangles underneath the curve, rectangles above the curve, and trapezoids. These were resolved by some computational problems showing that all techniques gave the same answer for the limit, but that it was computationally easier to use rectangles than trapezoids. Upper and lower sums were defined after students had computed the same answers for all the techniques with simple functions.

Situation 4

The following exploration was given as a preliminary step in computing integrals of simple polynomials: Find formulas for the sum of the first n even integers, the sum of the first n integers, and the sum of the first n integers cubed.

The following chart helped guide the students' work:

n	1	2	3	4	5	6
$\displaystyle\sum_{i=1}^{n} 2i$						
$\displaystyle\sum_{i=1}^{n} i$						
$\displaystyle\sum_{i=1}^{n} i^3$						

The hint was given to fill in the sums for the indicated values of n, to look for patterns, and to do the problems in the order stated. All groups successfully conjectured the results:

$$\sum_{i=1}^{n} 2i = n(n + 1) \qquad \sum_{i=1}^{n} i = \frac{n(n + 1)}{2} \qquad \sum_{i=1}^{n} i^3 = \left[\frac{n(n + 1)}{2}\right]^2$$

By using summation formulas, the students correctly computed

$$\int_{0}^{b} x \, dx = \frac{b^2}{2} \qquad \int_{0}^{b} x^2 \, dx = \frac{b^3}{3} \qquad \int_{0}^{b} x^3 \, dx = \frac{b^4}{4}$$

They then easily extended these results to an interval $[a, b]$ with $0 \le a < b$, obtaining

$$\int_{a}^{b} x \, dx = \frac{b^2}{2} - \frac{a^2}{2}, \text{ and so on.}$$

They noticed that each expression for the result of the first, second, or third integral, if it were rewritten with x instead of b, would be a function whose derivative is the integrand. In response, I then suggested for the first problem,

$$\int_0^b x \, dx = \frac{b^2}{2}$$

that they use the name $F(x) = \frac{x^2}{2}$. They picked up this suggestion for all the problems, and then conjectured that

$$\int_a^b f(x) \, dx = F(b) - F(a), \quad \text{where } F'(x) = f(x)$$

They were amazed when I labeled this result (with appropriate hypotheses) as the fundamental theorem of calculus.

Observations. For certain problems students found a variety of possible paths to the solution. For example, in evaluating

$$\int x \sqrt{1 - x^2} \, dx$$

the four members of one group suggested the following correct approaches:

   a. Let $x = \sin \theta$.

   b. Let $x = \cos \theta$.

   c. Let $u = 1 - x^2$.

   d. Write the answer by inspection.

The group members argued about which approach to take, without reaching agreement. I then commented as follows: "Let's agree to just pick one approach to start the problem. Then, whether it works or not, you can still try out those other ideas afterward. It might be interesting to see how many different ways you can solve the problem." The students then went on to solve the problem correctly using each of the four approaches in turn.

In evaluating $\int \tan x \, \sec^2 dx \, dx$, two students obtained different correct answers, namely, $\frac{1}{2} \sec^2 x + c$ and $\frac{1}{2} \tan^2 x + c$. Each student insisted that he was right and the other student was wrong. I then asked, "Is there any possibility that you're both right? Could the answers be equivalent?" The students then established the equivalence by using the identity $1 + \tan^2 x = \sec^2 x$.

Misconceptions, Difficulties, and Surprises

Through daily conversations with the students and daily observations of their work, I learned much about the student reactions to the subject matter. In addition to many strikingly successful experiences, there were also many misconceptions, difficulties, and surprising responses to the subject matter. If I hadn't seen the students working and heard their arguments, I would not have known these things; they don't normally surface in expository instruction.

The students frequently did not test incorrect identities or formulas by using specific instances of them. Examples of this included the incorrect formulas $1 + \sec^2 \theta = \tan^2 \theta$, $\cos(x + y) = \cos x \cos y + \sin x \sin y$, and $\frac{d}{dx} \sec x = \tan^2 x$. Each time the students wrote down such incorrect identities, I asked if there was any easy way to test the truth of their statements. It was usually necessary to suggest that the students try their statement with a particular value of x.

The students were not used to thinking in terms of definitions, and they tended to forget the definitions of the limit, the definite integral, and continuity. However, the definition of the derivative fared somewhat better than the others, perhaps because it was a simple formula that was frequently used. I often reminded students to write an appropriate definition and use it to approach a problem.

There was a noticeable tendency for the students to treat all problems as separate entities that were not related to one another. For instance, the groups first evaluated

$$\int \frac{dx}{a^2 + x^2}$$

by means of the substitution $x = a \tan \theta$. Instead of using this result, the groups then evaluated

$$\int \frac{dx}{9 + x^2}$$

by the substitution $x = 3 \tan \theta$. Although some repetition can be a useful aid in learning up to a certain point, I often had to remind people to use the result of one problem in order to solve another one.

In working with derivatives of composite functions, most students did not perceive the need for applying the chain rule in new situations. Although the student groups correctly developed the formula for the derivative of each major new function, they then made erroneous statements such as

$$\frac{d}{dx} \sin 2x = \cos 2x \qquad \frac{d}{dx} e^{3x} = e^{3x} \qquad \frac{d}{dx} \ln 4x = \frac{1}{4x}$$

In each instance it was necessary to remind students that they were dealing with a composite function.

In problems that could be solved in several different ways, the students often preferred to use the technique they learned first. For example, the technique of integration by trig substitution was first introduced by the problem of computing the area of a circle. In order to evaluate

$$\int_{-r}^{r} \sqrt{r^2 - x^2} \, dx$$

the groups used polar coordinates and set $x = r \cos \theta$. Then, in many other integrals involving the expression $r^2 - x^2$, the students always used the substitution $x = r \cos \theta$ rather than the more standard substitution of $x = r \sin \theta$. Several students said that $x = r \sin \theta$ would work but that they liked their first approach better.

The students' intuitive notions about sequences were surprising to me. Almost all the students believed initially that the listing 1, 1, 1, 1, . . . did not describe a sequence, since the nth term did not change and was not specified by a formula involving n. After resolving this issue, almost all students stated that the sequence 1, 1, 1, 1, . . . did not have a limit, since "it's not getting close to any number; it's there already." A similar response occurred with constant functions.

Most students stated that the sequence 0, 2, 0, 2, 0, 2, . . . converged to two different limits and were upset when I said that the sequence had no limit. Their discomfort was alleviated somewhat when I introduced the notion of a subsequence.

In trying to solve problems or write proofs using the formal $\varepsilon{-}\delta$ definition of the limit of a sequence or a function, the students encountered great conceptual and technical difficulties. Comments from several students indicated that they did not perceive the statement as a reasonable definition. "If that's a definition, it's the weirdest one I've seen in my entire life." Moreover, most students did not find the proofs of limit theorems to be useful. "There's no reason to prove a theorem unless there is some doubt about the result, and I never had any doubt about the sum of the limits being the same as the limit of the sum." Many students were not convinced by proofs of the limit theorems. "That proof is nothing but a bunch of equivalent statements with complicated notation. It doesn't prove anything to me." These attitudes and difficulties were not caused by lack of prior concrete experience; the students had spent several weeks working with a variety of sequences before encountering the formal definition of the limit.

The student concept of a function seemed to include several basic but unstated assumptions. Students invariably drew the graph of a function as a smooth curve with a small number of relative maxima or minima. A student said, and others agreed, that "there are only three possibilities at an endpoint of an interval. Either the curve comes in level or it comes in from below or from above." It appeared that students' concepts of a function on a closed interval actually meant a continuous, differentiable function with finitely many maxima and minima. Students viewed as "very peculiar" certain functions with infinitely many oscillations in their graphs, such as

$$f(x) = \begin{cases} x \sin \dfrac{1}{x} & \text{if } x \neq 0 \\ 0 & \text{if } x = 0 \end{cases}$$

Most students felt that there was something unnatural or artificial about functions with discontinuities. As they put it, these functions were "made up" by moving points out of their proper locations, by adding points that did not belong in the domain, or by putting in artificial steps.

The students seemed to think at times that all functions were differentiable. For example, for the function $f(x) = |x|$, the students stated that they were going to find $f'(0)$. When the right-hand and left-hand limits of the difference quotients turned out to be different, most students thought that they had made an arithmetic mistake somewhere. They found it hard to reconcile their belief with their correct computational result.

Many students made a distinction between theory and problems. As one student put it, "Calculus should be 25 percent theory and 75 percent problems." The distinction between theory and problems seemed to depend largely on the presence or absence of arbitrary functions. Although most students preferred problems over theory, they sometimes distinguished between useless theory and useful theory. Useless theory consisted of propositions intended to "prove the obvious" or "straighten out things we already know." Most students deemed as useless the definition of the limit and the development of the natural logarithm as an integral. Useful theory consisted of general propositions that had applications to interesting problems with specific functions. Many students accepted as useful theory the proof of the fundamental theorem of calculus and the development of the formula for the volume of a surface of a revolution.

In summary, the close contact with the students in the groups helped me gain much insight into the student perceptions of the calculus content. The difficulties that occurred should not obscure the success of the student groups in proving the major theorems of calculus, in developing techniques for solving classes of problems, in stating some insightful conjectures, and in coming up with problem solutions and proofs not previously known to me.

Evaluation of the Method

In studies of student achievement by Davidson (1971), Loomer (1976), and Brechting and Hirsch (1977), the experimental treatment was the small-group discovery method or a variation upon it, and the control treatment was the lecture-discussion method in calculus. Davidson and Urion (n.d.) compared these same types of experimental and control treatments in half a dozen courses ranging from general mathematics in junior high school through differential equations at the college level. In most comparisons there was no statistically significant difference in student achievement; when significant differences did occasionally occur, they favored the small-group treatment. Hence, it is safe to say that students taught by the small-group discovery method have performed at least as well as those taught by more traditional lecture-discussion procedures.

Over a number of years I have given attitude surveys to students and teachers involved with the small-group discovery method. The main problem areas reported most frequently by teachers and students include concerns about covering enough material, initial difficulties in forming effective groups, barriers to fostering cooperation among students, occasional conflict or frustration with overly difficult mathematical problems, and providing high-quality instructional materials. Although student attitudes toward the method of instruction are generally favorable, the degree to which they are favorable depends upon the teacher's experience and skill in handling the problem areas just described.

There are many advantages to learning mathematics in cooperative groups. The following positive points are frequently mentioned by teachers and students responding to attitude surveys. Students learn mathematics by working actively at a comfortable pace. They learn to cooperate with others and to communicate in the language of mathematics. The classroom atmosphere tends to be relaxed and informal, help is readily available, questions are freely asked and answered, and even the shy student finds it easy to be involved. Students tend to become friends with their group members, and the teacher-student relationship tends to be more relaxed, more pleasant, and closer than in a traditional approach. The usual "discipline" problems of talking and moving around are eliminated by definition. In addition, many students maintain a high level of interest in the mathematical activities. Many students like math more—or at least hate it less—than in teacher-centered approaches. Finally, students have an opportunity to pursue the more challenging and creative aspects of mathematics while they achieve at least as much information and skill as in more traditional approaches.

Attitudes of several students can be conveyed vividly by quoting their responses from a questionnaire given in a successful calculus class: (1) "Other students, no matter who, force you to learn more." (2) "Most classes stress being able to use formulas while this stresses total understanding." (3) "It is my most interesting and liked class. I enjoy coming to it." (4) I think I learned a lot more this year than in all three years of high school math." (5) "It showed me that I can do things that before looked impossible. All it takes is a little understanding. Math doesn't scare me as much now." (6) "I simply feel it was a great experiment (and experience) and more subjects should be adapted to this general method." (7) "This type of class was, in my estimation, the closest possible setup to an ideal learning situation."

References

Anderson, R.C. 1963. Learning in discussions: A Résumé of the Authoritarian-Democratic Studies. In *Readings in the social psychology of education*, edited by W.W. Charters and N.L. Gage. Boston: Allyn & Bacon.

Asch, S.E. 1960. Effects of group pressure upon the modification and distortion of judgments. In *Group dynamics: Research and theory*, edited by D. Cartwright and A. Zander. 2d ed. New York: Harper & Row.

Bales, R.F., and E.F. Borgatta. 1961. Size of group as a factor in the interaction profile. In *Small groups, studies in social interaction*, edited by A.P. Hare, E.F. Borgatta, and R.F. Bales. New York: Alfred A. Knopf.

Brechting, Sister M.C., and C.R. Hirsch. 1977. The effects of small-group discovery learning on student achievement and attitudes in calculus. MATYC *Journal* (2): 77–82.

Cartwright, D., and A. Zander. 1960. *Group dynamics: Research and theory*, 2d ed. New York: Harper & Row.

Chakerian, G.D., C.D. Crabill, and S.K. Stein. 1986. *Geometry: A guided inquiry*. Pleasantville, N.Y.: Sunburst.

Cohen, E.G. 1986. Designing groupwork: Strategies for the heterogeneous classroom. New York: Teachers College Press.

Davidson, N. 1971. *The small-group discovery method of mathematics instruction as applied in calculus.* Ph.D. diss., University of Wisconsin, 1970. Technical Report No. 168, Wisconsin Research and Development Center for Cognitive Learning, Madison, Wisconsin.

————. 1971. The small-group discovery method as applied in calculus instruction. *American Mathematical Monthly* (August-September): 789–91.

————. 1976. Motivation of students in small-group learning of mathematics. *Frostburg State College Journal of Mathematics Education* (11): 1–18.

————. 1979. The small-group discovery method: 1967–77. In *Problem solving studies in mathematics*, edited by J. Harvey and T. Romberg. The Wisconsin Research and Development Center for Individualized Schooling, University of Wisconsin, Madison.

————. 1985. Small-group learning and teaching in mathematics: A selective review of the research. In *Learning to cooperate, cooperating to learn*, edited by R. Slavin. New York: Plenum Press.

Davidson, N., L. Agreen, and C. Davis. 1978. Small-group learning in junior high school mathematics. *School Science and Mathematics* (January): 23–30.

Davidson, N., and F. Gulick. 1976. *Abstract algebra: An active learning approach.* Boston: Houghton Mifflin.

Davidson, N., R. McKeen, and T. Eisenberg. 1973. Curriculum construction with student input. *The Mathematics Teacher* (March): 271–75.

Davidson, N., and D. Urion. n.d. "Some results on student achievement in small-group instruction versus teacher-centered instruction in mathematics." (In press.)

Deutsch, M. 1960. The effects of cooperation and competition upon group process. In *Group dynamics: Research and theory*, 2d ed., edited by D. Cartwright and A. Zander.

Dewey, J. 1916. *Democracy and education.* New York: Macmillan. (Republished: Collier Books Paperback Edition, New York, 1966.)

————. 1938. *Experience and education.* New York: Kappa Delta Pi. (Republished: Collier Books Paperback Edition, New York, 1963.)

Gallicchio, A. 1976. The effects of brainstorming in small group mathematics classes. Ph.D. diss., University of Maryland, College Park.

Grant, S. 1975. The effects of three kinds of group formation using FIRO-B compatibility, sociometric choice with group dynamics exercises, and in-class choice on mathematics classes taught by the small-group discovery method. Ph.D. diss., University of Maryland, College Park.

Klingbeil, D. 1974. An examination of the effects of group testing in mathematics courses taught by the small-group discovery method. Ph.D. diss., University of Maryland, College Park.

Loomer, N.J. 1976. A multidimensional exploratory investigation of small-group heuristic and expository learning in calculus. Ph.D. diss., University of Wisconsin, Madison.

McKeen, R., and N. Davidson. 1975. An alternative to individual instruction in mathematics. *American Mathematical Monthly* (December): 1006–9.

Mills, T.M. 1960. Power relations in three-person groups. In *Group dynamics: Research and theory*, 2d ed., edited by D. Cartwright and A. Zander. New York: Harper & Row.

Moise, E.E. 1965. Activity and motivation in mathematics. *American Mathematical Monthly* 72 (4): 407–12.

Polya, G. 1965. *Mathematical discovery*, Vol. 2. New York: John Wiley.

Schutz, W.C. 1966. *The interpersonal underworld*. Palo Alto, Calif.: Science and Behavioral Books.

Slater, P.E. 1958. Contrasting correlates of group size. *Sociometry* 21 (2): 129–39.

Slavin, R.E. 1980. Cooperative learning. *Review of Educational Research* 50: 315–42.

Stam, P.J. 1973. The effect of sociometric grouping on task performance in the elementary classroom. Ph.D. diss., Stanford University.

Stein, S.K., and C.D. Crabill. 1986. *Elementary algebra: A guided inquiry.* Pleasantville, N.Y.: Sunburst.

Stein, S.K., C.D. Crabill, and G.D. Chakerian. 1986. *Algebra II/Trigonometry: A guided inquiry.* Pleasantville, N.Y.: Sunburst.

Thoyre, H. 1970. A pilot study on the use of small-group discussion in a mathematics course for preservice elementary teachers. Ph.D. diss., University of Wisconsin, Madison.

University of Maryland Mathematics Project (M. Cole, N. Davidson, J. Fey, J. Henkelman et al). 1978. *Unifying concepts and processes in elementary mathematics.* Boston: Allyn & Bacon.

Webb, N.M. 1985. Verbal interaction and learning in peer-directed groups. *Theory into Practice,* Vol. 24, 32–39.

Weissglass, J. 1976. Small groups: An alternative to the lecture method. *The Two-Year College Mathematics Journal* VII (February): 15–20.

———. 1977. Mathematics for elementary teaching: A small-group laboratory approach. *American Mathematical Monthly* (May): 377–82.

———. 1979. *Exploring elementary mathematics: A small-group approach for teaching.* San Francisco: W. H. Freeman.

White, R., and R. Lippitt. 1960. Leader behavior and member reaction in three "Social Climates." In *Group dynamics: Research and theory,* edited by D. Cartwright and A. Zander. New York: Harper & Row.

Neil Davidson *is Associate Professor of Mathematics Education in the Department of Curriculum and Instruction at the University of Maryland, College Park. He is the coauthor of* Abstract Algebra: An Active Learning Approach. *Dr. Davidson is currently president of the Mid-Atlantic Association for Cooperation in Education (MAACIE) and a member of the board of directors of the International Association for the Study of Cooperation in Education (IASCE). Dr. Davidson first developed procedures for small-group discovery learning over twenty years ago.*

12.

Implementing Group Work: Issues for Teachers and Administrators

LAUREL ROBERTSON, NANCY GRAVES,
AND PATRICIA TUCK

This chapter is a cooperative effort to confront issues affecting the integration of cooperative learning strategies in mathematics instruction. Using cooperative groups requires a different approach to planning and teaching mathematics than traditional methods do. We focus on steps for effective implementation appropriate for any of the various strategies discussed in previous chapters, and we address such issues as classroom environment, decisions teachers need to make when planning, and general factors that affect implementation. The chapter is intended for teachers of any grade level as well as for administrators wishing to support the implementation of cooperative learning.

Classroom Environment

We believe it is essential that teachers lay a foundation for cooperative learning by creating a cooperative classroom environment. This is particularly important if students have had little previous experience working cooperatively. The teacher can begin by implementing whole-class and small-group activities that build a sense of classroom community and group cohesion. These activities enhance student relationships, allowing students to know one another, accept and respect each other, and value their differences as resources. The experiences provided by these activities also strengthen students' be-lief that they will produce a better product and learn more as a group than individually.

The following scenario illustrates an elementary classroom with a cooperative classroom climate.

Let's imagine we are visiting the fourth grade classroom of an experienced cooperative learning teacher, Mrs. Baker (a composite person of the many excellent teachers we know). As we enter the door, we see a large handmade banner proclaiming that this is the "Ranch of the Rainbow Rangers." A student greets us, asking if we would like to sign the guest book. We notice other students clustering around groups of desks, above which such names as "Yellow Orioles" and "Orange Tigers" hang on coat hangers. These, our guide explains, are the family groups, in which the class begins and ends the day.

Margot, the Yellow Oriole's facilitator this week, is checking the daily schedule. She asks the group, "Has the play equipment been put away? Great, you guys! Now, let's go over our math homework together before we go to our math groups!"

"Don't forget we need to meet with the Orange Tigers before lunch to make out the food list for the class party," Jose reminds the Orioles. "Yeah, and our family gets to welcome visitors this week," adds Deanna, our guide. "Okay, let's get to the homework," urges Felix, the timekeeper for the group.

After individual math homework is compared, the group works together to decide on the best answer to each problem, using a consensus method learned by the class for their community meetings. The solutions are entered on a group answer sheet, stapled to the individual papers, and placed in the family folder. Seeing that Mrs. Baker has laid out folders for the math groups, the Orioles exchange secret handshakes and disperse to their heterogeneous math groups.

We follow Margot to her group to find that the member responsible for materials has already arranged them for the group in a central area. "Oh, there you are, Margot," smiles David. "Here's the problem Mrs. Baker explained to us yesterday. Here are some things we might use to help us figure it out."

"We have only 25 minutes in this work period," chimes in Laticia. "What do you think would be the best way to start?" Tuan asks the group members.

As they begin to solve the problem, each student suggests an approach or idea while the others listen. They try out likely strategies, stopping often to assess whether they are getting the group closer to its goal and to discuss the value of alternative strategies. When they finally all agree on a solution, they check to be sure that all members understand and everyone can explain the group's strategies and solutions. As we leave, the group is planning how to present their findings to the whole class.

Teachers (regardless of the grade level, student population, and student proficiency in mathematics) can use several types of activities to structure a cooperative environment such as Mrs. Baker's (see Graves and Graves, n.d.). These activities include:

1. Getting-acquainted exercises

2. Activities for creating a class identity

3. Activities for building whole-class unity

Getting acquainted involves using name games, icebreakers, and simple math activities to help students know one another better in an atmosphere of fun and safety and to disperse feelings of wariness and distrust. During this inclusion phase of group development, Mrs. Baker uses wall graphs to which students respond, showing a distribution of answers to questions about who we are (our families, cultures, households, and experiences), what we do and what we like (hobbies, interests, food, and pets), and the like. Younger students might work with real, picture, and bar graphs, practicing making mathematical statements about the results. Older students might use more sophisticated analytical techniques and generate and test hypotheses.

Creating a class identity helps to minimize factionalism that can occur between cooperative groups. Class symbols and mottos such as a class name, logo, and banner or crest help develop this sense of identity. Having a class space to display the banner in the auditorium or cafeteria can be part of an effort to create an "our school" atmosphere as well. Once the class community is solid, these activities can also be done with family groups (a further discussion of family groups can be found later in the chapter) or academic cooperative groups.

Whole-class unity events and activities utilize compelling projects, trips, or social occasions to unite the class in common goals, effectively preparing students for cooperative effort. Chanting or singing, class meetings, fund-raising, and cooperative sports and games also promote group cohesion. In the secondary classroom, short climate-building math warm-ups for the whole class can produce similar results (see Chapter 6 by Roberta Dees).

Another consideration when creating a cooperative classroom environment is developing shared responsibility for the operation of the classroom. In the traditional classroom, classroom management is almost entirely the responsibility of the teacher. The cooperative classroom is "our classroom" (Moorman and Dishon, 1986) because it is jointly managed by the students and the teacher. Feelings of ownership and participation are developed as the class establishes norms and standards of conduct and takes responsibility for the smooth functioning of the classroom. As we saw in Mrs. Baker's class, the Rainbow Rangers had divided the ongoing duties of classroom organization and management among the family groups. Academic groups were also expected to take maximum responsibility for organizing themselves for work.

Teachers can develop this "our classroom" atmosphere, the sense that we are all in it together, by:

1. Involving the students early in developing lists of appropriate norms, standards, or guidelines for behavior in the classroom and on school premises. This is particularly important for working together and for rapid and efficient movement between cooperative groups. Examples of such norms include: Use "indoor" voices, use encouraging statements, ask for help when you need it, and give help when you are asked.

2. Assigning on a rotating basis, to ongoing *groups* rather than to individuals, the following tasks: room maintenance, duty schedules, and checking and correcting homework assignments.

3. Establishing regular class meetings, to which individuals or groups can submit agenda items and where leadership and group responsibility can be practiced.

4. Making the class as a whole and subgroups within it responsible for planning, executing, and commemorating major unity events such as parties, trips, and fund-raisers.

Experiences such as these not only develop student self-governance but also lay the groundwork for the independent group problem solving that is important for cooperative mathematics activities.

Teacher Decisions and Role

Essentially, a cooperative lesson is divided into three phases, each of which includes several related steps.

I. Planning the Lesson

   A. Selecting the academic concepts or skills

   B. Selecting the lesson or activity and the cooperative strategy

   C. Selecting the cooperative skills to be specifically taught or practiced*

   D. Planning for group work: room arrangement, group formation, size of groups, group duration, group roles, materials preparation, extension activities

   E. Planning team-building experiences for newly formed groups or warm-up team exercises, which are content-appropriate, for ongoing groups*

II. Conducting the Lesson

   A. Providing background information, review, direct teaching, and an introduction to the activity

   B. Explaining the goals of the lesson and the task

   C. Establishing and discussing the cooperative skills to be specifically practiced*

---

* Not a formal part of every cooperative strategy

D. Monitoring group interaction

E. Intervening when necessary

III. Processing the academic and cooperative* aspects of the lesson

Planning the Lesson

When planning a lesson, the teacher first decides the mathematics skills and concepts to be addressed and then selects the appropriate instructional activity. This is also true when planning a cooperative lesson. Once the concepts to be taught or practiced have been identified, the teacher must decide whether a cooperative strategy is appropriate and which strategy to use.

Selecting a Cooperative Strategy. When deciding whether a cooperative learning strategy would be appropriate, some basic guidelines can be applied. Highly appropriate for cooperative group work are:

1. Lessons that are open ended, have many possible answers or solution strategies, require divergent thinking, or have many steps.

2. Lessons that provide opportunities for students to apply and/or extend skills and concepts.

3. Lessons where solutions or solution strategies are not readily apparent. If they are, little cooperative interaction will be needed and the value of students working together is lost.

Some cooperative strategies lend themselves well to specific uses, which can simplify the decision-making process regarding which cooperative strategy to use. The teacher might choose, for example, to implement peer practice techniques (see Chapter 3 by Robert Slavin) when the goal is for students to review previously learned material and skills. When problem solving (a natural partner with cooperative learning) is the goal, the Johnsons' "Learning Together" and

* Not a formal part of every cooperative strategy

Marilyn Burn's "Groups of Four" strategies are excellent choices, as are many of the other strategies described in this book.

Some cooperative strategies are useful for easing gradually into academic group work or fit well in a variety of situations.

1. *Think-Pair-Share* (Lyman, 1981): The teacher asks a question of the class, gives students time to think about it individually, and then has them share their ideas with the person seated next to them or with their assigned partner. After the pair discusses the issue briefly, they share their ideas with another pair or with the whole class.

2. *Numbered Heads Together* (R. Frank in Kagan, 1987): Students in a group are each given a number. They then put their heads together and discuss a question or problem posed by the teacher. The teacher calls a number, and students holding that number in any group may share their group's thinking.

3. *Consensus Strategies:* These strategies provide methods for students to come to agreement in ways other than ordinary voting or majority rule. For example, each student chooses a specified number of favorite solutions from a list of class-brainstormed solutions. Then, from those solutions picked most frequently, students choose their favorite or one they did not suggest but which they feel they could "live with."

Using these and other simple structures (Kagan, 1987), the teacher and students can easily move into more complex cooperative structures for problem solving or discovery.

After deciding to teach a lesson cooperatively and picking the appropriate cooperative strategy, the teacher has several other decisions to make.

How Will the Room Be Arranged? Room arrangement is an essential consideration for effective cooperative work. Students cannot cooperate easily in rows of individual desks. Generally speaking, the closer together students can be seated comfortably, the better. All group members need to have easy access to the materials and to be able to hear and speak to each other without difficulty. Noise problems will be reduced when the distance between group members is short and groups are separated from each other.

Sharing one desk or small table is a good arrangement for a pair; a small table is appropriate for a group of four. If tables are not available, desks can be clustered. Students can also be grouped around a flip chart or near the chalkboard for brainstorming or problem solving. The use of the chalkboard or newsprint helps the group focus on the task. Teachers should experiment with the available furniture to find out what works best.

Young students need opportunities to practice getting to and from groups when moving furniture is necessary. Older students can be involved in problem solving about space issues. Charts can be posted showing the arrangement of desks for different kinds of instruction (for example, paired work or jigsaw) so that valuable class time will be saved when rearrangement is necessary.

Another consideration when deciding on room arrangement is the issue of individual and group materials. Cubbies on one wall for individual possessions facilitate free movement around the room for different purposes. Some teachers encourage students to use portable backpacks or bookbags that can be slung over the backs of chairs. Since groups often share materials, it is a good idea to have a place in the room to store group supplies. Plastic wash tubs make excellent moveable, storable containers for group materials.

Bulletin board space is also an important consideration. Space will be needed for class "getting-acquainted" graphs, class unity and identity projects, and group work displays.

How Will Students Be Grouped? We suggest that teachers will have more success using random or teacher-selected learning groups rather than student-selected groups. (Some authors in this book, however, permit student-selected groups under certain circumstances.) Random grouping allows for heterogeneity and sends the message that all students are equally valued as group members. It is also difficult for students to argue with the "luck of the draw." They can, however, come to see the wisdom of working with everyone in the class. In *Circles of Learning*, Johnson, Johnson, and Holubec suggest many ways to assign students randomly to groups, such as counting off or drawing playing cards.

There are times when the teacher should consider selecting the groups. If, for example, reading is involved in the activity, the teacher will need to be sure that each group includes someone who can read. If several languages are a consideration in the class, the teacher may want to place a bilingual student in a group with monolingual students of two different languages. In forming groups, a wide range of academic and social abilities should be included and the groups should be as heterogeneous as possible in regard to sex and ethnicity. In other words, the groups should reflect the composition of the entire class.

There are two major types of groups that are found in cooperative learning classrooms:

1. *Families or tribes:* Groups of four to eight students that function mainly as support groups and perform responsible tasks for the ongoing management of the classroom. These are longer lasting than academic work groups; some teachers prefer to keep them all year. Jeanne Gibbs (1987) recommends that teachers form these groups sociometrically, so all students have at least one other person in their family group with whom they wish to work.

2. *Learning groups (or academic work groups or study groups):* Smaller groups of two to five students, depending on the nature of the task, the age of the students, and the complexity of teamwork required.

How Large Should the Groups Be? In addition to considering the type of group to be formed, teachers need to take into account the nature of the activity and the students' previous experience with cooperative group work. In general, teachers may find it is easier to begin with pairs than with larger groups, particularly if the teacher and the students have had little experience with cooperative learning. Pairs foster maximum involvement and may decrease the likelihood of exclusion or of one person riding on the coattails of the others. Once students have had an opportunity to work with many of their classmates in pairs, they may work more effectively when they are in larger groups.

We suggest using pairs for most structured cooperative activities in kindergarten and first grade. Larger groups can be formed for loosely structured activities such as free exploration of materials.

In other grade levels, after some paired experiences, students can begin working in groups of three or four. We suggest groups of two to four for most problem-solving experiences, even at the high school level. Most of the authors in this book suggest groups of four for problem-solving or discovery tasks.

How Long Should Groups Be Kept Together? Another decision teachers must make is how long to keep groups together. Giving students the opportunity to work with as many other classmates as possible is an important consideration at the beginning of the year to support successful group work later on. At this time, teachers might consider having students work in randomly selected groups that change frequently.

Once students have been paired with quite a few of their classmates, implementing longer-term groups encourages team building and the development of group skills. Teachers may then wish to structure or randomly select groups that work together for two or more weeks. Teachers who have the same students for more than one subject might consider utilizing long-term groups in one subject while frequently changing groups for other lessons.

In general, if social skill development is a goal, teachers may wish to keep groups together long enough for them to feel like a team. Group conflict is not often a signal to change groups but an opportunity to learn problem solving. Teachers become experienced at recognizing when teams have reached their peak effectiveness and are ready to be changed.

Will Group Roles Be Assigned? Before implementing a cooperative lesson, the teacher needs to decide whether or not to assign group roles (facilitator, reporter, recorder, encourager, and so on). Assigning group roles to younger or inexperienced students can help them learn about the different skills that group members need in order to accomplish their task, and may also ensure inclusion. As students grow in their understanding of how groups function, assigning roles to students may become unnecessary. Examples of lessons with assigned roles can be found in the chapters by David and Roger Johnson, Mary Male, and Rachel Lotan and Joan Benton.

If roles are assigned, it is important for teachers to provide opportunities for every student to experience each role. Leadership skills are thus learned by all in a safe, reality-based environment. Regardless of whether roles are assigned or not, the roles played by members during group work and the effectiveness of these roles need to be reflected upon and discussed at the end of the lesson.

The learning of roles can be viewed as a continuum. A teacher may wish not to introduce roles at all in kindergarten or first grade. In second and third grade, students might learn about and practice assigned roles. In upper grades, students might begin the year with assigned roles. As the year progresses, the teacher might begin a lesson by discussing the roles, asking each group to decide who will play each role, and at the end of the lesson asking how they made their decisions. After several experiences of this sort, roles might not be discussed at all during the introduction of the lesson. Instead, the teacher might ask at the end of the lesson how groups made decisions about the roles they needed.

What Materials Need To Be Prepared? Cooperative group work generally reduces the quantity of learning materials needed if one set of materials (manipulatives, construction paper, scissors, and so on) and one record sheet are prepared for each group. Commercially prepared materials may also ease preparation. (See the resource materials at the end of this book.) However, although cooperative group work may reduce the quantity of materials, preparation time may be as great or greater than when planning other types of lessons.

Group record sheets can facilitate group work. All members focus on the same problem and can check for agreement before writing. At times, however, it is important to provide individual record sheets for each student to record solutions or practice a skill in order to reinforce learning. Thus, when developing materials, care must be taken to ensure that the materials support both the cooperative and academic goals of the lesson.

What Extension (Follow-Up) Activities Will Be Available? It seems to be a law of nature that no two cooperative groups will complete their task at the same time. Thus, unless prepared with follow-up activities, the teacher can have a gigantic headache when seven groups finish at different times. Extension activities need to be considered carefully for their appropriateness to the students' cooperative and academic skills. They should extend the mathematical concept or provide opportunities to apply the concept in another context. Having planned extension activities before the lesson is important not only for student learning but also for teacher sanity!

Conducting the Lesson

Perhaps this states the obvious, but when presenting a lesson it is best to let students know what they are going to do, why they are going to do it, and how they are expected to work. Thus, during the lesson introduction it is important to explain the task and clearly state the academic and cooperative goals of the lesson.

When explaining the task, the teacher must walk a fine line. Saying too little about the task results in student confusion, lots of questions, false starts, and frustration. Saying too much robs students of problem-solving opportunities, leaving students little to discover on their own. Mathematics lessons require the introduction to include some structure and focus while allowing room for students to explore and discover.

Many teachers report they are reluctant to use cooperative group work of any kind on a regular basis because it is too noisy and out of control, because some students are happy to allow others to do all the work, and because students often treat each other unkindly. We believe if cooperative work is to be successful, cooperative group skills must be a focal point of the lesson. Many of the small-group methods described in this book include cooperative group skill development as an integral part of the strategy.

Cooperative Skills. During the lesson introduction, the cooperative skills to be specifically practiced (listening, paraphrasing, including everyone, disagreeing in an agreeable way, giving help without telling the answer, and so on) can be discussed and modeled— labeling each skill, identifying its importance, and discussing how it looks and sounds when in practice. Assigning specific roles to group members also provides opportunities to discuss and practice cooperative skills. The inherent structure of the lesson often allows for practice of a skill. For example, a lesson that requires a group record sheet lends itself to practicing the skills of agreeing before writing and checking for understanding.

When deciding on which cooperative skill to practice during a lesson, two factors should be considered. As mentioned earlier, the structure of the lesson often naturally lends itself to the practice of a specific skill. Additionally, the cooperative skill level of the class must be taken into account. Previous cooperative lessons will provide opportunities for assessment. Perhaps in the last cooperative lesson students had some difficulty staying with their groups. This skill could then become the skill to be discussed and practiced during the new lesson.

Monitoring Group Interaction. As groups begin to work, the teacher's role becomes that of observer and facilitator. The teacher monitors groups, looking for opportunities to extend academic and social learning. This is a golden opportunity to assess students' mathematical skills and their ability to apply concepts. Teachers often find cooperative group work reduces the number of paper-and-pencil tests they need to administer.

For teachers new to cooperative learning, it is often helpful to focus on one or two aspects of group work or to observe just one or two groups at a time. Taking notes when observing can provide focus and information for ensuing class discussions.

Intervening. When and how to step into a cooperative group is another fine point of the craft. Some methods emphasize that the teacher should stay out of the group unless the shedding of blood is imminent. Others make no recommendation. Thought needs to be given to the goal of the intervention and to whether the interruption will benefit or adversely affect the group.

One of the goals of cooperative learning is to allow group members to use each other as resources. A group norm that *all* members of a group must have the same question before asking the teacher for help encourages students to look to each other for answers. Students need opportunities to solve interpersonal and academic conflicts on their own and to use each other to answer questions.

With younger or less socially skilled students, intervention may need to occur more frequently. If the teacher decides to intervene to help the group work more effectively, a question can help students to focus on the group interaction and guide them toward finding a solution to their problem. It is important to turn the decision making back to the group as often as possible.

The teacher may consider intervening in several instances: to ask a question that will extend concept development or help the group work more effectively; to give a hint when a group is stuck; to give specific feedback to a student or to the group about their performance or interaction; to check for understanding; to explain a term or clarify a direction; to answer a question for a group; or to intervene with the whole class to clarify directions. After intervening, particularly if the intervention is a question to help students get back on track, the teacher should step away but let the group know that he or she will return later to see how they are progressing.

Processing the Lesson

Processing, giving students the opportunity to reflect on the academic and cooperative aspects of the lesson, extends and enhances the learning process and is integral to the power of cooperative learning. Students need to discuss their group experience, focusing both on their product and the way that they worked. Discussing how each group has solved the problem encourages multiple solutions and flexibility of thought. Similarly, discussing group interaction—both the difficulties and successes—significantly enhances development of group skills.

Good facilitation requires asking questions that get students to reflect and to talk with each other about their experience. For example, the teacher might ask, "How did your group include everyone?" or "How did you check for understanding?" or "How did your group decide what strategies to try?" Notes taken by the teacher during group work can suggest questions that get students to think and talk about their work. Teachers should talk less than students during processing.

The cooperative lesson is incomplete until it has been processed. Processing is most effective as soon after the lesson as possible. If the lesson is interrupted by recess, lunch, or changing of classes before processing has occurred, the teacher can declare unfinished business and facilitate the processing as soon as the group is together again.

Reflecting by the teacher is also important. In part, this will occur during the processing with the students. Peer coaching can also provide opportunities for the teacher to assess the lesson, its effectiveness, and needs for future lessons. Whether done with another person or individually, this teacher reflection contributes to the ongoing success of cooperative lessons.

Factors That Affect Implementation

Teachers and administrators wishing to implement cooperative learning strategies in their classrooms or throughout their schools need to be aware of several factors regarding innovation and change that impact the successful implementation in mathematics or any other subject.

Time

Learning to use cooperative techniques takes considerable time. It is our belief that cooperation in the classroom should be implemented slowly and at a pace that the teacher finds comfortable. It may take a year or more for a teacher fully to implement cooperative-learning strategies into regular classroom practice.

Teachers often have two concerns about time—how much class time is required for small-group activities and how often to use them. The use of cooperative groups can lengthen the amount of time needed for exploring a particular topic, especially when teachers and students are new to cooperative learning. Three actions may help reduce the added time: (1) selecting core topics for student exploration and emphasizing these in group work, (2) adjusting the balance between teacher presentation, group activities, and other methods, and (3) adjusting the challenge of the task and the amount of teacher guidance during group work. We suggest for maximum social and academic benefits, cooperative group work be implemented at least three times per week.

Teacher Involvement

Teachers can implement cooperative learning on their own. However, cooperative techniques are more likely to be used and maintained if several teachers or the entire staff, including the principal, is involved. Collegiality, sharing, group commitment, and support significantly affect personal growth and the level of implementation. The ideal situation is for cooperation to become part of the school climate and cooperative learning to be recognized as an integral part of the instructional process. Certainly a change toward the use of cooperation in the classroom is enhanced by a staff working cooperatively towards this end!

Staff Development

Staff development needs to be ongoing, with time to internalize and practice specific skills between in-service sessions. The content needs to include theory, demonstration, and an opportunity for teachers to experience and understand the benefits of cooperative learning. Cooperative-learning activities should be an integral part of the program, and teacher-teacher interaction should be encouraged. During the in-service sessions, teachers also need to have time to discuss and share their experiences, to ask each other questions, and to plan.

Between in-service sessions, collegial support groups and coaching provide opportunities to celebrate successes, problem-solve, and receive feedback. In order to be effective, time and space for coaching and support groups need to be made. Expectations as to purpose, process, content, frequency, and confidentiality need to be made explicit. Different models of coaching—expert, peer, and team—can be explored.

Coaching involves a preconference, a lesson, and a postconference. The coach and the person being coached plan the lesson during the preconference and agree upon what is to be practiced and observed. After the lesson has been taught, these observations are processed in the postconference.

Expert coaching is the collaboration of one educator already familiar with cooperative-learning techniques with a teacher who is at a less advanced stage of implementation. Peer coaching involves two teachers supporting each other as they are learning. Team coaching involves two teachers planning and teaching lessons together, first in one classroom and then in the other, with the opportunity to discuss and revise the lesson in between.

Principal Leadership

Cooperative learning is more likely to occur if the principal takes an active role. A supportive principal understands cooperative learning, encourages and facilitates teacher collaboration, sets an environment that values experimentation, helps teachers surmount obstacles, and is visible and accessible. To do this, a principal may need to arrange schedules to allow for peer coaching, release teachers for in-service or meeting with support groups, structure cooperative activities among staff members, provide resources, and tolerate initial problems and frustrations. The principal may also need to provide parent and community education about cooperative learning. Most of all, the principal needs to recognize the risk taken by teachers when making such a major change and to support and encourage them in as many ways as possible.

In this chapter, we have endeavored to outline the major issues affecting implementation of cooperative-learning. We hope teachers and administrators will recognize the need for collaborative effort when integrating cooperative-learning techniques into the instructional program and will plan, problem-solve, and support each other toward this end.

References

Gibbs, J. 1987. *Tribes: A process for social development and cooperative learning.* Santa Rosa, Calif: Center Source Publications.

Graves, N., and T. Graves. n.d. *Getting there together: A sourcebook and desk top guide for creating a cooperative classroom.* (In process.)

Johnson, D.W., R. Johnson, and E. Holubec. 1986. *Circles of learning,* rev. ed. Edina, Minn.: Interaction Book Company.

Kagan, S. 1987. *Cooperative learning: Resources for teachers.* School of Education, University of California, Riverside.

Lyman, F.T., Jr. 1981. The responsive classroom discussion: The inclusion of all students. *Mainstreaming Digest:* 109–112.

Moorman, C., and D. Dishon. 1986. *Our classroom: We can learn together.* Portage, Mich.: Institute for Personal Power.

Laurel Robertson *is Director of the Cooperative Mathematics Project and Co-Director of the Cooperative Learning Implementation Project, both programs of the Developmental Studies Center in San Ramon, California. She is also president of the California Association for Cooperation in Education (CACIE) and a member of the board of directors of the International Association for the Study of Cooperation in Education (IASCE).*

Nancy Graves *is an applied anthropologist and an educational consultant. Dr. Graves taught preschool and primary school and was a professor at the University of California, Los Angeles, and Auckland University in New Zealand. She and her husband, Ted Graves, researched the role of education in the modernization process of traditionally cooperative societies for the project Culture and Cooperation in the Classroom under a grant from the National Institute of Mental Health. Dr. Graves is on the board of directors of the International Association for the Study of Cooperation in Education (IASCE) and the California Association for Cooperation in Education (CACIE). She and her husband are joint editors of the IASCE newsletter.*

Patricia Tuck *is an educational consultant and a partner in Adventure Press. During her career in education, she taught at every grade level from kindergarten to graduate school. She has extensive experience with cooperative learning techniques, including curriculum development, teacher training and coaching, and classroom teaching. Ms. Tuck is coauthor of a chapter in* Learning to Cooperate, Cooperating to Learn.

Appendix

Sponsoring Organizations

This book is jointly sponsored by the International Association for the Study of Cooperation in Education and by the Math in Action Project of the San Francisco School Volunteers. The idea for the book was conceived at the meeting of the International Association in 1985. The structure of the book is a result of a seminar sponsored by the Math in Action Project of the San Francisco School Volunteers in September 1986.

The International Association for the Study of Cooperation in Education

The International Association for the Study of Cooperation in Education (IASCE) is a nonprofit educational association, dedicated to the study and practice of cooperation in education. This field includes the increasingly popular cooperative classroom methods where students work together in learning teams to master academic content and social skills. But cooperation in education also includes teachers working together to support and coach each other, to develop and share curriculum materials, and to join with students, parents, and business and community leaders to improve the physical, social, and intellectual quality of their schools.

IASCE Executive Board: Shlomo Sharan, President Emeritus; Robert Slavin, President; Elizabeth Cohen; Dee Dishon; Neil Davidson; Nancy and Ted Graves; Spencer Kagan; Laurel Robertson; and Mara Sapon-Shevin.

The IASCE has four regional branches, each of which provides regional and local support for practitioners of cooperative learning through conferences, workshops, classroom modeling, coaching, and a regional newsletter. In addition to the branch in Israel, there are three regional associations in North America:

California Association for Cooperation in Education (CACIE)

Mid-Atlantic Association for Cooperation in Education (MAACIE), based in Maryland

Great Lakes Association for Cooperation in Education (GLACIE), based in Toronto

For further information about the international association or any of its regional branches, write to:
Nancy and Ted Graves
International Association for the Study of Cooperation in Education
136 Liberty Street
Santa Cruz, CA 95060

The Math in Action Project of the San Francisco School Volunteers

Math in Action, funded by the San Francisco Foundation, teams pre-service and in-service teachers to participate in workshops that focus on cooperative learning and mathematics. The teams then plan and implement the activities in the classroom. San Francisco School Volunteers (SFSV) is a nonprofit agency that recruits, trains, and places volunteers in the San Francisco public schools. For information regarding SFSV or the Math in Action project, contact San Francisco School Volunteers, 135 Van Ness Avenue, San Francisco, CA 94102; telephone: (415) 864-4223.

Questionnaire Responses from Classroom Teachers

Survey Conducted by Marilyn Burns

The responses to a questionnaire sent to teachers implementing The Math Solution approach in their classrooms provide insights into teachers' experiences as they change their instructional practices. The responses reported are from nine teachers who teach in grades 2 through 9.

The first four questions on the questionnaire focused on the specific changes teachers made as a result of participating in The Math Solution courses. These questions were:

1. **What changes did you make in your classroom math instruction as a result of The Math Solution?**

2. **What was wrong with your old way of teaching, and why did you decide to make these changes?**

3. **What particular changes did you make first? Describe how you felt at the time and what happened.**

4. **What other changes have you incorporated?**

Responses from four teachers are as follows:

Grade 5: I have organized my classroom into groups of four and encourage group learning almost all the time. Cooperative problem solving has become the main focus of my mathematics instruction. I use manipulatives and emphasize process rather than quick right answers.

I had been teaching math the way I was taught. Mathematics to me was arithmetic. I taught algorithms symbolically with students working by themselves, focusing on getting the right answers by themselves. I seldom had time for measurement or geometry, and never taught probability and statistics. . . . I tried several cooperative problem-solving activities like pentominoes and was pleased with the results overall.

Grades 7, 8, 9: I stopped using the book as a means to teach a concept and started to rely on the textbook only as a source for practicing an already taught one. I tried to find ways to replace my telling students what to do with tasks that actively involved them. I started to ask students "why" for every answer they gave, whether it was right or wrong. . . . I felt children were imitating what I showed them to please me. I was never quite sure what they really understood. I was always surprised that on written tests they seemed to know less than in class. I felt bright children were not being challenged. . . . I wanted to be a better teacher.

I immediately changed the seating arrangement to groups of four and used the groups to check homework. I changed seats randomly with cards. (Once a week drove me crazy, but every two weeks was perfect.) I felt terribly nervous about the noise in my room. . . . The children, however, loved the room setup and the changing of the seats. Occasionally, when the noise got to me, I had everyone rearrange themselves in rows. This didn't last long because the students would do anything to be able to share again.

Grade 2: I began with groups of four and have students working cooperatively daily on math as well as writing and other areas. . . . So far I have used only the textbook in a cooperative way, where groups of four talk through problems on a particular page. I have always been concerned with developing positive attitudes toward math, and this new way is the best way I've found so far. Also the most important thing is that I am now working more on developing math concept understandings. Too often before, I ended up just teaching algorithms and skills at manipulating the numbers.

I have always tried to run a cooperative classroom and this approach fits into my already existing structure. . . . We began the first day with groups of four. Students learned the rules quickly and especially look forward to math menus.

Grades 3, 4, 5: I've changed nearly everything. I see the whole subject of math differently than I once did, which means that what I teach, when I teach it, and how I teach it have all undergone revision—and continue to. My old way of teaching was to use the approach of the textbook and to focus, as it did, on arithmetic. This was bad for those who had difficulty with such an approach, and it was basically dull, I think, even for the "good" math students. Our only excitement came from occasional extras, not from the total approach. I myself didn't really enjoy teaching math; it seemed cut and dried. I first tried a group-of-four activity, though in a language arts lesson rather than in math. The activity went well, the children enjoyed it, and I was pleased with how they worked together.

Question 5 focused on results from the changes implemented: **What benefits have you enjoyed from your changes?** Responses varied.

Grades 6, 7, 8: The extra time it takes to prepare each week and to supervise the groups is rewarded by the students' real involvement in math.

Grades 3, 4, 5: My children enjoy math, and I enjoy it, too. We are frequently explorers together, looking for answers because we really want to find them out. The feeling, I think, is more "math is often a matter of interesting things to figure out" rather than "math is just exercises to do." I think too that my children are learning more and are expecting what they do to make sense to them.

Grade 3: Students look forward to math. Their attitudes are definitely more positive and I think they are beginning to develop stronger math concepts.

Grades 7, 8, 9: I see students get excited about math. I hear math being discussed. I see peer teaching going on. I see youngsters no longer afraid to say, "I don't understand." The quality of conversation in my classroom is so much better than it was, and I never worry about having an answer key to the textbook. I purposely give problems for which I don't know the answers so I can work on them with my students. I have fun.

Grade 8: I feel much more confident as an educator. I have been inspired to look constantly for new ideas and to continue to learn math. My classes are more exciting to teach.

Grade 5: I enjoy and understand math more each year. My class seems to get along better and we've had fewer and fewer discipline problems since the changes. My class has had wonderful test scores to back up my new approach.

Grades 7, 8: The students are excited and look forward to class. Parents' remarks are: "Keep doing what you're doing—my child is excited about math." Kids are willing to try and work hard.

Question 6 asked for another view on the results: **What difficulties have you encountered? Describe any roadblocks and how you dealt with them.** The responses are from the same teachers who responded to question 5.

Grades 6, 7, 8: Difficulties have centered on individuals: (1) The kid who has difficulty interacting in cooperative learning and would rather be alone, (2) the one who would like to solve it for everyone, and (3) the one who would tend to sit back and let others do all the work. I have dealt with problems by trying to keep alert and discussing the situation with the individual students.

Grades 3, 4, 5: Materials were a difficulty at first, but I was able to persuade people that I needed them. A bigger difficulty has been trying to work out a balanced program that attends to all the facets of math that children need to explore, that really gets at the concepts in a substantial way, that challenges in productive ways, that avoids monotonous drill yet builds and maintains skills in estimation and computation. I've not found how to do this, and find my emphasis changing from year to year.

Grade 3: I really haven't encountered any roadblocks so far. However, I have played offense by communicating very clearly to parents and to the administration. First, I wrote a description of the math program to my principal before school started. Then I wrote weekly newsletters to the parents in which I often described our math program.

Grades 7, 8, 9: Adjusting to a fluctuating noise level—a major difficulty at first—seems to have become less of a problem, possibly because I have become more confident that it is good and it is necessary for learning. Also slowly disappearing is the worry that everyone isn't working and the complaints like "I don't want to sit with him." Difficulties I'm still dealing with are giving good directions (though I'm getting better), how to summarize well, and a lack of parental, peer, and administrative interest.

Grade 8: I find it difficult to motivate all students to really get involved; there are always some holdouts.

Grade 5: I had difficulty seeing how these problem-solving experiences fit into my curriculum. It just took time for me to understand how much my students learn from those activities and how that learning was what they really needed. The more I did and the more I watched my kids, I began to realize that it helped them learn how to think and that would enable them to master any objective the district could come up with.

Grades 7, 8: Students are reluctant to think and fear being wrong. They continue to second-guess what they think I want them to say. Also, students do not work cooperatively naturally. Learning to support one another is difficult. I have dealt with these problems by continually asking students what they think, what they are learning. It's the building of trust that is crucial. . . . I also spend time on activities that students are generally successful on and use those to foster the cooperative spirit.

Question 7 asked: **What reactions have you received from students?** The responses again are from the same teachers who responded before.

Grades 6, 7, 8: Student reactions have, for the most part, been very positive. . . . I have a few students who actually admit that they like math.

Grades 3, 4, 5: Most of my students like math, enough even that they're moved to say they like it. One of my current students, who transferred this year from a school for the gifted, said one day to another student, then later to me, "I didn't really like the math they taught in my old school, but I like math here." It seems sometimes that they actually think there are different maths like there are different languages. I guess there are. But what they're really noticing is more a difference in approach, I think.

Grade 3: They look forward to math time and some math activities are particularly popular. They really do have their favorites.

Grades 7, 8, 9: Ninety-nine percent positive! The aspect liked by just about everyone is sitting in groups because they "don't have to wait for the teacher to help, and sometimes even get to give help."

Grade 8: My students tell me that they like the problem solving, and they even bring problems for me to solve.

Grade 5: My students love math class. They know that I respect their thinking and the process of problem solving. They like working in groups and are more ready to take chances than before. They love working with materials and are eager to try new experiences.

Grades 7, 8: Students are positive! They appreciate the caring I exhibit. (They see being allowed to work cooperatively, to be supported by others, as caring.) Students are more willing to give and push themselves when working for a group. They feel comfortable for the most part. Numerous students express the fact that, for perhaps the first time, math is all right.

The final question in the questionnaire was concerned with advice to other teachers: **What are the most important things you would tell a teacher who was going to start teaching math as recommended by The Math Solution?**

Grades 6, 7, 8: Assuming they had taken the course, I would say, "It works!" Computational skills still have to be taught and to some extent drilled. However, problem solving and the ability to apply concepts is essential to math literacy. Checking to see that the kids got the right answer is not enough. We teachers need to be certain that they know how and why.

Cooperative learning is a great tool. Groups need to be set up randomly and not left to student choice. Four to a group is an ideal number. Also, I would recommend that a teacher begin with problems that require manipulative materials and are interesting but simple enough to ensure the groups' success.

Grades 3, 4, 5: I feel I'd probably tell them that they need to keep thinking constantly—questioning the value of what they choose to do, its appropriateness to their students' needs and development, the best ways to approach it, worthwhile ways to extend it, etc., etc.; and that they need to remember to watch their students rather than some long-range plan as they do their day-to-day planning.

Insofar as cooperative learning is concerned, I'd tell teachers that I feel a cooperative group approach is important in all areas of the curriculum and that they should give such an approach a good, long try so that they can see for themselves its benefits. And I'd remind them that such an approach is more in keeping with the way the world works than is the situation we've set up in school.

Grade 3: Before beginning, look closely at your philosophy of teaching and learning. If you believe that people learn better when they are in an emotionally safe, cooperative environment, then here is one way to work in math. If you believe that math concepts are of central importance to develop rather than the skills and algorithms that we learned, then here is a way to get at concepts in an ongoing way. If you believe that each child is responsible for his or her own learning and that you are to act as a facilitator rather than a dispenser of knowledge, then here is a super way to proceed.

Grades 7, 8, 9: Go slow! Make only one change at first and pick a change you think you are comfortable with. Try an activity you've done, but expect the results to be different from your experience in the course. Expect lots of questions, expect noise, expect conflicts you don't have in adult groups, expect a lower quality of discussion in the summary. Then try another activity with the same students. Compare the experiences.

Work on the change inside you. Tell your students about your feelings on how learning happens. Let them know you are committed to your room being a place that will be best for them to learn in. Explain the choices they have and why.

Don't quit when you get discouraged.

Grade 8: Begin slowly. Use what makes most sense to you first. Don't expect to be able to do everything. When you begin cooperative learning, tell your students what you are doing and why. Evaluate the learning experiences in terms of cooperative learning.

Grade 5: I would tell a teacher to try some of all the types of activities but to start with whatever feels most comfortable. Good planning is a must, especially at the beginning. Things can and will go wrong, but the benefits are there beyond the foul-ups.

Grades 7, 8: Take time to help students learn cooperative learning. This year I began by asking students what cooperation was, what were important components, and we listed and posted these. Then we concentrated three full weeks on group work. I did problem-solving activities and arithmetic review and continuously processed how the group worked and the way the problem was tackled. This has been the most successful beginning I've experienced, so I would pass this information along.

Survey Conducted by Julian Weissglass

1. What changes did you make in your math instruction in order to use small groups?

Grades 5, 6: I have changed the seating to facilitate students working together. I've made groups working together more dependent on each other by only answering questions that no group member could answer. I've made answer keys/books more available. My lessons are much more frequent and much shorter. I spend more time circulating among the groups. The noise level and feeling tone of the room—while, in my opinion, never oppressive—is much more frequently warm, friendly, and productive. . . . a place where humans can grow and thrive.

Kindergarten: I set aside part of two to three math periods per week for a cooperative learning/manipulative activity. The time spent teaching math needed to be increased in order to do this.

High School: I devised activities for the students to do without my doing any class instruction. The more I did this, the more I learned how to come up with active learning lessons rather than listening learning lessons. I also set my expectations at good, solid basic learning rather than also thinking that the kids would learn some of the "fancy" extras just because I had talked about them!

Grade 4: This year I am trying to use small groups in my instruction. So far I haven't been too successful, but I still am trying to alter my teaching style. I feel I have not done as much as I would have liked, because I have not had the time to develop lessons. Those I have done have been fairly successful. Wouldn't it be nice if the text I use in math was designed to help me?

Grade 5: I have always used groups and cooperative learning; however, the number was flexible and children were grouped by me according to skill level or by children based on friendship. Now the groups are groups of 4 (except one group of 5 because I have 33 children) formed by pulling numbers from a hat.

Grades 4–6: I changed the content of the math lessons from focusing on basic arithmetic skills to focusing on more general problem-solving skills. This allowed for more discussion and interaction as to what was the "answer" rather than a simple clear-cut "2 + 2 = 4" answer. I also changed the grouping of children from homogeneous to heterogeneous abilities. This also allowed the children to "experience" different learning styles and abilities than their own and hopefully an integration on their part of some of the other kids' strategies. When I do use small-group instruction for the purpose of teaching basic skills, the children are grouped in more homogeneous groups and very little, if anything, is different in my math lessons in terms of how I prepare for them or the subject matter.

High School: I now have my desks arranged in groups of five students, and use cooperative learning all the time except during tests. I regularly incorporate some group problem solving into all levels from algebra II to calculus.

Grade 4: Less talking *at* the students, more presenting what I want them to work on and then letting them get started. If we believe in the groups, then we have to be quiet and let students listen to each other.

2. **What was wrong with the old way, and why did you decide to make these changes?**

Grades 5–6: Probably, as implied above, that students, while getting along well with me, were not too terribly turned on to math. Too much drill piled on.

Grade 6: I noticed many individuals fell through the cracks.

Resource: I began using cooperative learning because I was unhappy with the unkind and uncaring ways that the kids treated each other.

Grades 4–6: Too much time spent telling the kids to stop talking to each other; now they have a reason to talk to each other. . . . Math was boring for many of them and now very few consider it boring except for work on basic skills or when they work in workbooks. . . . There were always some kids who just did not understand. Now I find that often other children can explain concepts to them in language they understand. . . . So many different abilities and styles—now the differences seem to enhance and complement each other.

High School: I was frustrated by the traditional teaching techniques in several ways. I never had time to get to each student to answer his or her questions or just observe how the work was going. Both I and the students were bored by the routine of correcting the previous day's homework.

Grade 4: They were learning too many recipes for computation and not doing enough problem solving. Also they couldn't get started on problem solving without my intervention. Now they have lots of people who can help them—each other.

3. What particular changes did you make first? Describe how you felt at the time and what happened.

Grade 4–6: Changes in seating, adjustment in noise level, playing some music, making answers available. Felt good about it but found, initially, that students too eagerly were willing to talk/visit, etc. While on a "number" of things, mathematics was often not the subject. It took a while (one of the reasons for my increased circulation—I worked hard to be positive, friendly, etc., while still trying to maintain standards) to get what I felt was a good working "hum." It takes work to keep it there, but it's well worth the effort.

High School: The first thing I did was to reorganize the room using tables that four students could sit around. I decided to let the first groups be friends, i.e., let students choose where they would sit.

Grade 5: My first change was to rearrange tables (I had previously gotten rid of those terrible flip-top individual desks that "all" upper graders have). My next change was to number the tables and to have each child as he or she entered the room on the first day pull a number from the hat. I felt so strongly from my experiences at UCSB that when parents would say, "Please move my child because he or she can't work with _____," I said, "Trust me. It'll work." Every four or five weeks we have a "big move." The move is based on numbers pulled from the hat. The children look forward to the challenge of working with someone new.

Grade 4–6: First I had kids pair up in partners to solve problems. After a few weeks of partners we went to two partnerships working together. Then I went through the rules for groups of four a la Marilyn Burns and had kids do several cooperative exercises that were nonverbal, i.e., cooperative puzzles and squares, trust walks, etc. I scheduled this activity for once a week when no other adults would be in the room. This helped the kids rely on each other and get the format and rules straight.

High School: When I first put all student desks into groups, I was frightened that students might talk all the time about social life, or refuse to work with people other than their friends. I had them do a cooperative logic activity from *SPACES* to begin with. They all enjoyed both the problems and the interaction and thought that it couldn't possibly be math.

Grade 4: We physically moved the desks into groups of four and gave the students activities to work on while we stressed what we would see and what we would hear if a group was cooperating. Both of us (teachers) were scared. Change is scary—what if it all falls apart. And it has, many times. But classes fall apart when students sit in straight rows and don't interact, too. It took about a month before the groups could function to get *anything* done. They argued, they sulked, they worked alone, they walked away from their group. Gradually they have learned to work with the people within the group.

4. What other changes have you incorporated?

Grades 5–6: Use a lot more student sharing (word problems they've written), career awareness, tie-in with science, computer awareness; much more nontext activities including manipulatives—

I believe that manipulatives done in a group, with each person participating, is far less threatening than working alone.

Resource: I have spent time teaching students how to be cooperative and to complete a cooperative task; this is very necessary as many have never worked cooperatively at school.

Grade 4: I have purchased many manipulatives and intend to continue to try to incorporate them in my teaching.

High School: I have also incorporated manipulatives into my instruction—not as often as I'd like, though.

5. What benefits do you perceive from your changes to small-group cooperation?

Grades 5–6: Generally a nicer feeling tone; more enjoyment *and* covering more difficult tasks/lessons/activities. . . . Students feel more pride, at times, about what they've done.

Grade 5: Example: Math problems to do at the board are given to a group—not individuals. My only instruction is, "If you worked on the board yesterday, let someone else from your table go today." Even the shyest, most insecure children go willingly because the work they are doing or showing was done cooperatively and if it is "wrong," it isn't a reflection on *you*—you're just the recorder. Everyone in the group needs to reanalyze it.

Grades 4–6: Kids teaching each other. . .learning of cooperation skills. . .learning of interaction skills. . .heightened awareness of each other. . .higher interest in math. . .stronger verbal abilities. . . stronger problem-solving abilities. . .more sharing of ideas rather than "guarding my answer" from the other kids.

High School: The benefits I've found range from intangible things like improved classroom environment and improved mental health (for me) to the virtual elimination of discipline problems. Along with that I see more tolerance of students who are different.

Grade 4: They learn from each other. Many times one of them can explain something much better than I can and they now see each other as sources of help. I'm free to watch and listen to see what other learnings I need to give them to help them (a group or the class) move on, or give an extension. The arguing and bickering has disappeared. Interpersonal relationships appear to have improved. In one early group we had two girls who *almost* had a fist fight over who was going to record the information. They can now do verbal give-and-take to settle such things. Four students who at the beginning of the year would *not* interact or make eye contact with anyone in their group (only with people they chose) now willingly participate. They have become willing to take the risk of interacting in a group. Two students who felt they were above the level of the others are now listening to the opinions of the rest of the group and not working alone.

6. What difficulties have you encountered? Describe any roadblocks and how you dealt with them.

Grades 5–6: Letting students work with a group (checking their own work, etc.) too long without my checking for understanding/mastery—in other words, for some of them, I was having them work too independently. I was lulled into this by how nicely everything seemed to be going. It worked for many, but others had gotten lost without realizing it. Now I monitor much more carefully groups and individuals.

High School: The biggest difficulty that I have encountered is my getting used to a higher noise level in the classroom and monitoring the noise level so that the students/friends working together are working on mathematics and not just visiting.

Grade 6: Class size remains a problem. Small-group cooperation is a big help, but 36 students is still too many. The noise level can also be a problem. This is due partly to the fact that the school in which I teach has partly closing movable walls. One of the teachers in the building has a quiet traditional classroom. My teaching partner and I try to cooperate with her when we can and ignore her protests when we can't. The proper facilities are extremely important to cooperative learning.

Grade 6: My greatest roadblock or difficulty continues to be having administrators recognize the value in taking time to establish these familylike groups. Once a caring class has evolved, all else is possible. I continue to be questioned about my motives and congratulated at year's end for the *unexplained* success.

Grade 5: Difficulties have been when children (from my class) have gone to other classrooms and been required to sit in silent rows of single desks. I likewise have difficulties when I first get children from other classrooms and require them to sit together randomly and work together.

Grades 4–6: More of my time is spent on helping children interact and solve interpersonal problems than on actual teaching of math. Sometimes, when kids are in a group with someone they do not like, the experience is less than satisfactory for all involved. The noise level of the room sometimes goes sky-high when everybody is really talking and involved.

High School: The main difficulty I've encountered is parent understanding of cooperative learning. Since it doesn't look like the math teaching they've been through, some of them don't like it. The principal has handled this problem, for the most part. I also had parents at our last school open house actually go through a cooperative, manipulative activity, and that worked extremely well.

7. **What reactions have you received from students, teachers, your principal, parents?**

Grades 5–6: Extremely positive all the way around—this includes the junior high teachers who comment favorably on my former students. My principal is especially supportive.

High School: Parents are receptive to small-group learning when it is explained to them from a positive approach.

Grade 6: During parent conferences several parents commented how positive their children are this year and how they seem genuinely anxious to go to school. This attitude had not prevailed before. My principal has stated that this year's sixth graders don't seem to explode on to the playground at recess. I believe that part of the reason is that they are more actively involved in their learning in the classroom.

Resource: The principal believes in cooperative learning and thought it was great; other teachers told me they've tried it before but it "never works for them" or that their students couldn't handle it. The parents had little to no reaction. Students were not too happy to begin with.

Grades 4–6: By far, most of the kids like cooperative groups. They enjoy working together and have a lot of fun talking. Feedback from parents has been most positive. Parents who are able to observe the process in the classroom are impressed with the variety of types of learning going on from one lesson. It also becomes very obvious to the parents that children have different ways of learning and of solving problems. Other teachers who have observed are exited by the quality of interaction among the children. They have also commented how it (the observation) gave them the impetus to go back and keep trying with their kids.

8. What would you describe as your greatest success with group work?

Grades 5–6: Discovery lessons (Pick's rule, etc.), manipulatives, and so on.

Grade 6: I feel successful with small-group cooperative learning because more students understand what they are doing and are able to achieve more.

Grade 5: I think the greatest success is getting the reluctant participant to feel good about himself or herself and to become an active participant knowing that his or her table (group) is behind him or her.

Grades 4–6: Working together with others seems a very important life skill, indeed a "basic skill," and seeing children learn this has been the greatest success. Second would have to be seeing how profoundly it increases the awareness of parents and teachers about children's learning styles and the variety of approaches one must take to help kids understand.

High School: My greatest success was in the affective, not cognitive, domain. Two years ago, I made up the groups and put together many strangers in assuring heterogeneity. After a quarter, I changed the groups, again making them heterogeneous. I had each student write, anonymously, something nice about everyone in his or her old group as the new groups were formed. Many of the students who had complained ("I can't work with that weirdo") said they were sad to leave their new friends.

Grade 4: Giving the class a problem-solving situation and seeing them start to work within 20 seconds, to *discuss* it with each other, and offer to the whole group their strategies. Then when each group had a different answer, not being upset, but going to work again to figure it out *and* figuring out why their strategy hadn't been successful.

9. What are the next steps you feel you need to take?

Grades 5–6: I feel I need to be communicating more with parents (I do some but not enough); I would really like to use a text even less than I'm using it. Do more outdoor (and other science-related) math.

High School: I'd like to develop a curriculum to have more cooperative, manipulative activities for college-prep mathematics.

Grade 4: I need to know how to intervene to get a group going again when it has hit a snag, without taking over. I need help in teaching cooperation. I can point out what I can see when people are cooperating, but what specific help can I give the students? What specific skills do they need to concentrate on? I need to know how to help them be more responsible for their actions and how to differentiate between group work and time for individual work. I need to rethink my curriculum to decide which techniques are most appropriate for such tasks.

10. What are the most important things you would tell a teacher who was going to start teaching math with cooperative learning in small groups?

Grade 6: There are three things to look for. One, the positive level of enthusiasm. Two, the results—mainly the real long-term understanding that is developed. Third, there is a natural acceptable noise level that can be expected. I am not forgetting good planning because I believe good teachers always plan.

Grade 6: Show a concern for all students' problems, discuss with them your own fears and concerns, value their feedback, and assist them in teaching one another.

Resource: To spend *at least* a month doing team-building activities and giving the students the opportunity to build trust and caring for their fellow students. Deemphasize competitive activities, even in P.E. Don't get discouraged if at first it seems difficult!

Grade 5: I tell other teachers:

1. Don't worry about the noise level.

2. Don't worry about copying (this is a concern that is expressed to me by parents, other teachers, and principals).

3. Don't worry about someone "riding along free," because they soon realize each one will be held accountable; if concerned, designate each one for a specific task, e.g., recorder, reporter.

4. Use concrete materials rather than pencil-and-paper activities—especially when beginning.

Grades 4–6: Go slowly. . .try it maybe once a week. . .tell the kids why you are doing it.

High School: If the teacher were nervous about the idea, I'd encourage him or her to start with students in pairs. Beyond that I'd share some activities I've found successful and offer to come in and observe and/or teach a sample lesson. I'd stress the need for patience and flexibility with the students. This all seems to add up to a support group, which, of course, is the only way to go.

High School: I would try to impress the teacher with the idea that the classroom is probably going to be more noisy. Be aware of the change in noise level and don't stop because of the noise before the process has a chance to work. Be patient, let the small-group instruction have a chance. Don't go back to our old methods because you are uncomfortable. You have many years of structure behind your changing. The students can handle almost any structure that you want to try with them; don't let yourself kill a structure that can improve the learning in your classroom.

Resource Materials*

General Introduction to Cooperative Learning

Glasser, William. *Control Theory in the Classroom*. New York: Harper and Row, 1986.

Psychiatrist William Glasser presents an analysis of problems with traditional schooling and identifies four needs that must be satisfied in order for students to choose motivated behavior. He demonstrates how cooperative learning teams can help students meet these needs.

Johnson, David W., Roger T. Johnson, and Edythe Johnson Holubec. *Circles of Learning: Cooperation in the Classroom*. Edina, Minn.: Interaction Book Company, 1986.

This book provides an introduction to cooperative learning for parents, teachers, and administrators. Three alternative goal structures—competitive, individualistic, and cooperative—are described, and the four basic elements of cooperative learning recognized as essential by most trainers are identified: forming face-to-face learning groups, creating a sense of positive interdependence among them, ensuring the individual accountability of each group member, and explicitly teaching the requisite collaborative skills for working together effectively.

Kohn, Alfie. *No Contest: The Case Against Competition*. Boston: Houghton Mifflin, 1986.

This book describes several harmful effects of competition shown by research in the social sciences. Also included is a critique of four prevailing myths about competition.

* Some of the references in the Resource Materials are from *Cooperative Learning: A Resource Guide* by Nancy and Ted Graves, 1987, published by IASCE.

Specific Cooperative Learning Strategies

Aronson, Elliot, et al. *The Jigsaw Classroom*. Newbury Park, Calif.: SAGE Publications, 1978.

This is the basic text for learning the "jigsaw" method of cooperative learning. Jigsaw is applicable to subjects in grades 4 and up that can be divided into discrete segments, issues, or questions. Each team member learns a different piece of information in "expert" groups. Students then teach each other what they have learned so that when all the information is shared with the group, the jigsaw is complete.

Cohen, Elizabeth G. *Designing Groupwork: Strategies for the Heterogeneous Classroom*. New York: Teachers College Press, 1986.

At each step in implementing groupwork, this general introduction to the field devotes particular attention to strategies for promoting status equalization and full participation by all group members, regardless of sex, ethnicity, socio-economic background, or previous academic achievement. Particular attention is given to the problems of the bilingual classroom, including a description of the Finding Out/Descubrimiento math/science program.

Dishon, Dee, and Pat Wilson O'Leary. *A Guidebook for Cooperative Learning: A Technique for Creating More Effective Schools*. Holmes Beach, Fla.: Learning Publications, 1984.

A clear, step-by-step guide to implementing the Johnsons' approach to cooperative learning, written by two experienced classroom teachers. The book stresses basic principles, cooperative skills training, and the teacher's role at each stage. Practical advice for handling a variety of typical classroom problems is also included.

Johnson, David W., and Roger T. Johnson. *Learning Together and Alone: Cooperative, Competitive, and Individualistic Learning*. 2d ed. Englewood Cliffs, N.J.: Prentice Hall, 1987.

The revised edition of this 1975 classic emphasizes basic principles of cooperative learning, group processes, and monitoring the development of social skills. This edition devotes more attention than the original to the appropriate use of competition and individualization within a basically cooperative classroom.

Kagan, Spencer. *Cooperative Learning Resources for Teachers*. 4th ed. 27402 Camino Capistrano, #201, Laguna Niguel, Calif.: Resources for Teachers, 1987.

This is a comprehensive general manual on structures for cooperative learning. It covers the major cooperative learning approaches, plus several innovative adaptations, team building, classroom management, cooperative skills training, and coaching.

Sharan, Shlomo, and Yael Sharan. *Small-Group Teaching*. Englewood Cliffs, N.J.: Educational Technology Publications, 1976.

Besides providing a general introduction to cooperative learning, this is the earliest full exposition of the authors' Group Investigation method, a project/research approach that is particularly well suited for intermediate, secondary, and tertiary students for promoting higher-order thinking skills.

Sharan, Shlomo, et al, eds. *Cooperation in Education*. Provo, Utah: Brigham Young University Press, 1980.

Based on proceedings of the first International Conference on Cooperation in Education, Tel Aviv, Israel, 1979, the first four chapters provide useful teacher manuals for implementing Group Investigation (Sharan), Jigsaw (Aronson), Student Team Learning (Slavin), and an introduction to the use of small-group methods in teaching mathematics (Davidson).

Slavin, Robert E. *Using Student Team Learning*. 3rd ed. Baltimore, Md.: Center for Research on Elementary and Middle Schools, The Johns Hopkins University, 1986.

Complete instructions are provided for implementing two general team learning methods: Student Teams Achievement Divisions (STAD) and Teams-Games-Tournaments (TGT). Descriptions of two new programs, Team Assisted Individualization (TAI) for arithmetic, and Cooperative Integrated Reading and Composition (CIRC) for language arts, are also included, as well as brief descriptions of other cooperative learning methods.

Cooperative Learning and Mathematics

Baratta-Lorton, Mary. *Mathematics Their Way*. Menlo Park, Calif.: Addison-Wesley, 1976.

This activity-centered and manipulative-based program is designed for grades K–2. Students are engaged in explorations at learning stations. Although the materials are not designed for cooperative learning, they are well suited for sharing materials and discussions in pairs or small groups.

Burns, Marilyn. *The Good Times Math Event Book*. Oak Lawn, Ill.: Creative Publications, 1977.

This book contains 70 "events," graded by difficulty, in geometry, numbers and operations, measurement, statistics and probability, and functions and graphs. The author encourages their use as discovery techniques in learning groups, but they can also be used as independent enrichment activities.

———. *A Collection of Math Lessons*. New Rochelle, N.Y.: Cuisenaire Company of America, 1987.

A collection of 14 exemplary math lessons for grades 3–6 that illustrate Burns' problem-solving approach to math education. Each is fully scripted as a classroom vignette, complete with unedited examples of the students' work. Includes an introduction describing her cooperative learning strategy: Groups of Four.

———, and Bonnie Tank. *A Collection of Math Lessons from Grades 1 Through 3*. The Math Solution Publications. Distributed by Cuisenaire Company of America, New Rochelle, N.Y.

This book offers a series of cooperative learning lessons for grades 1–3 in four topic areas: number sense, place value, measurement, and geometry. Vignettes describe how lessons are introduced, how children respond, and what a teacher might do.

Clark, Clare, Betsy Y. Carter, and Betty J. Sternberg. *Math in Stride*. Grades 1-6. Menlo Park: Addison-Wesley, 1988.

This series is a manipulative-based approach for learning mathematics, following a developmental sequence from concrete to representational to abstract. Many of the lessons involve small-group discussion and learning stations.

Cook, Marcy. *Scavenger Hunts for Math*. 1986. Available from Marcy Cook Math, 312 Diamond Avenue, Balboa Island, California 92662.

Twenty-eight math activities for elementary and junior high students working cooperatively in groups of 2–4. Each scavenger hunt involves matching 12 answers to 12 questions that require a variety of math concepts and skills—estimations, approximations, visualizations, and computations—to increase students' number sense.

————. *Talk It Over*. 1987. Available from Marcy Cook Math, 312 Diamond Avenue, Balboa Island, California 92662.

Ninety problems for upper elementary and junior high students working in cooperative groups of two to four. Designed to engage students in a "pursuit" rather than a routine procedure.

Davidson, Neil, and Frances Gulick. *Abstract Algebra: An Active Learning Approach*. Boston: Houghton Mifflin, 1976. (Out of print: for information on obtaining the book, contact Neil Davidson at the Department of Curriculum and Instruction, College of Education, The University of Maryland, College Park, Maryland 20742.)

This college-level text is designed for use with the small-group discovery method. Students in groups solve problems, prove theorems, make conjectures, work out examples, and construct counterexamples. This book contains more than enough material for a one-semester course in abstract algebra.

Downie, Diane, Twila Slesnick, and Jean Kerr Stenmark. *Math for Girls and Other Problem Solvers*. Berkeley, Calif.: Lawrence Hall of Science, University of California, 1981.

Seventy-three activities and problems for small groups and whole-class instruction designed to provide hands-on experiences in logical thinking and problem solving that stimulate curiosity and interest in mathematics and encourage girls to consider math-related careers. Creating a cooperative and supportive atmosphere for working is an important part of the authors' strategy for overcoming "math anxiety."

Fraser, Sherry, et al. *SPACES: Solving Problems of Access to Careers in Engineering and Science*. Berkeley, Calif.: Lawrence Hall of Science, University of California, 1982.

This volume is part of the *EQUALS* program, which was designed to foster increased participation of young women in mathematics and math-related occupations. Thirty-two cooperative activities that foster problem solving in grades 4–10 are arranged in categories, including design and construction, visualization, mechanical tools, attitudes and personal goals, and careers.

Kaseberg, Alice, Nancy Kreinberg, and Diane Downie. *Use EQUALS to Promote the Participation of Women in Mathematics*. Berkeley, Calif.: Math/Science Network, Lawrence Hall of Science, University of California, 1980.

One focus of the *EQUALS* program is overcoming "math anxiety" among women. Cooperative small-group learning is an important strategy used. This handbook describes the rationale for the *EQUALS* program and the activities and materials needed to conduct an *EQUALS* in-service workshop or introduce *EQUALS* into the classroom.

Lane County Mathematics Project (Richard Brannan and Oscar Schaaf, directors). *Problem Solving in Mathematics* (Grades 4–9), and *Alternative Problem Solving in Mathematics* (Grades 4–6). Palo Alto, Calif.: Dale Seymour, 1983.

This series of books provides a set of problem-solving activities intended for a classroom atmosphere that fosters openness, creativity, communication, and cooperation. Students learn to employ a set of problem-solving skills, which can be combined into strategies for problem solving.

Langbort, Carol, and Virginia Thompson. *Building Success in Math.* Belmont, Calif.: Wadsworth, 1985.

This book is designed to help people who feel uncomfortable with math. It presents a variety of approaches to problem solving to show that there is not just one way to solve a problem. Working in pairs or small groups is encouraged to foster talking about math.

Lappan, Glenda, William Fitzgerald, et al. *Middle Grades Mathematics Project.* Consists of five books: *Mouse and Elephant: Measuring Growth; Factors and Multiples; Similarity and Equivalent Fractions; Spatial Visualization;* and *Probability.* Menlo Park, Calif.: Addison-Wesley, 1986.

This curriculum project for grades 5-8 fosters a problem-solving approach using small groups and manipulative materials where appropriate. The instructional model includes three phases: launch, explore, and summarize. A scripted format provides teacher action, teacher talk, and expected responses from students.

Meyer, Carol, and Tom Sallee. *Make It Simpler: A Practical Guide to Problem Solving in Mathematics.* Menlo Park, Calif.: Addison-Wesley, 1983.

This year-long course in problem solving for grades 4–8 takes about 15 minutes of class time per day, working in groups of four. Students learn to write story problems, as well as apply five basic strategies applicable to nonmathematical problems.

Slavin, Robert E. *The Johns Hopkins Student Team Learning Project.* Center for Research on Elementary and Middle Schools, The Johns Hopkins University, Baltimore Maryland.

The Center offers two elementary mathematics programs for grades 3–8 designed for small-group learning: Student Teams

Achievement Divisions (STAD) and Team Assisted Individualization (TAI). Emphasis is on the mastery of basic algorithms, and the programs follow the approach of most standard textbooks. In-service training is available. For information on Student Team Learning, contact:

Center for Research on Elementary and Middle Schools
The Johns Hopkins University
3505 North Charles Street
Baltimore, MD 21218
Telephone: (301) 338-8249

Team Assisted Individualization (TAI) is distributed under the name Team Accelerated Instruction by Charlesbridge Publishing, 85 Main Street, Watertown, MA 02172.

Souviney, Randall J., Tamara Keyser, and Alan Sarver, *Mathmatters*. Santa Monica, Calif.: Goodyear Publishing Company, 1978.

This book offers a series of activities for individuals and small groups, based on stages of intellectual development as described by Piaget and Bruner. Developmental activity sequences involve student understanding of a concept at the concrete level, representational level, or symbolic level. Students all work on the same concepts, but perhaps at different developmental levels.

Stein, Sherman K., Calvin D. Crabill, and G.D. Charkerian. *The Stein Series (Geometry: A Guided Inquiry; Elementary Algebra: A Guided Inquiry; and Algebra II/Trigonometry: A Guided Inquiry)*. Pleasantville, N.Y.: Sunburst Communications, 1986.

This series of high school math texts is specifically designed for small-group instruction as part of a coordinated math curriculum, including computer applications.

Stenmark, Jean K., Virginia Thompson, and Ruth Cossey. *Family Math*. Palo Alto, Calif.: Dale Seymour, 1986.

Designed to give parents ideas and materials for helping children in mathematics, the one hundred hands-on activities in this book are also well suited for group activities in the classroom.

Szetela, Walter. *Mathematics: Problem Solving Activities* (Grade 6). Palo Alto, Calif.: Dale Seymour, 1982.

This book offers a collection of word problems designed to be appealing to students. Fourteen units are organized around a series of problem-solving heuristics. The author suggests that students work in pairs to solve the problems. Although the book is intended for grade 6, many of the challenging problems are useful for grades 7 and 8, and some for algebra students.

University of Maryland Mathematics Project (Mildred Cole, Neil Davidson, James Fey, James Henkelman, et al). *Unifying Concepts and Processes in Elementary Mathematics*. Boston: Allyn and Bacon, 1978. (Out of print; for information on obtaining the book, contact Neil Davidson at the Department of Curriculum and Instruction, College of Education, The University of Maryland, College Park, Maryland 20742.)

This is a text for a two-semester course in mathematics for elementary teachers. It emphasizes mathematical processes, small-group learning, and discovery. Topics are unified by fundamental concepts of sets, operations, relations, mappings, groups, and fields.

Weissglass, Julian. *Exploring Elementary Mathematics: A Small-Group Approach for Teaching*. 1979. For information about this book, contact the author at Tri-County Math Project, Department of Mathematics, UC Santa Barbara, Santa Barbara, California 93105.

Covering topics from addition through probability theory, this is a college math textbook that shows teachers how to use a discovery/laboratory approach to teaching elementary mathematics in cooperative groups.

Whimbey, Arthur, and Jack Lochhead. *Problem Solving and Comprehension*. Hillsdale, N.J.: Lawrence Erlbaum Associates, 1986.

This handbook outlines a structured "thinking aloud" method for pair problem solving. A systematic approach for problem solving is designed to sharpen students' thinking skills.

Cooperative Learning and Computers

Male, Mary, David W. Johnson, and Roger T. Johnson. *Cooperative Learning and Computers: An Activity Guide for Teachers*. 3rd ed. Santa Cruz, Calif.: Educational Apple-cations, 1986.

This manual contains a rationale for using cooperative learning methods with computers and 27 step-by-step lessons in math, language arts, and social studies that illustrate three different cooperative learning models: Teams-Games-Tournaments, Jigsaw, and Learning Together. Descriptions of 29 useful software packages applicable to many subjects are also included.

Cooperative Learning and Math/Science Education

Cooperative Mathematics Project (CMP). Project of the Developmental Studies Center, 111 Dearwood Place, Suite 165, San Ramon, CA 94513; telephone: 415–838–7633 (contact Dr. Laurel Robertson).

A project to develop cooperative mathematics problem-solving materials for Grades 2–6.

DeAvila, Edward A., Sharon E. Duncan, and Cecilia J. Navarette. *Finding Out/Descubrimiento*. Northvale, N.J.: Santilla Publishing Company, 1986.

This is an integrated math/science discovery learning program for grades 2–5. It includes 130 lessons designed for cooperative small-group use. All learning materials are presented in Spanish, English, and pictographs.

Wiebe, Arthur, et al. *Project AIMS*. Fresno, Calif.: AIMS Education
Foundation, 1982–1988.

The Project AIMS (Activities for Integrating Math and Science)
books were written and field-tested by 120 teachers under a
National Science Foundation grant to Fresno Pacific College.
There are over 20 books for kindergarten to grade 9 including *Glide
into Winter with Math & Science; Seasoning Math & Science;
Overhead & Underfoot;* and *Math + Science, A Solution.* The books
are designed for small-group instruction and are being adapted to
the Johnsons' model of cooperative learning. Each book contains
20–25 lessons, a teacher's manual, and student worksheets for
duplication. An index of math skills and science processes helps
teachers integrate the lessons into their own curriculums. The
AIMS Foundation also provides in-service training.

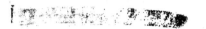